HERE COMES TROUBLE

The life and times of a
very English schoolboy 1936-1954

Published by Mountnessing Publishing
England

Copyright © 2025 Brian Hughes

All rights reserved

Brian Hughes has asserted his right
under the Copyright, Designs and Patents Act 1988
to be identified as the author of this work

ISBN 978-1-84396-695-1

A catalogue record for this
book is available from the British Library.
and the American Library of Congress

Cover design by Creative Covers

This book is dedicated to
Karen Fordham, who has played such
a vital role in its production.
Without her co-operation and unfailing
assistance it would not have
been published.

HERE COMES TROUBLE

The life and times of a
very English schoolboy 1936-1954

Brian Hughes MA MBE FRGS

MOUNTNESSING PUBLISHING

Contents

1
PROLOGUE

3
CHAPTER 1
Self-examination: Who are we?

5
CHAPTER 2
Britain in the 1930s

10
CHAPTER 3
A Visit to a Lyons Corner House

13
CHAPTER 4
1936: A Year of Change

16
CHAPTER 5
Our Genes

19
CHAPTER 6
My Father: His Early Years

23
CHAPTER 7
My Father's Early Working Life

29
CHAPTER 8
My Paternal Grandfather

34
CHAPTER 9
My Paternal Grandmother

37
CHAPTER 10
My Mother

41
CHAPTER 11
My Maternal Grandfather

48
CHAPTER 12
"Grannie" Somers

55
CHAPTER 13
Uncle Gerald

58
CHAPTER 14
The Relationship between My Parents

60
CHAPTER 15
My Birth and First Near-Death Experience

64
CHAPTER 16
Kettering, Northamptonshire

67
CHAPTER 17
Kettering: The First Year

74
CHAPTER 18
1940-42

83
CHAPTER 19
My Conversion to Being Better Behaved

93
CHAPTER 20
Kettering Grammar School

100
CHAPTER 21
Clothes Rationing

107
CHAPTER 22
Life at Home During the War: Part One

111
CHAPTER 23
The Arrival of the Americans

114
CHAPTER 24
Life at Home During the War: Part Two

124
CHAPTER 25
Kettering to Ramsden Bellhouse

135
CHAPTER 26
Brentwood Preparatory School 1946

137
CHAPTER 27
Hornchurch 1946

141
CHAPTER 28
Brentwood Upper School 1946

149
CHAPTER 29
The School Rules

158
CHAPTER 30
My First Year in the Main School

166
CHAPTER 31
Wearing the School Uniform

173
CHAPTER 32
The Move to Billericay

183
CHAPTER 33
The Journey to School from Billericay

188
CHAPTER 34
Billericay: Centre of the Web

200
CHAPTER 35
Billericay Urban District

208
CHAPTER 36
Upper Two: Dinky Toy Dealer

213
CHAPTER 37
My Father's Operation

217
CHAPTER 38
Billericay High Street: 1946 to the Present

226
CHAPTER 39
Classical Three: A Fateful Decision

230
CHAPTER 40
Healthy Mind in Healthy Body

236
CHAPTER 41
Extramural Activities

241
CHAPTER 42
The Teachers at Brentwood School

255
CHAPTER 43
The Festival of Britain 1951

265
CHAPTER 44
Leisure Time Activities 1949-1952

275
CHAPTER 45
The Brentwood School CCF

283
CHAPTER 46
Lullingstone Roman Villa, 1953

289
CHAPTER 47
To Greece as a Boy Scout 1954

299
EPILOGUE

Photographs

i
My father, age 19
My mother, age 18

ii
My parents playing leading
roles in St. Martin's Church pageant, 1935
Lyons Corner House "Nippies"
Copyright © PA Images\Alamy

iii
My father's Scout Troop, early 1920s
A teenage Dudley Moore, age 15, with female friend
A teenage Dudley Moore, top left with his
mother Ada and cousin Richard

iv
My grandfather, John Somers, centre, with his brothers, c.1905
My grandmother Gertrude Evelyn Somers, c. 1910

v
My maternal grandparents, 1940
Uncle Gerald and self, 1939

vi
Young Brian, age 3
Young Brian, age 7

vii
3 Broadway, Kettering
Brian and Gillian Chapman, age 8 and Angela

viii
Ralph, the GI, with mum and Angela, 1944
GIs with father, Angela and me, 1944

ix
Message from King George VI to boys and girls, 8th June 1946

x
Brian in Kettering Grammar School uniform
Romford Market, 1950 © The Francis Frith Collection

xi
Pink Cottage, Billericay: our former family home
Brentwood Old Big School (much as it was in my time)

xii
Charles Allison, MA, Headmaster

xiii
Brian in Sea Scout uniform, 1948
Billericay High Street, early 1950s Copyright © The Francis Frith Collection

xiv
On holiday with KV8557 and caravan at Corton, 1950
The Skylon at the Festival of Britain, 1951
Copyright © Chroma Collection/Alamy

xv
Message from Queen Elizabeth II to takers of evacuees

xvi
Mr. Rennie, Mr. Nicholls
Mr. Higgs, Mr. Hodgson

xvii
Peter Preston with his father's Jaguar, 1954
The Bean Library, Brentwood School

xviii
Mosaics at Lullingstone Roman Villa, 1953
Copyright © Historic England Archive

xix
London Transport Coach, TF7c
Copyright© TFL from the London Transport Museum collection

xx
Boys queuing for milk outside the Tuck Shop, 1950
Brian in Scout uniform, age 18 (1954)

xxi
Messrs Benson, Cluer, Rowswell and Barron, Greece, 1954
Dignitaries at Scout Camp, Vouliagmeni 1954

xxii
School production of "1066 and All That".
Brian, far right, in CCF uniform
Angela and I, summer term 1954

Prologue

Anyone who writes a book with a view to inflicting it upon the general public should have a valid reason for doing so. It should inform the reader in some way or tell a good story, preferably both.

Having miraculously survived a brain haemorrhage in a swimming pool at the age of 71 I felt I had that reason when I wrote "A Law Unto Myself". Although autobiographical, it was meant to be informative and contain some interesting anecdotes which might prove helpful to others when assessing their own hopes and ambitions for the future.

On reflection, however, it left a lot unsaid. It disclosed little about the experiences during childhood that helped shape me as a person and led to the way in which I approached adulthood. It told only half a story and was a bit like a travel guide which describes a place but does not tell one how to reach it.

Not many people survive into their eighties and most leave unsaid, unexplained or undocumented details of their lives that would be of interest to their children, grandchildren and future generations.

When, moreover, we look back to our own grandparents there is so much we could have learned from them. We invariably leave the questions we would have liked to ask about their lives and experiences too late. They are no longer there to answer them.

In the circumstances and in view of the fact that I have throughout my life been blessed with an elephantine memory I proffer as an excuse for a second book answers to a number of those questions before they are asked and thereby fill in some of the gaps in our family history. At the same time, I hope to set out in as readable a manner as possible the experiences and events that so influenced me as a young person between 1939 and 1954.

I cannot deny that memory is selective and admit that I have doubtless consigned to my mental wastepaper basket incidents that I have chosen consciously or unconsciously to forget. But that does not invalidate what I can accurately recall, and I hope the reader will find what I have to tell about my life and surroundings, during the War and post War, of interest as social commentary, if nothing else.

1
Self-Examination: Who Are We?

In writing anything with an autobiographical content it is sensible to consider the background to our existence and what has contributed to who we are and how we present ourselves to the world.

We are all born within a specific historical and sociological time frame. Of that there is no question. Within that time frame a number of factors influence our lives the most important of which are our genetic make-up, our family environment and the attitudes, social, political and moral of the people closest to us during childhood.

Aristotle, the famous philosopher, who wrote on most branches of learning and who was tutor to Alexander the Great, concluded that it was possible to predict the behaviour in adult life of anyone by looking at his or her early years and the influences brought to bear upon him or her during that period.

By way of simple analogy, if you point an arrow in the air, draw back the bow and fire it in a particular direction then, depending on the force you apply to doing so, you will have a good idea of its trajectory and where it will land. The same applies, metaphorically, to a child. Examine the forces imposed on it during its early life and you will be able to deduce what sort of person it will become as an adult.

Centuries later, Jesuit priests refined and built upon Aristotle's perceptive observation saying, "Give us a child until he or she is six and we will mould his or her behaviour for life." Other religious orders and oppressive regimes have not been slow to adopt this concept of moulding the young and it has become prevalent in the modern world as the power of the State and its ability to control the actions and thoughts of its citizens has grown. Independence of thought and freedom of speech have been systematically curtailed in many parts of the globe as a result.

Given the above it is undoubtedly true to say that, over and above our genetic make-up and family environment we as adults, very much reflect the times in which we grew up as children. We absorb the culture, including regretfully the prejudices of those around us, when we are young.

2
Britain in the 1930s

Into what culture was I born? Let me set the scene for you.

The 1930s were a remarkable period in Britain's history. Against the ominous backdrop of National Socialism and rising intolerance and oppression on the continent of Europe and isolationism on the part of the United States of America the country nevertheless appeared to be heading towards a more prosperous and enlightened future.

Prejudices still abounded within our society but we had not, mercifully, gone down the paths of Communism or National Socialism like our continental neighbours despite the clear divisions in wealth and privilege that existed.

By the end of 1935 the nation had, moreover, survived the ravages of the Great War, the war to end all wars, or so it was thought at the time, and had emerged from the Spanish flu epidemic of 1918 and 1919 and the Depression of the late 1920s and early 1930s. Notwithstanding the massive loss of life and wealth that had resulted from these three calamitous events there was an admittedly cautious feeling of optimism in the air.

The Equal Franchise Act of 1928 had finally put an end to suffragism. All women over the age of 21 had at last been given the vote and politicians were reluctantly conceding that they should also have a voice in Parliament and a say in the destiny of the country.

There remained pockets of resistance to the concept of universality and equality and it was not until 1947, for example, that Cambridge University decided to award degrees to women. Despite their ability to vote in parliamentary elections women were regarded in many respects as "second class" citizens until the late 1940s.

Prior to the outbreak of the Second World War in 1939 which "rebadged" the Great War as "The First World War" class structures were, moreover, as rigid as they had been for the previous 50 years and wages for most people were very low. You were either lower or working class, middle class or upper class. The upper class comprised professionals of whatever kind (doctors, lawyers, scientists, etc.), wealthy industrialists and merchants, intellectuals of differing persuasions, including academics, and what one might describe as "The Establishment". Within the Establishment one would find the aristocracy, the military and the Anglican clergy.

There was still a lot of poverty, injustice and hypocrisy in our much-vaunted democratic society. Everyone was expected to know their place and the Church, of whichever strand of Christianity, exerted considerable influence over our moral and social attitudes. In terms of health and well-being, medicines and medical treatment, including dental treatment, were available but only, for the most part, if one had taken out an "approved" insurance policy with the Cooperative Wholesale Insurance Society, the Liverpool Victoria Insurance Company or similar to cover the potential cost, or could afford to pay for them out of one's own pocket.

Nevertheless, patriotism was strong despite the fact that the Oxford Union Society on 9 February 1933 voted in favour of the motion that "it would under no circumstances fight for its King and Country" and politicians were, by and large, respected. We still had an Empire and the United Kingdom, as a nation, was admired throughout the world for the role it had played and the sacrifices it had made during the Great War.

Although unhealthy nineteenth century living conditions were gradually being replaced for many but not for all by council housing developments the concept of a period of leisure time for everyone had taken firm root. It was reflected in a growing range of entertainment and sporting activities.

Books and magazines which catered for all tastes had existed since Victorian times but there was now the immensely popular phenomenon of the Cinema with "talking pictures" in black and white and, towards the end of the decade, in colour also. Another exciting source of leisure and relaxation from the rigours of employment was the "wire-less" radio system, recently developed and operated under Royal Charter by the British Broadcasting Corporation, known by its initials, the BBC. It brought news, music and entertainment into one's home as if by magic. The system captured radio waves transmitted across the length and breadth of the country by the BBC thereby enabling one to listen to what was being broadcast by it. Nowadays we take radio for granted but in the 1930s it was exciting to be able to tune in and listen to the Home Service or the Light Programme and other radio stations on the continent of Europe. Television, (TV) was on the horizon in the 1930s although it was not really developed commercially until some time after the Second World War.

In addition to these ground-breaking innovations there were the pre-existing dance halls and ballrooms, the most famous of which was under the Blackpool Tower, West End and provincial theatres, venues offering everything from classical concerts to "Variety" shows, church socials where many young people including my parents found lifelong partners, circuses and fetes of all kinds. There were swimming pools within municipal baths which had also been built in the 1920s and 1930s in many towns, given the absence of bathrooms in so many homes, and for most working-class people there existed the exciting opportunity of being able to spend time, however brief, at the seaside.

In terms of sport, moreover, there was something for everyone whether it be watching or playing football (soccer, rugby union or rugby league), cricket and tennis. Nor should we forget the popularity of horse, greyhound and pigeon racing, playing darts, angling and visits to one of the many thousands of public houses in which these activities could be discussed in congenial surroundings over a pint or two.

These leisure activities of whatever kind acted as a sort of antidote to the low wages and onerous working conditions endured five or six days a week by most working class and many middle-class people and were consequently extremely popular.

On a national level Fred Perry, adored by the general public but disliked by many members of the upper class, had restored our international reputation in lawn tennis, our cricketers appeared to have the measure of pretty well everyone who played the game apart from Don Bradman, the Australian batsman, and our footballers were considered the best in the world on home turf. This somewhat complacent assumption persisted through the pre and immediate post-Second World War years until the "Galloping Major" Ferenc Puskas, and his Hungarian team, nicknamed the "mighty Magyars," shattered it in 1953 by beating England at Wembley. But that prospect was unthinkable in the 1930s and 1940s!

In terms of technical excellence and engineering we were, for example, holders of the Schneider Trophy for the fastest seaplane ever (the precursor to the Spitfire), our Rolls-Royce and Bentley cars were acknowledged to be the best in the world and great strides were being taken to bring low-cost family cars to the middle-class market. For example, a recently introduced and popular model, the Ford Eight, manufactured at its Dagenham plant in 1939, cost only £115.

The upper class, apart from the lower echelons of the Church of England and of the Armed Services, already possessed the more expensive models and during the late 1930s owning a car, however inexpensive, became a potent status symbol for any aspiring person or family in the lower levels of society. The working class had to get by for the most part, with motor bikes and sidecars but the desire to acquire something more prestigious never left them.

By the end of 1937 many young middle-class couples, like my parents, could, for the first time, contemplate the purchase of their own freehold house. The economy of the country was in reasonably good shape boosted as it was by the production of defensive armaments as a precautionary measure on the part of the Government against the threat of war and a possible invasion by Germany, following Hitler's bold annexation of Austria, the Saar, the Rhineland and Czechoslovakia.

Given the improving nature of the nation's finances, the increasing opportunities for leisure and gainful employment and the growth in civic pride evidenced by the laying out of parks and the construction of public buildings more people were feeling, despite the threat of war, that life offered much better prospects for themselves and their families than it had in the preceding two decades of the twentieth century.

This sense of optimism was abruptly brought to an end on 3 September 1939.

3
A Visit to a Lyons Corner House

Although living conditions were basic for most people throughout the 1930s and wages remained low there was one outstanding experience that many people, whether rich or poor, could enjoy. It was a visit to a Lyons Corner House or Tea Room.

They were a "cross" between a restaurant and somewhere for a cup of the nation's favourite beverage and a piece of cake and had steadily been growing in popularity since the 1920s. By 1939 there were over 200 Tea Rooms, for the most part in London and the Home Counties, but also in places like Cambridge and major northern cities,

There were three very impressive Corner Houses in Central London, tastefully decorated in the Art Deco style. The best known was in Coventry Street, close to theatreland, and it was to this Corner House that my impecunious nineteen-year-old father took my eighteen-year-old mother whom he had met at a church social early in 1930.

These "flagship" Corner Houses had multiple floors: each had a delicatessen on the ground floor selling, among other things, sweets, chocolates, cakes, fruit, and flowers, also a ladies hairdressing salon. On the upper floors there were restaurants with musicians in each one playing the popular tunes of the day.

The Corner House in Coventry Street, in particular, could seat 2000 people at any one time with 400 hundred staff serving over 5000 covers daily. Like the two other "flagship" Corner Houses and all the Tea Rooms it offered good quality food at reasonable prices. It catered for the lunch time needs of the massive number of daytime office workers in the vicinity, also for meetings of all kinds during the day and for those going to the theatre at night.

For one shilling and six pence (7 1/2p) my father told me that he and my mother had a pot of tea for two and two delicious pieces of cake before heading off on their first outing to a cinema in the West End.

But Lyons Corner Houses and Tea Rooms had not only a "classy" atmosphere with which to impress one's prospective partner: they had another major attraction. They had waitresses called "Nippies". These young women were chosen for their pleasant appearance and personalities and you can imagine what young men in London and elsewhere thought about that! The Nippies had a very smart and distinctive uniform. They wore black alpaca dresses with a double row of pearl buttons down the centre to a white square apron at dropped waist level with white cuffs and collars and white starched caps, with a black headband, similar to the headbands worn by maids in the houses that could still afford to employ them.

Suffice to say that of the 7,600 Nippies employed at any one time in the Corner Houses and Tea Rooms between 800 to 900 each year married young men who came in for pots of tea or similar in the hope of finding an attractive partner with a pleasant appearance and personality! In fact, Lyons themselves claimed that the marriage rate was higher among Nippies than any other class of working girl.

For lower and middle-class people a visit to a flagship Corner House was like stepping into a different world. It brought a touch of glamour and "high living" within their reach. It was an experience not to be missed as it nearly was by my parents. My father apparently arrived early and stood at the Shaftesbury Avenue end of Coventry Street while my mother, as eager as himself, also arrived early and stood at the Piccadilly Circus end.

My mother who was of a somewhat fiery disposition, was becoming distinctly irate when, after forty minutes, he had not appeared as arranged and was about to depart. Fortunately, my father had the good sense to walk to the Piccadilly Circus end of the street and found her. Once they had met all was well, but had he not done so I might conceivably not have existed.

This incident was recounted to me on a number of occasions during my childhood. I was told by my mother how lucky he was not to lose her but who was standing at the wrong end of the street I never discovered. On the basis of the often repeated maxim that a woman is never wrong it was doubtless my father!

4
1936 – A Year of Change

It was on the sixth day of the second half of the decade that I was born. Quite a lot also happened in 1936! A fortnight after my birth King George V who had celebrated his Silver Jubilee at St. Paul's Cathedral on 6 May the previous year, died at Sandringham on 20 January 1936, aged 70.

Referring back for a moment to the King's Silver Jubilee it is interesting to note some predictions for the 25 years to 1960 in the Daily Mirror, the newspaper which claimed "the largest net sale in Great Britain" at the time.

Sir Robert Hadfield, a famous scientist and engineer, said: "I think the next twenty-five years will see a wonderful development of the League of Nations from whose work the world should greatly benefit. It seems to provide the way out of this present situation of doubts, difficulty and suspicion between the nations of the world."

Lady Houston, speaking for the Establishment stated: "during the next twenty-five years England might easily be swamped and blotted out and become an annexe of Russia, if things continue as they are going on now." One can almost hear her patrician accent!

C.R. Nevinson, a well-known artist and intellectual, felt that the best thing to do was to transfer the seat of government from England to Canada, "Only this way will this country – the only decent country left – be able to keep clear of petty racial antagonisms. I feel that, if the heart of Empire were to be removed from the British Isles, the other European nations would go off the boil." How deluded that man was!

These strands of thought and opinion were subsequently crystalised in the abject failure of the League of Nations to maintain peace, and the setting up of the United Nations after the Second World War, the anti-Communist sentiment which neutralised any serious pretensions the Communist Party might have had to political representation in the Parliament of the United Kingdom and the refusal of King George VI and his consort, Queen Elizabeth, to move from England with their children to Canada at the beginning of the Second World War.

Within a day of the death of George V, the 42-year-old Prince Edward was proclaimed "King Emperor" (Rex Imperator). He was the first bachelor monarch to ascend the throne although Queen Victoria was not married until two years after her Coronation.

"While we lament the passing of a great King" declared the Daily Mirror "our grief is tempered by the knowledge that this brave and popular son will preside over the destiny of the Empire. He takes the sceptre with the united love and confidence of his people."

It is not too difficult, therefore, to understand the shock everyone felt when a monarch who had made a rousing speech on the radio on 1 March, promising "to continue to promote the well-being of his fellow men" abdicated in favour of a relationship with an American divorcee on 10 December, some nine months later.

During the year Adolf Hitler marched his troops into the demilitarised Rhineland, a significant portent of things to come. He declared that it was "impossible to keep an honest and brave people forever as slaves", a way of living he imposed upon the rest of Europe when he enslaved most of it a few short years later.

The RMS Queen Mary, a magnificent cross Atlantic liner upon which my uncle John served as an anti-aircraft gunner during the War sailed on her maiden voyage on 27 May and won the Blue Riband for the fastest ship across the Atlantic, in August, Jesse Owens, the black American athlete, broke the existing world records for the 220 yards, the 220 yards hurdles and the long jump, much to the annoyance of Adolf Hitler, at the Berlin Olympics, and the Crystal Palace, a really impressive glass structure built on the outskirts of London to house the Great Exhibition of 1851 burned down. The loss of this magnificent landmark affected Londoners deeply at the time. A football club has been named after it but that is all we have to remind us of its former existence.

Civil war raged in Spain throughout the year, the Italians were busy invading Abyssinia whose Emperor was Hailie Selassie, Mrs Beryl Markham, the pioneering Aviatrix and explorer, was the first solo woman pilot to fly the Atlantic from Britain to the United States and Squadron Leader (later Air Commodore) Ronald Swain beat the altitude record by flying a monoplane in a specially adapted flying suit which nearly killed him, to a height of 49,967 feet.

The first Imperial Airways Empire flying boat with an incredible, at the time, range of three thousand miles, the precursor to the RAF Short Sunderland flying boat, made its initial appearance and last, but by no means least, Arsenal won the F.A. Cup, courtesy of the legendary Ted Drake, beating Sheffield United 1-0.

It is only by looking at 1936 in the round that one can obtain a flavour of the national mood at the time. It was one of adventure, innovation and hope for a better future. The threat posed by National Socialism in Germany and Italy was apparent but the likelihood, at the time, of another war was not yet serious enough to cause real concern. The mood changed perceptibly as we got closer to 1939 and conflict with Germany became more likely.

5
Our Genes

As previously stated we are all the product of our genetic imprint. Characteristics that we often believe are personal to ourselves in terms of habits, likes and dislikes, and reactions to the situations we encounter in life, are in fact, usually hereditary. They have been lodged inside us from birth and have been passed on to us by previous generations.

These inherited characteristics are, of course, no more an excuse for bad behaviour than they are a reason for good. We all possess a "moral compass" irrespective of them and an understanding of what is right and wrong.

We readily accept physical and facial similarities brought about by our parentage and it should not be surprising that the imprint goes deeper than that. On a superficial level Winston Churchill is famous for saying "all babies look like me" but most parents, of whatever race and colour, spend time on working out which of their own facial characteristics are reflected in their infant offspring at birth. Later on, they tend to attribute the worst behavioural aspects of their children to their spouses but that is another story.

I had no idea about my genetic imprint until I had a mitochondrial DNA test in my seventies. By this time it was far too late to determine which parental line was responsible for my behaviour as a child and I would not wish to lay it at the door of either. The test revealed my maternal and paternal genetic history.

On my mother's side it would appear that her "reference sequence" indicated an unbroken family line for well over a thousand years. This is not, apparently, unusual because the maternal reference sequence does not change a great deal. It remains constant for generations.

Her genes were classified as predominantly Celt which is a bit of a misnomer, with an element of Anglo Saxon and Viking. I say "misnomer because "Celt" is the designation given to the native bronze age population of England prior to the Saxon and Norman invasions.

During the Ice Age huge glaciers covered vast areas of Europe and, as a result, the sea was one hundred metres lower than it is today. Magdalenian Tribes from Europe could walk across land now covered by the waters of the English Channel during the summer months to the Southern parts of the country and return to what is now the south of France before the harsh winters made Britain completely uninhabitable once again.

Once back in the south of France, after travelling such a long distance on foot, they would spend the winter in rock caves like those close to the River Dordogne before returning again to the north in the Spring. Their motivation for travelling such immense distances was doubtless the existence of wild animals, like reindeer, which could survive the colder winter temperatures and which they could hunt for food. As the ice gradually receded and the Magdalenians disappeared with it they were replaced by Neolithic tribes who ventured and stayed further north: some settled in Britain, becoming the native population.

These settlers are sometimes referred to as "Beaker" people because their culture was similar to that of tribes in the Middle East and it is more than likely that some 20,000 years ago there was a migration of people from the Middle East to Southern Europe. We tend to refer to these people generically as Celts and now associate them with Wales, Scotland, Ireland and Brittany in France but the entire native population of Southern Europe stemmed, in the dim and distant past, from the same racial origins.

One might well ask why the Roman invasion and occupation of Britain for nearly four hundred years has left no discernible genetic markers. The answer could be one of two reasons. The first is that the native population of Italy was very much the same as that of the rest of Southern Europe. The second is that the Romans, very much like the British during the Raj and the Normans, during the first three centuries of their occupation of England and Wales kept themselves to themselves.

My father's paternal DNA was similarly predominantly Celt with traces of Anglo Saxon and Viking ancestry. His maternal DNA, however, had a Norman element which I have researched and which I will refer to in a later chapter.

6
My Father: His Early Years

My father, Alfred Robert Hughes, whom I loved and admired was born on 20 August 1911. He was born at a time when motor cars had not completely supplanted horses as a means of transport and aviation was in its infancy: in fact, it was only three weeks after his birth, on 9 September, that the first UK aerial post was flown the 26 miles from London Hendon airport to the Postmaster-General's Office at Windsor Castle by Gustav Hamel in a Bleriot monoplane.

His parents and their rapidly growing family lived at the time at 53 Gordon Road, Wanstead which is now close to Eastern Avenue, Ilford. My grandfather, William Owen Hughes, a qualified company secretary, must have been of comfortable means because Wanstead, then in Essex, was a popular residential area for well-paid, middle-class, workers in the City of London less than ten miles away.

The town lay on a ridge between the Rivers Lee and Roding and was close to Woodford and to Epping Forest: it had quick and easy access to London and was pleasantly rural. The rural nature of Wanstead and neighbouring Woodford was to change dramatically after the First World War. Massive urbanisation took place between 1918 and 1939. As a result, the urban districts of Wanstead and Woodford were amalgamated in 1934 to become a borough in 1937. The borough was subsequently merged into the London borough of Redbridge.

From its inception the borough of Wanstead and Woodford was staunchly Conservative and the Woodford parliamentary constituency was for some years represented by Winston Churchill after the crushing defeat of his Government in the 1945 General Election.

My grandparents continued to produce more children than could be accommodated at their home in Wanstead and moved before my father was five years old to Leigh-on- Sea. My father was the sixth of nine children. He had an older brother, William Owen George Hughes, presumably to differentiate him from his father, and grandfather, a younger brother, Bernard, and six sisters, Ada, Edith, Eva, Alice, Marjorie and Joan, five of whom survived into adulthood. The sixth, Edith, would also have survived had she not been trapped on her bicycle between two tramcars on the seafront at Southend-on-Sea. Although not physically injured she was so traumatised by the incident that she developed diabetes and died, sadly, at the age of 20 in 1918.

My father was baptised on 8 October 1911 at the Wanstead Congregational Church. This came as a surprise because I had always thought of him as a lifelong member of the Church of England, but it did explain an aspect of his ancestry which had previously puzzled me. Records show that his father and grandfather were Wesleyans.

It is clear, however, that his move to the larger family home in Leigh on Sea and his desire to emulate the upper-class people with whom he associated in the City of London led my grandfather to abandon his Wesleyan roots and transfer his allegiance to the Church of England. He began to worship at St. Clement's Church in Leigh-on-Sea and purchased burial plots for his family in its churchyard. Paradoxically, my father would not have met my mother if his father had remained a member of the Congregational Church and had he not deserted it in his desire for upward social mobility.

By the time he was five my father was at Leigh North Infants School. He moved on to Leigh North Boys School and, at the age of 12, secured a place at Westcliff High School for Boys. He left the High School just before his 16th birthday in 1927 and it would appear that my grandfather was not prepared, and probably financially unable to pay for his further education.

According to his final school report he does not appear to have concentrated overmuch on his classwork during his final year. My father told me that not only had his father been unwilling or unable to pay for further education he had also been unwilling to buy him white shirts or a school tie or blazer throughout the four years he was at the school. My father had to wear his Scout jersey at all times which earned him the nickname of "cabbage". This could not have helped his sense of self-respect, and he was probably relieved to be able to leave school to look for employment, and earn sufficient to buy some decent clothes.

Nevertheless, my father achieved his General School Certificate with passes in English language and literature, French, German, mathematics and science with credits in German, which he enjoyed a lot, and arithmetic, and a distinction in mathematics. Although he was not robust enough to play contact sports at school, he nevertheless enjoyed swimming long distances and was awarded a number of certificates for doing so. In the words of his headmaster in his final report he was "regular and punctual in attendance, a quiet and reliable boy whose conduct throughout has been excellent."

In terms of social and leisure activities he was a regular attender at St. Clement's Church and a keen Boy Scout. He had joined the local Scout group in 1922 at the age of 11 and went regularly to camps where he paraded with other Scouts in his Baden-Powell hat, very much the same as the hat now worn by the Royal Canadian Mounted Police, the RCMP, and with a wooden staff or stave which was presumably a substitute for the rifles issued to adult members of the armed services.

Robert Baden-Powell (later Lord Baden-Powell) was an inspirational figure to many young boys like my father. As a junior army officer in India in the 1870s he had specialised in scouting, map-making and reconnaissance. He had set up small units or patrols which worked under a single leader and he had made sure there was special recognition for those who did well. He awarded them proficiency badges, a forerunner of those he later introduced into the Scouting movement.

As a result of the skills he had acquired and his natural aptitude for living and surviving in the open Baden-Powell had published a small handbook for the soldiers under his command: it was entitled "Aids for Scouting". The handbook may never again have seen the light of day but for the outcome of the siege of Mafeking.

Baden-Powell, by now a Lieutenant General, had been posted to South Africa at the beginning of the Second Boer War in 1899 and shortly thereafter found himself in charge of a small British garrison defending the besieged town against some 5000 Boers.

Although vastly outnumbered he managed to give the Boers the impression that the town was more heavily defended than it actually was, and held out against them for seven months until a relief column arrived and lifted the siege on 16 May 1900. He had used the youth in the town to good effect as observers of the Boers and as message carriers from his command post to the soldiers under his command.

Baden-Powell returned to England a couple of years later a national hero and his handbook attracted the attention of youth leaders all over the country.

As a result of the interest generated by the handbook in scouting and looking after oneself in the open Baden-Powell undertook to produce a handbook that not only instilled in young boys the concepts of patriotism and loyalty to the Crown but also gave them a sense of adventure and a desire to participate in outdoor activities of all kinds. An experimental camp was set up on Brownsea Island, off the coast of Dorset, in 1907 and proved a great success. Shortly thereafter "Scouting for Boys" was published and the rest, as they say, is history. The Scout Association was formed and Scouting took off in a big way, not only in England but across the world.

The point of my mention of scouting is that my father acquired, during the many Scout Camps he attended, the skills of putting up tents, cooking meals on primus stoves and living in the open that proved of great value to us, his family, on camping holidays in later years.

7
My Father: Early Working Life

Leaving school at just under 16 years of age and finding a job in 1927 was not going to be easy but my father asked the Rector of St. Clement's Church for a character reference and it read as follows:

"I have much pleasure in giving my testimony to the very excellent character of Alfred Hughes. I have known him intimately for some seven years or so and, during the whole of this period, he has been in close touch with me both as a member of my choir, a communicant and also as a Scout.

I have never known him to be anything other than strictly honest, truthful and straightforward. He is 16 years of age but well advanced emotionally. The boy has a good future before him."

It is a pity that the word "intimately" has gained a suspect connotation where priests and young boys are concerned but, in 1927, it meant "very well" and I am sure it was meant to convey that to the reader of the glowing reference.

As a result of the reference and a satisfactory interview my father was appointed in September 1927 to a junior clerkship vacant at the time in the office of the borough accountant of Southend on Sea borough council at a salary of £40 per annum, just under 16 shillings per week (80p per week in decimal money) rising by annual increments of seven pounds ten shillings (£7.50) to a maximum of £65 per annum. I am no mathematician but four annual increments of £7 pounds 10 shillings gives a final figure of £70, not £65.

The council would pay the cost of a fidelity bond which protected the council from any dishonesty on the part of an employee and which was quite normal in those days and, within his salary, he would receive two weeks' paid holiday each year. The concept of an employee actually being paid when taking a holiday had been introduced during the late Victorian era. Paid holidays are taken for granted nowadays but they were not taken for granted then. Even allowing for wage inflation one can only wonder at the salaries young people received in the 1920s. But in 1927 this poorly paid clerkship did at least represent employment, the first step on the career ladder for a 16-year-old.

Fate was now to play a hand. As I will explain in a later chapter, his father ran out of money by the end of 1928 and was forced to apply to Dagenham borough council for a council house. My father, who had lived with his parents, had no option but to move with them and give up his job in Southend. Nevertheless, he used his initiative and secured employment as clerk and typist to the headmaster of the Ilford County High School for boys. It was the move of his family to Parsloes Avenue in Dagenham that led indirectly to his first meeting with my mother.

Although he enjoyed working at the school he knew he had to find himself a long-term career and applied successfully for a post in the general and legal department of Dagenham urban district council. The headmaster had clearly been impressed with him and in a reference dated 10 March 1930 he wrote as follows:

"Mr A.R. Hughes has been my clerk and typist since January 1929. He has been extremely helpful to me. He is regular and punctual, interested in his work and extremely pleasant to deal with. The work in a Headmaster's Office is varied and confidential. He quickly picked up the essentials of his duty and appears to have treated matters within his ken with the greatest discretion. His personal character leaves nothing to be desired."

The headmaster followed this with a second reference on the school's notepaper shortly after my father joined the council in which he stated: "Mr A.R. Hughes was Headmaster's Clerk at Ilford County High School from January 1929 until May 1930. While he was with me his devotion to duty left nothing to be desired. He spared no pains in his efforts, his very successful efforts, to be of assistance to me and I am very sorry to lose him. I recommend him warmly as I have always found him honourable and reliable, Alfred Diggens, B.A. LLB."

I quote these references because they do rather sum up my father and his attitude to work, his reliability and integrity. But he had many other qualities and I will mention them later.

When he obtained employment at Dagenham urban district council the council and the district were expanding rapidly. In fact, its development was unequalled in Britain at the time. The population of Dagenham increased tenfold in ten years. In 1919 the London County Council whose population was bursting at the seams took powers to buy 3,000 acres of land in Essex which, from the name of a former hamlet in the area, became known as "the Becontree Estate".

In a "Garden City setting", circular in shape, the six years between 1919 and 1925 saw the erection of 25,000 houses of 85 different types "modestly but effectively comfortable together with all the public buildings, open spaces and communications which twentieth century life requires."

More than 100,000 Londoners many of whom lived in run-down properties in Stratford and the east end of London, attracted by this forward-looking development, found a new life there. In 1891 the population of Dagenham had been 4,324 people but by 1931 it had soared to 89,365. It was expected in 1931 to have reached 150,000 by 1940.

The attraction of employment with Dagenham council must have been a powerful one. My father would be working for a dynamic urban district council, which was expanding rapidly and at the forefront of new town design. There was also the prospect of being able to exchange his bedroom in his parent's home for a brand-new council house should he marry while working for the council.

Although it is unlikely that this was a material consideration when he obtained employment with the council in May 1930, its proximity to his parents' home probably being the most important factor, there is no doubt that he had met my mother some five months earlier and that they appear to have fallen in love instantaneously. They had met at a social event in the temporary building that housed St. Martin's church, Goresbrook Road, Dagenham at the time.

My mother attended St. Martin's because her father, John Somers, my grandfather, was a member of the parochial church council and a sidesman. My father probably found his way there because of its proximity to his home. Within weeks of attending his first Sunday service he had joined the choir and shortly thereafter was appointed an assistant Scoutmaster, thereby maintaining his interest in and commitment to Scouting.

A newly built church replacing the temporary building was consecrated on 23 January 1932 and it would appear that my parents became "leading lights" among the younger members of the congregation, organising youth pageants and similar. They both spoke very warmly of the Rev. Ashley Turner, the first vicar, whom they liked a great deal and who christened me on Easter Sunday, 1936.

With the encouragement of my mother to whom he was now engaged my father joined the National Association of Local Government Officers (NALGO) and attended a summer school in July 1932 at Selwyn College, Cambridge. The summer school was opened by the inspirational Sir Edward Hilton Young (later Baron Kennett), the Minister of Health, and included visits to the colleges and a social gathering in the Guildhall. My father was so impressed by the university that he constantly urged me during my childhood to go there as an undergraduate if I possibly could.

When he was at the summer school he could not resist the temptation to go for an early morning swim in the Cam, much to the annoyance of the anglers! In a letter to my mother mentioning this he also told her that the only thing he found disconcerting at the college was the way the waiters in the dining hall hovered behind him, eager to snatch away his plate immediately he finished each course. He commented on the rather superior attitude of the senior members of the university and the humble nature of the waiters and other menial employees. I have to admit that I noticed something similar when I was at Cambridge, although not among the undergraduates. In July 1932 they would have been on their summer vacation as we were in the 1950s. He went on to take and pass a NALGO qualifying examination in local government, thanks, undoubtedly, to the encouragement given to him by my mother.

My parents were married at St. Martin's church on 22 September

1934, four days after my father, as an employee of the council, had entered into a tenancy of 43 Warrington Road, just off Green Lane, and not far from Chadwell Heath station. My mother and father appreciated that they would have to relinquish their tenancy when my father left the council and that if they were to have any flexibility in where they lived and where my father worked in future, they would have to save hard and buy, rather than rent, their own home.

Three years later they had saved enough, and it was time to move on. My father successfully applied for the post of general and legal assistant at Hornchurch urban district council. Whereas Dagenham consisted for the most part of council-owned property, houses in Hornchurch, not more than five miles away, were predominantly private and freehold. With a great sense of pride and achievement they moved into a newly-built three-bedroomed semi-detached house, 46 Alma Avenue, on 29 September 1937. My paternal grandfather meanwhile had purchased a newly built bungalow in the same road only a few months earlier.

Although my parents wanted to live as close to their respective families as possible and although the prospect of a German invasion of Britain itself was not seriously contemplated by politicians and the general public it had become increasingly apparent to my father by early 1939 that living in a house so close to an RAF fighter base was not a good idea. In the event of an "all-out" war with Herr Hitler the aerodrome and the area around it might well be bombed as London had been bombed indiscriminately by Gotha bombers and Zeppelins during the Great War. The German dictator had already demonstrated how little care or respect he had for civilian life during the Civil War in Spain where he had aligned himself and his mighty air force, the Luftwaffe, with General Franco.

My father therefore contacted one of his colleagues from his Dagenham council days, a John Rook, who had become head of the legal department at Kettering borough council in Northamptonshire and, through his good offices, joined him as a legal and general clerk on 1 June 1939.

By this time, thanks to my mother's remarkable talent for spending my father's limited income in the most cost-efficient manner, my parents had saved enough to be able to acquire a second-hand Morris Minor, KV8557, which subsequently served the family faithfully for many years.

I do not think my father minded handing supervision of the family finances to her: he appreciated her ability to make the most of what he earned, and she kept accurate, neatly written, records of every penny spent. For him it was almost like being married to a full-time accountant! She was very capable where money was concerned, and he left her to deal with money matters while he concentrated on his work and his career.

8
My Paternal Grandfather

To me, as a child, my paternal grandfather, William Owen Hughes, was a distant, disapproving and somewhat austere figure. Although my parents were living in the same road as my grandparents between September 1937 and June 1939 he never once, to my recollection, visited them at our home. In fact, I can only recall meeting him and my grandmother once, just before we left for Kettering, and him once thereafter at the Diamond Stores in Hainault.

According to my father he only had time for two of his children, his daughter Ada who ran off and married John (Jock) Moore and his son, Billy (William Owen George Hughes) who was born in 1903 and who died of abscesses on the lungs at the age of thirty after working in a Missionary bookshop in Dar es Salaam. Ada fell out of favour with him until she and Jock produced Dudley whose meteoric career as a musician, comedian and Hollywood actor is well documented. I will mention him later in this chapter.

My grandfather's other children were not particularly well regarded or looked after by him. The children, for example, had to share one swimming costume between them, although they were of different ages, sexes and sizes, when they wanted to go for a swim from the small beach at Leigh-on-Sea where the family lived until the early 1920s. Fortunately, it was a one piece garment which could be worn by boys and girls alike. My grandfather appeared to expect affection from his children but offered little in return.

As for his character he was entrepreneurial, ambitious, pretentious and insofar as he wrote and self-published in later life books on such subjects as "Self Healing by Divine Providence" and similar (in the back of which he advertised correspondence courses) appeared content to prey very much on the hopes and fears of a small but vulnerable section of the general public. I could see that his spiritualist books might have had appeal to elderly widows and people with diseases or conditions for which, at the time there was no known cure or treatment, but they really imparted little of significance or merit to their readers.

To me he appeared, in the words of Joseph Addison, the 18th century editor of *The Spectator*, rather like "the mountebank who sold pills which (as he told the country people) were very good against an earthquake". My cousin Richard who lived with my grandfather until he died told me that on his death he, and his mother Eva, one of my aunts, dug a six foot hole in the garden and buried a great stack of them. "That", declared my aunt, "is where the family's former fortune is being laid to rest." And to the extent that he had any remaining wealth after a turbulent financial career, she was probably right.

His background, however, appears to have been much more interesting. Family tradition has it that his ancestors lived in Llangedwyn in North Wales and that his great grandmother, one of the daughters of the mill owner there, had gone to work as a lady's maid at Llangedwyn Hall, the home of Sir Watkin Williams Wynn: the mill was virtually opposite the Hall and I suspect that she and her parents wanted her to learn more about the gracious style of living of the aristocracy in such a splendid household.

Be that as it may she must have been an attractive young woman because it was not long before Sir Watkin "had his way with her". When she told him she was pregnant he paid her to leave Llangedwyn and live elsewhere on the understanding that he would offer her financial support, in the form of an allowance until she died, provided she never returned to Langedwyn. It was, apparently, quite a common arrangement among members of the aristocracy who made their female servants pregnant.

She went to Liverpool where her baby son was born. She called him William Hughes, so far as I can ascertain from research carried out subsequent to my first book. Her son, William Hughes, moved south from Liverpool when he was old enough to do so and subsequent male heirs were named William Owen Hughes. They became boilermakers for the then revolutionary steam powered ships being manufactured in the dockyards near the city of London. Boiler making was probably a reasonably well-paid occupation at the time demanding, as it did, an advanced level of mechanical skills.

My grandfather was a draper's assistant when he married in 1900 according to his marriage certificate but, being ambitious, studied hard and managed to qualify as a Company Secretary. Thereafter he became the Company Secretary of the Anglo Baku Oilfield Corporation which exploited the production of oil from wells in the area of Russia close to the Caspian Sea.

There were a number of eminent aristocrats with influence on the Board of the Company and my grandfather became quite wealthy: it was during his spell as Company Secretary that he moved to Leigh-on-Sea, became a member of the Church of England and, in a fit of breathtaking "hubris", bought a Victorian "mock castle" believed to be Tadershad Castle near Bangor in North Wales and approached the College of Arms for a family crest. At this point, however investigation of his lineage revealed that his grandfather had been conceived "on the wrong side of the sheets". The Castle was sold to an American during the Great War at a substantial profit, the family crest which had actually been commissioned and produced, was consigned to an attic cupboard and his grandiose projects were quietly shelved.

Unfortunately, the Bolsheviks and the Soviets after them did not approve of the foreign control of one of their country's most important resources and took over the Baku Oilfields leading to the collapse of the Company. In the early 1920s the Russian Revolutionary Government gave my grandfather and the other shareholders in the Company Bonds to the value of their respective shareholdings but the Bonds were never redeemed and when, as a small child, I visited my grandfather at his home in Hornchurch I can just recall seeing a pile of splendidly ornate Bond Certificates in the bottom drawer of his writing desk. Being an inquisitive three-and-a-half-year-old I had started to open all the drawers, much to his annoyance. I have noticed my own grandchildren doing exactly the same and I admit it can be nerve wracking!

On the loss of his position as Company Secretary he had moved his family from Leigh-on-Sea and used the bulk of his remaining financial resources to purchase two large houses in Canewdon Road in Westcliff-on-Sea. One was intended to accommodate his family, the other to provide an income from holidaymakers spending time in the area. The 1920s, however, were not a good time economically for the owners of boarding houses in Westcliff and Southend-on-Sea. Times were hard and the depression of the late twenties dug deep into the pockets of those who might otherwise have been able to afford a few days by the seaside. With no income from guests and with bankruptcy looming he was forced to sell both properties, pay off his creditors and apply, cap in hand, to Dagenham Council for a house in which he and his family could be accommodated. He and my grandmother still had a number of children, including my father, living with them at the time.

But he was nothing if not resourceful and shortly after my parents married, he rented a property in Aldeburgh Road in Upminster and moved out of Dagenham. In 1937 as previously indicated he purchased a freehold bungalow in Alma Avenue, Hornchurch where he lived with my grandmother until she died of cardiac asthma in 1940.

He remained an entrepreneur for the rest of his life and in 1947 he sold the bungalow in Alma Avenue and purchased shop premises, the Diamond Stores, in Hainault which had a spacious first floor flat. There was a derelict bomb site next door when he moved in and, being astute, made enquiries as to its ownership. Since the former owners and members of their family could not be traced he fenced the site, incorporated it into his own garden and applied for a Possessory Title at the Land Registry.

He was joined at the store by Eva, one of his daughters whose husband George had died tragically during the war by falling out of the back of an Army lorry in Cairo, and by her son, his grandson Richard. It was Eva who helped him run the store, thereby providing them both with an income and a home for Richard, who as previously stated, assisted in the burial of his books when he died.

The whereabouts of the family crest are unknown but cousin Richard can recall, before he emigrated to New Zealand, that grandfather Hughes had kept it in an upstairs cupboard at his flat in Hainault as a reminder of what might have been!

Although when I was born, our parents lived in Council houses less than a mile apart, I do not recall seeing my cousin, Dudley, in my early years. After the War, however, on our return from Kettering to Essex my father made a point of taking us round to see his older sister, Ada of whom he was very fond.

Dudley's precocious musical talent had been obvious from the moment he could put his infant hands on a piano keyboard and "auntie Ada", who was quite musical herself, would insist on poor Dudley playing something for "uncle Alfred and auntie Gertie". I can vividly recall the reluctant and embarrassed look on the face of the teenage Dudley as he was obliged to play part of a Chopin prelude or similar, quite beautifully on the family piano. Performing for relatives on behalf of his doting parents was clearly not an experience he enjoyed!

Although it is not well known he was born with a club foot and from, infancy in 1935, had a number of operations on it which his parents undoubtedly found it difficult to afford prior to the setting up of the National Health Service in 1948.

I do not know whether this disability, his innate talent or the taunts of other children at his school, spurred him to outperform them, but in the early 1950s he won an Organ Scholarship to Magdalen College, Oxford. I am aware that his school, the Dagenham County High School, gave every child in the school a day's holiday to mark his achievement.

9
My Paternal Grandmother

Although my paternal grandfather's ancestry might be open to question my paternal grandmother appears to have had the most extraordinary lineage, all conceived "on the right side of the sheets" and traceable back to 980AD. I only found out about it in my late seventies when Dudley Moore's niece, my second cousin, presented me with an authenticated copy of it, going back as far as 1123AD. I did some further research and took the genealogy back to 980AD. After studying various sources, I concluded that I had gone off course in tracing lineage between 1040AD and 980AD but I am now reasonably satisfied that I have located the correct ancestors for that period.

My paternal grandmother's name was Ratford and by tracing her maternal line through the Ames, Deex, Stanton and Cardinall families my second cousin arrived at the Knightleys. Lettice Knightley had married a William Cardinall in the sixteenth century. She was the great granddaughter of Richard Knightley who died in 1442AD. Her name might strike us as odd nowadays but it was popular in Tudor times and was derived from "Laetitia", the Latin word for "joy" or "happiness". By way of further example, the name of the mother of Robert Devereux, the second Earl of Essex, a favourite courtier of Queen Elizabeth I until he joined a conspiracy against her and literally lost his head, was also Lettice.

Richard Knightley's father whose name was also Richard and who lived at Gnosall in Staffordshire was married to Joan Giffard, the daughter of Sir John Giffard of Chillingham Hall, Codsall Wood, near Wolverhampton, not many miles away. It would appear that, like the Romans, the Normans kept themselves aloof and apart from the native Celtic and Anglo Saxon populations. Both families had Norman forebears. There would have been no love lost between the Normans and the people they enslaved and that is doubtless why Normans married Normans and why they built so many impregnable castles to defend themselves when they first arrived.

On the Knightley side of the family, the male line goes directly back in time from Richard Knightley, senior, to Nicholas Maucovenant de Knightley whose grandfather Rainauld de Baliol, the younger son of Baron Giudo de Baliol sailed with his two brothers, Hugh and Wydo, as part of William the Conqueror's invading army. Baron Guido had been born in 1012 AD at Bailleuil, not far from St. Omer in Picardy, as had his son in 1040 AD.

Shortly before the invasion Rainauld, the modern version of which is Reginald, had married Amilia, the niece of Seigneur, subsequently Earl Robert de Montgomery and it was as a result of the family connection that Rainauld was granted a subtenancy of considerable property including the hamlet of Chenistelei, also known as Knightley. Rainauld adopted Knightley as his family name instead of Baliol. The hamlet of Knightley still exists just outside Gnosall.

Rainauld's grandfather was Wydo de Baliol, born in 980AD, and there the trail goes cold. Some historians suggest a family link with an aristocratic lady by the name of Mabile (from which Mabel is derived) D'Alencon and the Kings of Creil. Suffice to say that, if the genealogy produced by my second cousin is accurate, I am quite content with a lineage that can be traced back to 980AD! Should the name Baliol ring any bells it is probably because Hugh de Baliol created a family dynasty a member of which, by way of penance for misdeeds, endowed a house for the maintenance of poor Scholars in Oxford in 1260.

With the aid of that endowment Balliol College was established in 1263: it would go on to house and nurture the formidable talents of an array of famous writers, economists and scientists including Adam Smith who wrote "The Wealth of Nations" and Lord Beveridge, an architect of social reform whose Report led to the creation of the Welfare State. In addition to five Nobel Laureates it has produced four Prime Ministers: Boris Johnson, Harold MacMillan, Ted Heath and Herbert Asquith and a host of other politicians including Dennis Healey, Roy Jenkins, Yvette Cooper and Chris Patten, the last Governor of Hong Kong. There must be "something in the water" at the College because well-known Balliol alumni can be found in virtually every area and in every decade of our society. In the current decade familiar names include TV presenters Robert Peston, Peter Snow and his son Dan Snow, the former Head of the Metropolitan Police, Dame Cressida Dick and Ghislaine Maxwell, the daughter of the late and infamous Robert Maxwell.

Rainauld had a number of children and one, his son Bernard, was granted lands near Durham, a pretty lawless area as far as the Normans were concerned. He therefore set about building his own "Bernard's" castle, now known as Barnard Castle. A member of his family, John Baliol, subsequently became King of Scotland for a short time.

If we then look at the Giffard family, we discover that Walter Gautier Giffard, the Seigneur of Longueville, close to Dieppe and son of Osborn de Balbec was a cousin of William, Duke of Normandy, and, like Baron Guido de Baliol, was one of William's close companions. He was not only a relative but one of Williams's trusted advisers and provided 30 ships for the invasion of England.

Although Walter was hereditary Standard Bearer to his cousin, William, and was offered the privilege of carrying the family standard into battle at Hastings he politely declined, saying that because of his age he needed both hands free to fight. He was subsequently granted the feudal Barony of Long Crendon in Oxfordshire with 107 Manorial incidents. His descendant, Peter Giffard, in all probability acquired Chillington Hall in a marriage settlement from a Peter Corbusson and decided to live there. It is as a result of that decision that Joan Giffard met and married Richard Knightley.

Sadly, my paternal grandmother, Ada, died in 1940 before I was old enough to get to know her.

10

My Mother

My mother, Gertrude Evelyn Hughes, formerly Somers, was never really happy with her Christian or forename but it happened to be her mother's name and there was a tendency before the first World War to give the first born the forename of his or her parent. Evidence of this can be found in the fact that the name of my paternal grandfather was William Owen Hughes, as also was his father.

My grandfather carried on the family tradition by naming his son William Owen George Hughes, presumably adding "George" to avoid the confusion that would otherwise have resulted at the beginning of the twentieth century when all three would have been alive. I escaped "William" but not "Owen" because both grandfathers wanted to contribute to my forenames, as also did my father. Mercifully they all conceded that, in addition to their names, I should have one of my own. By the time they had finished I had four first names, one English (John), one Scottish (Robert), one Welsh (Owen) and one Irish (Brian)! This made me distinctive at School and probably added to the generally held perception that I must be eccentric in some way.

The name of Gertrude, therefore, was completely acceptable and normal at the time it was bestowed on my mother. In fact it had peaked in popularity in 1906 when it achieved number twenty two spot in girl's names for that year. Gertrude was the name of a Goddess in Norse mythology, of the Patron Saint of Cats (believe it or not) and, of course, of the infamous Queen mother in "Hamlet". In old German the word meant "strength" or "spear" and the name probably appealed to my father with his enthusiasm for the German language though not, I have to say, for the Germans themselves. It's diminutive "Trudi" or "Trudy" became popular in its own right in later years.

Having done some research on the early years of her life I discovered that she was born on 2 April 1912 and baptised on 1st May 1912 at St. Columba's Church, Wanstead, in what is now known as Leytonstone. She was born less than a fortnight before the Titanic hit an iceberg and sank on 15 April and four days after the tragic death of Robert Falcon Scott, known as "Scott of the Antarctic", who with his four companions attempted to be the first ever to reach the South Pole on foot. News of their proposed attempt had attracted the attention of a Norwegian explorer, Roald Amundsen who decided he would compete for the crown of being the first to do so. He used dog sleds to carry his food and equipment for his attempt whereas Scott used ponies all of whom died. To the chagrin of Scott, Amundsen reached the South Pole five weeks before him and left a letter for Scott in a tent which marked the precise position of it.

On their arduous return to their base camp one of Scott's group lost his life in a tragic accident and after encountering unusually bad weather Scott and his three remaining companions were forced to pitch their tent in a blizzard only 11 miles from the "One Ton" food store containing the provisions that would have saved their lives. One of the group, Captain Lawrence "Titus" Oates, described thereafter as "a very gallant gentleman", being aware that the gangrene and frost bite from which he was suffering was slowing down his companions and compromising their chances of survival, chose self-sacrifice. He walked out of the tent, into the blizzard, saying "I am just going outside and may be some time". His companions died nevertheless in the tent. Captain Oates body was never found but he epitomised "the British stiff upper lip" for which we were known and famous. The story of Scott and Oates inspired me as an 11-year-old, as I will explain in a later chapter.

Given the middle-class nature of Wanstead at the time it is probable that John Somers, her father and my grandfather, also had a reasonably well-paid job before he was conscripted, at the age of 35 five, into the Royal Artillery in 1916. At the time of his conscription my mother had a younger sister and brother. The forcible loss of his employment and the meagre soldier's pay upon which she was expected to maintain herself and her three children obliged my grandmother to leave Wanstead and move in with her own mother. From a comparatively large and comfortable home in a semi-rural location she found herself and her young family living in her mother's terraced house in the much more densely populated Borough of East Ham.

In 1916 East Ham was by no means an unpleasant place to live, with its Central Park, Plashet Park and Royal Victoria Gardens. The Borough boasted an impressive Town Hall, a Magistrates Court and a Boys Grammar School. In later years it added a Technical College, a Central Library, a Fire Station and, like many other Boroughs, Municipal Baths. By 1939 its docks, the Royal Albert Dock and the George V dock, comprised, between them, the largest sheet of enclosed dock water in the world until the Nazis bombed and virtually destroyed them during the Blitz.

My mother, who was very bright, went initially to Brampton Road Junior Mixed School where she excelled: in her School Report for the half year ending on 31 March 1921, two days before her ninth birthday she gained 171 marks out of a maximum of 180 despite being absent on 29 occasions. In her subsequent Report for the half year ending 30 September 1921 she gained 133 marks out of 140 and came fourth in a class of 50 children. At the age of 10, she moved on to Brampton Road Girls School where according to her school report for the half year ending 31st March 1922 she gained 78 out of a maximum of 85 marks coming 12th in a class of 57 girls. It is interesting to note class sizes in each school at the time.

When her father was demobilised, he was unfortunately unable to return to his former occupation. Unemployment of soldiers returning from the Western front and other theatres of war was rife. Just days after the end of the war Lloyd George, the Prime Minister and hero of the hour, told a crowd outside the Grand Theatre in Wolverhampton "the work is not over yet. What is our task? To make Britain a fit country for heroes to live in. There are millions of men who will come back. Let us make this a land fit for such men to live in. Don't let us waste this victory merely in ringing joy bells".

The joy bells rang but, sadly, Lloyd George's bold vision of the creation of a land fit for heroes never came to fruition. His speech turned out to be nothing more than the characteristic rhetoric of so many politicians before and since. Years of low wages, poor housing conditions and unemployment for those returning heroes followed. In fact, the only employment my grandfather could find was that of a commercial traveller, a sack salesman for the company that produced them. The sacks were made of jute and he travelled the length and breadth of the country in a "T" type Ford selling them to Brewers, Farmers and Coal Merchants.

In my earlier years he recounted to me a ghostly encounter during these travels, details of which I will relate in the next Chapter.

By the time my mother was twelve my grandparents had added another daughter and a son to their family and were able to rent a Council House on the newly built Becontree Estate at 160 Broad Street, Dagenham. The switch of schools to Marsh Green School in 1924 must have unsettled my mother but despite the interruption in her education she came 20th out of a class of 45 at the age of 13. Academically she was very bright, as I discovered later, but like my father, was unable to progress any further than General School Certificate level and left school at 15.

On leaving school in 1927 she appears to have worked as a general junior clerk, for Companies in the City of London including British Ropes Limited, whose Head Office was at 52 High Holborn. The company manufactured steel wire for a vast range of industrial, commercial, agricultural and domestic purposes and had factories in Cardiff, Wakefield, Liverpool, Gateshead and Glasgow. Her employment culminated in 1934, at the age of 22, in appointment as a clerk for the Ministry of Labour at its Ilford Employment Exchange. Her commencing salary was 36 shillings and six pence per week of 44 hours: this was the equivalent of £1.82 and a half pence in decimal currency, £94.90p per annum. She proved to be so capable and efficient that the Manager of the Employment Exchange was sorry to see her leave in the latter part of 1935. But by then she was becoming heavily pregnant, and I was due to arrive early in January 1936.

11

My Maternal Grandfather

My maternal grandfather, John Somers, was the son of Henry Bolton Somers, who lived in Tyrells Pass, County West Meath in what is now Eire. According to my grandfather he was a Schoolmaster who taught at Wilson's Hospital School, a Church of Ireland School for the sons of local gentry in Mullingar. Tyrells Pass is due west of Dublin on the road leading to Moate and Athlone.

Henry Bolton Somers was, so far as I can gather, of "Old English" Protestant stock: he was born in Moate, the son of a schoolmaster, in 1837 and had married a young lady some years younger than himself by the name of Alice Billen, the daughter of a well to do sheep farmer in Hendon, Middlesex.

Henry's family had never lived "beyond the Pale", the former dividing line between the English and the Gaelic controlled areas of Ireland: in fact they appear to have settled in Ireland some time before the "New English" settlers brought in by Oliver Cromwell.

The mid nineteenth century was a disastrous time for those living in the south of Ireland: the potato famine of 1848, the attitude of the Government at Westminster towards the predominantly Catholic small farmers and the destitution they suffered had done nothing to heal the wounds inflicted on them by the English in Elizabethan and Cromwellian times: It had caused immense resentment towards those who were perceived to be the Protestant ruling class. As G.K. Chesterton sagely observed "the tragedy of the English conquest of Ireland in the seventeenth century is that the Irish can never forget it and the English can never remember it".

Being, it would appear, a member of an Orange Lodge in Moate,

Henry was a natural target for this resentment and was threatened with death in the 1870s by local Fenians if he did not relinquish his post as schoolmaster. On hearing of the threat his fellow Lodge members and local farmers raised thirty guineas between them and urged Henry to move back to England with his family as quickly as possible – which he did.

He settled in Stratford where my grandfather was born in 1881: my grandfather was the third of his four sons, having two older sisters. Henry's own brothers and sisters, not being so prominent in Protestant circles, remained in Southern Ireland and their descendants are there to this day.

Henry could not find employment as a teacher but he did manage to obtain employment with Arthur Boake, another Protestant who had emigrated from Dublin to London in 1869 and who had founded "A Boake & Co." producing brewing chemicals. Arthur Boake was quite an entrepreneur and in 1876 a Francis Roberts joined him as an equity partner. The business was later incorporated and became Boake Roberts & Co., a company that expanded enormously thereafter into many types of chemical products.

Henry got on extremely well with Arthur Boake and remained with him until retirement: in fact, on his retirement Arthur Boake presented my great grandfather with a comfortable armchair in which he could relax and read books to his heart's content.

The only unfortunate aspect of the return of Henry and Alice to England was that when Alice asked for her share of her deceased father's silverware, with a view to raising some money for her children's maintenance, her brothers told her that they had already sold it and divided the proceeds between themselves some years previously. They had done so in her absence in Ireland from which they had not expected her to return: this irked her a great deal and she made sure her children, including of course, my grandfather never forgot it. As a Solicitor, who has dealt on many occasions with the Estates of deceased people and who has seen the avarice displayed by members of their families this sort of behaviour does not surprise me at all.

Quite where Henry's ancestors came from I have absolutely no idea.

Unfortunately, the family Bible which might have revealed a great deal about his ancestry was left in Tyrell's Pass with Henry's brothers and sisters. Although attempts were made in the 1960s to trace it the Bible had disappeared. All one can say is that "Somer" is an Anglo-Saxon baptismal name and that the additional "s" means "son of Somer". The most references to it as a family name which it later became are, not surprisingly, in Somerset.

Although I have no knowledge of the education my grandfather received in Stratford, I confirm that he was a very intelligent and well informed man. He must have had a reasonably well-paid occupation before conscription notwithstanding the fact that he could only find employment as a sack salesman after demobilisation.

I used to sit at my grandfather's knee and he told me one very interesting story about his time as a commercial traveller selling jute sacks. He drove the length and breadth of the country in his "T" type Ford and although it was normally very reliable it did break down late one snowy night on the outskirts of Doncaster.

He felt he had no alternative but to walk to Doncaster, put up somewhere for the night and return to the vehicle next day. As he set out on his walk the moonlight lit up the road between the hedges: it was almost like daylight. He could see, walking towards him, an elderly lady in dark clothes and wearing a shawl. As they passed he said, "Good evening," and she replied, "Good evening." There was something strange about her, however, and he wondered what it was. He turned round to have another look but there was no sight of her.

All he could see, in the moonlight, was the imprint of his shoes in the snow behind him. He resumed his walk, somewhat perplexed and then suddenly realised with horror what was strange about her. She had left no footprints in the snow behind or in front of him. My grandfather who had seen active service on the Western Front said that, at this point, he panicked and ran all the way to Doncaster!

Despite the hard times through which everyone was living in the early 1920s he had managed, by December 1923, to move his family from my great grandmother's house in East Ham into a new Council House at 160 Broad Street, Dagenham.

By 1933 he had been able to upgrade the family accommodation to another newly built house in Sheppey Road on the Becontree Estate with front, side and back gardens. It was in the back garden that, some six years later, he was to build the Anderson shelter in which I spent a couple of hours during the Bliz: it was cold and damp, and I did not enjoy the experience.

Even though I was very young when I stayed there in January 1940 I can recall that 227 Sheppey Road had the luxury of an upstairs toilet but not an upstairs bath. As a result, having a bath was more complicated than stepping into a white enamelled bath with hot and cold taps in the type of bathroom we know and expect today.

In the kitchen there was a grate for a coal fire with a large inbuilt tub above it. Into the tub which had quite a large capacity – probably three or four gallons – one poured cold water from the tap. When the water in the tub was heated it could be used for washing clothes or washing oneself: clothes in the sink and oneself in a large tin bathtub on the kitchen floor. There was no central heating in the house and there were no pipes taking hot water upstairs.

An upstairs bathroom was subsequently installed but in 1933 an upstairs toilet, rather than a brick built "privy" in the back garden, was a big advance as also was the means of heating water for washing clothes and having a bath. Quite how my mother and her two sisters coped with having to have a bath in the kitchen I have no idea but it certainly must have kept "bath time" to a minimum! Most people nowadays, living in centrally heated homes with bathrooms, have little conception of living and working conditions in the 1930s.

When Briggs Motor Bodies built a plant at Dagenham in 1931 to make bodies for the Ford vehicles being produced at the adjacent factory my grandfather obtained employment in their Accounts Department and stayed with them and subsequently the Ford Motor Company, which absorbed the former into its massive car producing complex, until his retirement in 1946.

I stayed with my grandparents for a short time after my release from Old Church Hospital following my recovery from Scarlet Fever in January 1940: I will mention this incident again later. Even as a four-year-old I can remember my grandfather coming home from work in the evening, removing his black bowler hat, brushing it methodically and putting it on the hat stand in the hall, then taking off his black jacket and waistcoat, brushing them equally methodically and putting them on a coat hanger. After this he would take off his starched collar, placing his front and rear collar studs in a drawer of the dresser before disappearing upstairs to remove the rest of his attire and change into something more comfortable. It was a daily ritual and I was fascinated by it. In retrospect he probably took such care because he could not afford or, on the outbreak of war, would have been unable to buy another suit. This thought would not have occurred to me at the time.

When he retired from Fords at the age of 65, my grandfather took up painting as a hobby and either painted real life country scenes by visiting beauty spots like Epping Forest or still life objects like "Chinese style" blue and white vases or street scenes taken from postcards of the places he had visited during his life, including Belgium and France during the First World War.

He was, of course, a complete amateur but he did manage to achieve a sense of perspective in his paintings and they were relatively good. He framed them himself and gave them to members of his extended family.

When, after the Second World War and between the ages of 10 and 18 I visited Sheppey Road after school on Saturdays he regaled me with accounts of life in Stratford and the East end of London in the 1880s and 1890s, of the lamplighters, the "knockers up" and the street vendors, like the muffin men. The lamplighters had to go up and down the streets to light the gas street lamps (and presumably turn them off later), while the "knockers up" had to knock on doors or tap on windows to wake people up in the morning: there were no alarm clocks in those days. When the strawberry season came along there would be women selling fresh strawberries from the carts they wheeled through the grimy and somewhat down at heel parts of the area in which he lived.

He told me that the street vendors had different cries and I can myself recall in the late 1930s and 1940s the "rag and bone" men who would wend their way through Kettering on their horse drawn carts, ringing their bells and shouting "rag and bone man, any old iron". They would pile on to their carts pretty well any unwanted item you cared to throw away and were immortalised by Wilfrid Brambell and Harry H. Corbett in the "Steptoe & Son" series on BBC Television in the 1960s and 1970s.

The other horse drawn carts one would see a lot belonged to the coal merchants who regularly delivered coal in jute sacks to your front door in the 1930s and 1940s. Each sack would be carried from the cart to one's house on the shoulders of a well-built man, too old to be called up for service in the Armed Forces, who would empty it where directed, in the case of my parents behind the side gate of our house. One bought coal by the hundredweight (cwt) and I can recall my parents usually ordering three or four sacks full at a time.

I remember this so well because as a four-year-old I was a bit of a nightmare to my parents and used these fascinating shiny lumps of coal to effect my escape from the garden by piling them up against the gate and climbing over it on more than one occasion until my father "got wise" and broke the coal into much smaller lumps. But we all have to face up to the fact that four-year-olds are curious about the world outside the confines of their own homes. I was just more curious and adventurous than most.

As previously indicated my grandfather was very intelligent and well informed and one of my favourite games with him was to ask him questions from Whitakers Almanac. The Almanac, a bulky red-covered reference book, was full of information on a wide variety of subjects and I believe my uncle Gerald who lived with my grandparents, had purchased it in a sale when the local Public Library replaced it with a more up to date edition. "Open it at any page" he would say to me "and ask me a question on anything on that page", which I did. He could answer nearly every question and I was extremely impressed. Perhaps I acquired my photographic memory from him and his side of my family.

He also exhibited the traits of an Army quartermaster because, just to the left of the front door as one entered 227 Sheppey Road, was a large pantry cupboard with rows of shelves. Inside the cupboard he would store tins of all types of meat, fruit and vegetables. An inventory on a hook inside the panty door showed what was in stock and, for the purpose of replenishment, what had been used.

Once again I feel sure I acquired my desire never to run short of food (which my children find rather amusing) from him. He and his family, however, had doubtless been obliged to go short after the First World War and in the 1920s and 1930s and it was his aim always to have a "reserve supply" in the house if at all possible.

He was a well-built man who, throughout his life, took regular exercise and looked after himself physically. In addition to cycling to beauty spots like Epping Forest to do his painting he used to cycle about once a fortnight the approximately 18 miles from Becontree to Billericay, between 1948 and 1956 on the ex-Post Office bicycle he had acquired, to chop down the Silver Birch trees in our woodland garden and dig out their roots, also the roots of the Spanish Chestnut trees that once stood in it. Some of the roots were massive and he would work on them all day having arrived quite early and then cycle back to Becontree late in the afternoon. In 1956, at the age of 75 he turned to my mother one day and said that he was sorry he could not continue to cycle down to Billericay. "Why is that, Dad?"

"The traffic is too bad," was his reply. It had nothing to do with the state of his health or the removal of tree roots.

In his later years he suffered from eyesight problems and not being able to paint or read or cycle or enjoy what he considered mediocre television programmes he sadly died of what one can only describe as boredom at the age of 95. He just passed away in his sleep, probably thinking and feeling that there was not much more to live for.

12
"Grannie" Somers

There is no doubt that I loved my maternal grandparents and that I was particularly close to my grandmother until the outbreak of war, and consequent shortage of petrol, prevented my parents from driving to Sheppey Road from Kettering in Northamptonshire on a regular basis.

Petrol rationing for private motor vehicles was announced as soon as war was declared on 3 September 1939. Car owners were to be allowed a modest ration of petrol each month depending on availability. By mid-1942, however, so many ships carrying petroleum to Britain had been sunk by German "U" boats that the use of petrol for any private purpose whatever was terminated. From then on it was only available for essential work: special permits were required for its consumption by, for example, Doctors visiting patients, ambulance, fire and police services, buses and farm and goods vehicles.

Being unable to drive a car because of a shortage of petrol is doubtless inconceivable to people born from 1950 onwards, but petrol was, in fact, rationed until 1950, some five years after the end of the war.

How did rationing work? The first coupons were issued on 16 September 1939. On production of his or her car registration book at the Post Office, the owner received dated coupons for use during two specified monthly periods. They could not therefore be hoarded: it was a matter of "use them or lose them". Each coupon was for one unit of "motor spirit", as petrol was then called and one unit represented one gallon, just over four and a half litres. Coupons were allocated according to the rating (horsepower) of each vehicle.

As a child I did not mind petrol rationing too much because, although I could not travel to Sheppey Road to see my grandparents,

I could play happily and safely in the street outside our house with no concerns about traffic. But not being able to buy petrol must have been extremely frustrating for people who had to "jack up" their cars on wooden blocks or household bricks (in order to prevent deterioration of the tyres) and leave them in a garage for three or more years. In the pre-war years it was necessary to have a garage for one's car to protect it from the elements. Anti-rust treatment was not as good as it became later: a car left permanently in the open would deteriorate rapidly. There were consequently no cars parked in streets as there are now.

Of course, car production ceased on the outbreak of war because the factories that had previously made cars were converted to produce military vehicles and aircraft.

But I digress and must return to Grannie Somers. Although I do not expect most readers to accept what I say about her and will probably dismiss it as complete nonsense I had, for many years, the feeling that, even after her death in 1956, she was concerned for my welfare and "kept watch" over me.

Those who have already heard about my ghostly and paranormal experiences will more readily believe me than others but the sensation of shock in the air when I once criticised her after her death for not letting my cousin take the "11-plus" exam was palpable. I have expressed my apologies to her many times since, although she may no longer be around to hear them. It was at that moment, however, that I realised her spirit was still present.

My first memory of her was when my parents celebrated Christmas at Sheppey Road in 1939. I was coming up to my third birthday and I probably remember her because she intervened decisively in what could have been a lifesaving incident for me. My parents had put me in a high sided wooden cot, one side of which could be released and lowered, in the dining room so that they could keep an eye on me during the festivities. Somehow I got hold of a boiled sweet and swallowed it whole. It stuck in my throat and I began to choke.

My observant grandmother rushed over to the cot and hooked out the sweet with her little finger. It was her quick reaction that possibly saved me. My father encountered a similar situation with my 18-month-old sister, which I will describe in a later chapter.

My second memory is the way she looked after me just after Christmas the following year. Having moved to Kettering in June 1939 and having carefully saved their petrol for the journey to Sheppey Road and back my parents had decided to drive up early on Christmas Day 1940 and return early on Boxing Day morning. They did not want to leave our diminutive Fox Terrier "Jum", short for Jumbo, at home on his own for too long. It was, incidentally, my father's sense of humour to attribute the name of an elephant to such a small dog!

After a very gratifying Christmas Day as far as I was concerned, with lots of presents from my parents and relatives I was terrified when my grandmother spotted a red rash on my body and pointed it out to my parents. They all thought the rash looked serious and my father decided to drive round to the house of the local GP and ask him if he would be so kind as to pay an emergency visit to my grandparents' home. There were no telephones in those days in Council Houses and it was a day upon which few Doctors would want to leave their own homes to see patients.

Nevertheless, he came round and immediately diagnosed scarlet fever, a notifiable illness, which required me to be taken to the Isolation Ward of the Old Church Hospital in Romford. I was not at all happy at the prospect of having to go to a Hospital at Christmas and hid under the dining room table which had cross beams beneath it. When the Ambulance arrived a frightened young boy had to be extracted forcibly by his father from the quarter section of the crossbeams, closest to the dining room wall to which he had retreated.

Scarlet fever was and remains an infectious disease which in 1940 took about a week to 10 days to be treated with the aid of the newly discovered antibiotic, penicillin. There was therefore no question of my parents taking me back to Kettering. They would have to return there without me.

During the week I was in hospital my grandmother visited me every day bringing me colouring books and puzzles and stayed with me as long as she could. There were other children in the Ward and we played with the nurses. I must have been a bit too exuberant because one of the nurses opened a window, scooped up a handful of snow from the windowsill and put it down the back of my pyjamas, much to the amusement of the other nurses. I, however, will never forget the feeling of cold snow melting on my back and wearing a wet pyjama top!

When I was discharged from the Hospital my grandmother took me back to Sheppey Road on big red buses which I had never encountered before and by which I was completely captivated. Everything about them was, to me as a four-year-old, wondrous – a big metal pole on the passenger boarding area to swing on, the inside or outside stairs to an upper deck and the "tinging" of the bell when passengers wanted to get off. This experience led me into becoming an avid London Transport "bus spotter" when, at the age of ten, I was able to travel on them alone.

My grandmother's background was as interesting as that of my grandfather. Her maiden name was Langley. The Langley family lived in St. Helens in Lancashire, were Roman Catholic and her father, Henry Langley, had at one stage been very wealthy. John Langley, her grandfather had a glass works in the town and, according to my grandfather, had invented and produced the system of glass tubing used in siphoning beer from barrels or casks to the taps from which it was dispensed in public houses across the country.

Before John Langley died his son Henry had shocked the family by marrying a young lady by the name of Elizabeth Anne Roberts who had been born in Colchester but whose father, Charles Roberts, had served in the Lancashire Militia. Charles had run away from his home in Northmoor in Oxfordshire at the age of sixteen and in view of his "copperplate" signature on his enlistment papers it is more than likely that he came from a "well to do" family and had rebelled against his parents and his upbringing by joining the army.

The reason for the shock, however, was that Elizabeth was a member of the Church of England. She was obviously prevailed upon to convert to Roman Catholicism because her six children of whom my grandmother was one were all brought up, initially, as Roman Catholics in St. Helens.

Although John Langley was sober and hardworking and undoubtedly a shrewd and successful businessman, his son Henry was not. Within a couple of years of his father's death and, notwithstanding the fact that he had a wife and six children, he apparently gambled away the entire family fortune, mortgaged the factory to pay off his gambling debts and sold the factory and the business without disclosing the existence of the mortgage to the purchasers.

In order to avoid arrest and prosecution Henry fled to the Stratford area of London with his wife and children, changed his surname from Langley to Clare and converted himself and his family to the Church of England. He found employment in a glass works there but unfortunately died of work induced lung disease, pneumoconiosis, leaving his widow destitute. She was, however, a woman of some character and resilience and survived as best she could with her growing family.

My grandmother, therefore, had a disturbing and difficult childhood and it is not surprising that her upbringing had a profound effect on her and upon the attitudes of her daughter, my mother.

Fate clearly brought my maternal grandparents together in the Stratford area. They met, married and appear to have moved to Wanstead where my mother, the eldest of their children was born in 1912. In view of their similar family experiences they were determined to provide a stable and secure home for their children. It must have come as a heart stopping moment for both of them when, in 1916, and at the age of 35, my grandfather received his "call up" papers, forcing my grandmother, like so many young mothers, to raise and look after their, by then, three young children on her own.

My grandfather was conscripted into the Royal Artillery and was sent to the Western Front where, after serving as a member of a team responsible for bringing horse drawn guns up to the battlefront, he was assigned to laying telephone lines across "no man's land" to forward observation posts (FOPs) from which an officer would, during daylight, be able to direct artillery fire onto enemy positions. It was a highly dangerous task and he told me that he was very much aware of what would happen to his wife and three young children if he was killed. He realised that German snipers would be on the "look out" for any British soldier who had ventured out beyond his own trenches and took as few risks as possible. He had, in fact, been lucky to survive given the hazardous nature of what he had to do.

On his return from the Western front my maternal grandparents had two more children, making up the five children I have previously mentioned. Thanks to the combined efforts of my grandparents, my mother, her two sisters and two brothers were a happy close-knit family during their younger years and kept in close touch with each other once they had grown up and had moved away from Sheppey Road,

Although I am stepping outside the time sequence of my autobiography, not having yet mentioned my birth, I feel compelled at this point to comment on the Somers family as a family unit. Saturday evening was "family evening" and to the best of my recollection my parents, two aunts and two uncles congregated every Saturday, apart from the Second World War years, with or without partners and subsequently with their children at Sheppey Road.

Between the ages of 10 and 18, therefore, I would head there after School late on Saturday afternoon. We had lessons on Saturday mornings at Brentwood School, followed by sport, either cricket, rugby or soccer in the afternoons. But more of that anon. My parents and sister would normally arrive by car at about the same time as myself and I really looked forward to seeing my kind hearted grandparents and to the lively company of my uncles, aunts, cousins and their boyfriends, later husbands, who would make a point of turning up weekly to talk, to laugh, to express their views on everything from football to politics, to debate history, my uncle Gerald's favourite subject, to enjoy the splendid "fry up" courtesy of my grandmother and uncle Gerald and to drink gallons of tea!

Because there were not enough chairs or sofas for everyone in the lounge and dining room which had folding doors between them my cousins, all female, had to sit on their boyfriends' laps – not that they seemed to mind. Occasionally my grandfather would get out his accordion, if pressed to do so, and play tunes we could all sing along to – as doubtless had his comrades in the Royal Artillery.

There was consequently a terrific sense of family at all times and Saturday nights at Sheppey Road were probably very much the same as a typical Irish family gathering in the 1940s and 1950s minus the Guinness! It is quite possible that echoes of my great grandfather's family can be found in them, and it is not surprising that my father so readily accepted and was absorbed into the warmth of the Somers family: it must have been so different from the coolness displayed by his own parents towards their children.

Saturday evenings constituted stimulating entertainment of the most natural kind and such a change from lessons and homework as far as I was concerned. They were enjoyable, fun evenings in which everyone participated. There was no need for television. In fact, my bachelor uncle Gerald ("Gerry" to everyone) who lived with and supported my grandparents financially bought a television set in 1953 in order to watch the Coronation, but the set was rarely turned on. Any television programme would have had to be fairly momentous to compete with and drown out the noise and laughter generated by my talkative family.

13

Uncle Gerald

My mother's younger brother, Gerald, was born in 1924, 12 years after my mother and 12 years before myself. Gerry, as he was known, was my favourite uncle, a good looking, charming and kindly young man, also a generous one during my time at Brentwood School.

One of the reasons I was happy to go to my grandparents home so regularly in those days was the half-crown (two shillings and six pence) he always gave me. It was a welcome boost to the pocket money I received from my mother and would equate in modern parlance to about seven full size Mars Bars. Not that I spent it on Mars Bars!

He had suffered from meningitis when he was about 10 years old and, as a consequence, had missed out on vital years of secondary education. Nevertheless, he was intelligent and personable and secured skilled employment at an oil refinery near Dagenham producing different grades of petroleum by his monitoring of the production process. He became so proficient at it that he could read a book a day while sitting at his control desk.

He took out, on average, six books a week from his local Public Library and became passionately interested in all aspects of British, European and American history, particularly the life and exploits of Napoleon Bonaparte, and in geology, including the study of the formation of rocks and the types of gemstone found within them.

He constantly and wistfully told me that his ambition was to go prospecting in Brazil but that he could not do so because of his overriding responsibility to look after his parents. I suspect, however, that, apart from the financial contribution he made to household expenses, they looked after him rather than the other way round. While expressing my regret that his ambition was sadly unattainable I secretly doubted whether he would ever have got further than Southampton had he ever attempted to fulfil it.

When he left School in 1940 he became a local Defence Volunteer in the ARP (the Air Raid Precaution Service). He told me that he was stationed on the roof of St. Paul's Cathedral during the second Great Fire of London and tasked with several other Fire Guards in extinguishing the flames from the incendiary bombs that landed on it. He subsequently volunteered for service in the RAF but his childhood illness counted against him and he was discharged, much to his disappointment, on medical grounds.

Like all young men he respected "Winnie", Winston Churchill, as a Leader but was very much in favour of social change which led to improved living and health conditions for the poorer and less privileged members of society. He did not believe that Churchill would be able to deliver them. As an earnest supporter of Clement Atlee, Ernest Bevin and Aneurin (Nye) Bevan he could become quite vociferous on the subject of politics, not, he constantly assured me, that he ever wanted to see the abolition of Grant Maintained Grammar Schools or Independent Public Schools. He would just like to see them opened up to all bright children, with the children of wealthy parents getting into them on academic merit alone.

It was always best to let him have his say and then resume playing gin rummy, pontoon or drafts with him or alternatively steer the flow of his oratory towards less contentious subjects, like the Duke of Wellington or his favourite character, Napoleon Bonaparte. We gambled, incidentally, with matchsticks lest anyone should feel he was leading me astray!

His other abiding interest was in ghosts and ghost stories and he made a point of visiting "haunted houses" whenever he was able. I am quite sure, however, that he never saw a ghost: if he had done so he would have told me.

He would have made a splendid teacher had he been able to obtain better educational qualifications in his earlier years. He was humorous, knowledgeable and had the ability to transmit the passion he felt about history and so many other subjects to the listener. He was, moreover, generous in spirit and proved equally popular with my children and stepchildren all of whom loved "Uncle Gerry's" perceptive, witty and often irreverent views on life.

14
The Relationship Between my Parents

As a result of my experiences of life, both personal and as an observer on the lives of others I have come to the conclusion that a happy and contented childhood is almost entirely attributable to a loving relationship between one's parents.

There is no doubt that my parents fell very much in love when they met at St. Martin's Church early in 1930. My father was 18 years old and my mother seventeen at the time. He was a romantic and sociable young man, outgoing and humorous. As a teenager she was reserved in public until she met him and somewhat insecure in the company of adults as a result of the mixed fortunes of her family between 1916 and 1930.

She had been deeply affected by the life changing experiences of her mother and grandmother and their need to economise and keep everything they possessed in as pristine a condition as possible. My father, on the other hand, appeared less affected by what had happened to him and by his parents decline from comparative wealth to genteel poverty. He was ever the optimist, looking forward, not back.

They were both highly intelligent, also committed Christians and, although their personalities were very different, they complemented each other. My mother was strong-willed, fiery and adept at getting her own way. My father, on the other hand, was placid, kind and easy going, prepared, to a large extent, to go along with her hopes and ambitions for them and subsequently their family. He was well aware that she would only do what was in the best interests of them both.

In fact, my mother turned out to be a remarkably capable manager of the family finances once they married, controlling expenditure to the penny. It is not surprising that the Manager of the Employment

Exchange in Ilford was sorry to lose her. She was ambitious for my father in his early years but, as time passed, she came to appreciate the limitations placed on him by his poor health, his lack of professional qualification and consequent inability to progress his career. She made it her task to manage their joint resources as effectively as possible and was remarkably successful in doing so.

Because she could be quite dominating, I was told by Gerry, my uncle Gerald, that he and his siblings warned my father against marrying her. My father was such a nice young man that they felt they should do their best to put him off! Fortunately for me, they failed. She was, of course, their older "bossy" sister and this must have influenced their attitude to her and hers towards them.

My father who was hardworking, long suffering, honest and kind could make friends with anyone because he had no "side", no social pretensions. As a teenager he appears, in their courting days, to have thought of himself as a knight of old and my mother as a damsel locked in a castle tower. He wrote her passionate love poems which I have been able to locate among her papers along these chivalric lines.

He also wrote humorous poems for her about his favourite character Sir Pinto Bere who always popped into a local Inn for refreshment before going off to fight dragons. Sir Pinto's encounters with them were comic, to say the least.

I was consequently fortunate enough to be born into a loving parental environment. They, on the other hand, knew nothing of the pickle I would turn out to be on that fateful day in January 1936.

15
My Birth and First Near-Death Experience

Having given what, to the reader, may well be considered a rather one-sided view of the culture into which I was born, my genetic make up and family environment I now return undeterred to 1936, and the circumstances of my birth.

My parents eagerly anticipated the birth of their first child and as soon as she left the Employment Exchange in Ilford in September 1935 at the age of 23 my mother set about "nest building". That meant getting a bedroom ready for its arrival in January.

Her favourite department store was Harrison Gibsons in Ilford, and nearly all the furniture in our family homes in Dagenham, Hornchurch and subsequently in Billericay until the mid-1950s was purchased by way of hire purchase agreements with the store. She invariably called into Harrison Gibsons on her way to my grandparents on Saturday afternoon until it was virtually rebuilt and lost its former traditional image and "genteel" atmosphere, becoming very much the same as any other modern department store, doubtless in a bid to expand its clientele. Thereafter she developed a similar attachment to Bolingbrokes in Chelmsford until that, again, was overtaken by modernity, the need for innovation and its merger with Wenleys, the adjoining ladies' clothes and fashion store.

On 28 September 1935 my parents therefore visited Harrison Gibsons and for eleven pounds, nine shilling and one penny (of which five shillings was interest) purchased everything necessary to cater for a growing infant of whichever sex it might turn out to be. This included a crib, a three-foot oak bedstead, a hair mattress, bolster and feather pillow, also a baby bath, bath mat, Lloyd Loom basket, rug and linoleum for the floor. The purchase was to be paid off at £1 per month.

I mention this particular purchase by way of illustration of how far small sums of money, in modern terms, went such a long way in those days and how my mother took advantage of extremely low interest rates to furnish our various homes.

My mother, so far as I am aware, had an uneventful pregnancy, but I came uncomfortably close to death during the process of being born. In fact, I was very lucky to enter the world alive. It was the first of my many close encounters with the "other side".

I made my entrance feet first in the maternity unit of Old Church Hospital in Romford on 6 January. Quite why I failed to turn into the correct "head down" position as most babies do and be born in the usual way I have no idea, but my failure to do so posed a substantial risk to my mother and myself.

In fact when my legs appeared rather than my head the Doctor declared that he would have to concentrate on saving my mother. He could not guarantee that I would survive birth, but he would do his best to deliver me alive.

I was, however, safely delivered by forceps to the great relief of my mother and the Doctor. I had emerged from what must have been a traumatic experience for everyone apart from myself, undamaged with, I am told, a healthy pair of lungs.

Unfortunately, my mother was diagnosed shortly after my birth with puerperal fever, a severe blood infection which had previously killed so many mothers when giving birth. It is believed, for example, that Jane Seymour, the third wife of Henry VIII, may well have died from it. Had it not been for the recent discovery of the antibiotic, Penicillin, the proximity to Romford of the May and Baker factory producing it and the ability of my father to fund the purchase of it she could have died within weeks of my birth.

Because my mother became so ill, she could not breast feed me and the task of looking after a newly born baby fell on the shoulders of her mother, "Grannie Somers". I suspect that she and subsequently my mother were pretty liberal with the Cow and Gate baby milk and the Farex because I laid down fat cells in my first few months with which I have had to contend in later life. Well, that is my excuse!

I weighed seven and a half pounds at birth and rapidly put on weight. Apart from the fact that my mother had become very ill my childhood got off to a good start. I was baptised with two other babies on Easter Sunday at St. Martin's Church, having been born at Epiphany. It is unusual to be baptised on one of the busiest days in the Christian Calendar but my parents and my grandfather, John Somers, were stalwarts of the Church and the Reverend Ashley Turner, the Vicar at the time, decided to recognise their commitment and that of two other couples by carrying out the Baptism Service on that particular Sunday. Baptism may have secured my place in the Church of England to which I still belong but it is questionable whether the blessing I received at the time did anything to affect my nature or the course of my life.

Fortunately, my parents appreciated from the outset that I was inquisitive, energetic and adventurous and I am deeply indebted to them for their forbearance in tolerating the mischievous and independently minded little boy they had brought into the world. Like all young babies I was completely self-oriented. The combination of a strong-willed mother and an equally strong-willed child did occasionally lead to a battle of wills, but so far as I can recall persuasion and inducements to be good were the only stratagems my mother adopted in order to control me.

I do not remember much of my first three-and-a-half-years but my mother told me I was quite a handful. At eighteen months I would sit on the back doorstep of our new house in Hornchurch and grab our dog's tail. Jum would growl and snarl as I held on to it but he never bit me. My mother said she wished he had because it might have taught me not to be so naughty but, fortunately, Jum was extremely patient with me and would wait until my mother came to his rescue and released him from my grasp.

At the age of three-and-a-half I can distinctly remember eating a bowl of bananas and custard: bananas disappeared from dining tables at the end of 1939 and, just before we moved to Kettering, I can also recall jumping up and down on a neighbour's sofa where, to my mother's great embarrassment, I tore up a Peter Rabbit book which was supposed to keep me occupied while she and the pleasant young lady next door had cups of tea together.

Not long after that I was taken to see the "Wizard of Oz" and recall hiding under the cinema seat when the Wicked Witch of the West appeared! Having watched the film many times as an adult I can fully appreciate the terrifying effect it must have had on a child who was not yet four years of age.

16
Kettering, Northamptonshire

My parents moved from 46 Alma Avenue, Hornchurch to 3 Broadway, Kettering on 7 June 1939, just three months before the outbreak of the Second World War, when I was nearly three and a half years old. Pickfords, a national removals company, charged eight pounds and ten shillings (£8.10 -) to transport all their furniture and other possessions from Hornchurch to Kettering.

They rented our new home for thirty shillings (£1.50) a week from Mr & Mrs Izzett who owned the corner shop next door. They were offered the freehold at the time for £350 but did not have the wherewithal to purchase it. They already had their own house in Hornchurch, subject to a mortgage, and could only afford to rent the property.

As previously mentioned my father had come to the conclusion that war with Germany was inevitable and living so close to the RAF aerodrome at Hornchurch would expose his family to unnecessary risk. Despite Neville Chamberlain's assurance that the written promise he had secured from Adolf Hitler at Munich in 1938 guaranteed peace between the two Nations my father, like so many others, was sceptical. He and they were right to be so.

Although the fighter base was indeed attacked it was not the bombing of it by enemy aircraft that damaged our home. During the latter stages of the war the Germans had developed a flying bomb, the V1, and a fearsome rocket, the V2. As with the Blitz, Hitler intended to demoralise the population of London by destroying as much of the capital as he could with them.

Londoners nicknamed the V1 the "doodlebug". It was a winged bomb with a jet engine on top which would cut out when its supply of rocket fuel was exhausted and when it was ostensibly over its target. The moment its engine gave a final splutter and fell silent, was the moment to run for cover and the moment at which the doodle bug would crash to earth and explode.

Doodle bugs were quite indiscriminate in what they hit, adding to the fear factor. It was quickly found, however, that the latest and fastest models of fighter aircraft could intercept them by flying alongside, flipping them over with their wing tips and steering them off course into open countryside,

The V2 was even more terrifying. It travelled at supersonic speed and was impossible to divert, once launched. Whereas a V1 could destroy more than one house, a V2 could destroy almost an entire street. Indeed, a German V2 destroyed a number of houses in the street beyond our back garden in 1944 and caused "blast damage" to our own home. I will refer to this in a later chapter.

When my parents moved to Kettering they let our home to a Mr & Mrs Steadman for, I believe, thirty five shillings (£1.75) a week. The Steadmans paid the rent until a few months before the outside of the house suffered blast damage from the V2 rocket but did a "moonlight flit" in mid-1946. when my father pursued them in the County Court for nearly two years unpaid rent.

Kettering was quite a change from Hornchurch. Whereas Hornchurch had, by 1939, become a residential suburb of Metropolitan London, on the London Underground system and served by London Transport buses, Kettering was a self-contained town, set in the Northamptonshire countryside with a population of about 35,000 inhabitants and its own successful industries, the foremost of which was the manufacture of boots and shoes.

In 1700 Kettering was described as "a well traded populous market town" and there was indeed a busy cattle market at the beginning of the War which I remember. Prior to the arrival of the railway in May 1857 the town had a number of small factories producing boots and shoes but production soared when large orders for them were received from the French Government during the Franco Prussian War in 1870. From that time onward huge orders for army boots were received from the British,

French, Italian and Russian governments and considerable quantities of army clothing were also manufactured. The town became prosperous as a result.

In addition to the wealth generated by the manufacture of a vast range of leather goods and clothing for the army Kettering was also fortunate in having a good deal of ironstone subsoil. The ironstone located in the Borough and in the surrounding area made it an important source of supply to iron and steel works, particularly Corby, only a few miles away.

The Heraldic arms to which every successful Borough has aspires tell the story of the town. On a black shield appears a gold-coloured animal hide indicative not only, in my view, of the widespread use of leather but the wealth it generated. On either side of the hide are gold circles with blue and white wavy lines inside them, symbolising, apparently, the formation of the Baptist Missionary Society in Kettering in 1792 while, superimposed upon the circles are martlets (birds) taken from the Arms of the Watson family of Rockingham, some nine miles distant, who with the Montague family were Lords of the Manor of Kettering. The gold cross between the circles is taken from the See (Diocese) of Peterborough under whose Ecclesiastical jurisdiction Kettering falls.

Supporting the shield are the golden Griffin of the Montague family and a figure in black with a broken chain symbolising the triumphant work of William Knibb, a resident of Kettering in the cause of freedom from slavery. The flames in the crest of the heraldic arms and the iron chain encircling them represent the iron ore industry while the skein of silk below the iron chain refers to the clothing industry.

By the time my parents arrived in Kettering in 1939 the town had lost most of the historic buildings it might once have had. It was nevertheless a pleasant, attractive, self-contained and forward looking place with every modern amenity.

Although I have lived in Essex for most of my life my character and outlook was formed in Kettering during the following seven years.

17

Kettering: The First Year

One cannot expect a three-and-a-half-year-old, even one with a photographic memory, to remember much about his or her surroundings. The description I now give comes, therefore, from my recollection of living at 3 Broadway as a child for nearly seven years. I can nevertheless, vividly recall certain incidents before I went to Primary School at the age of four years and nine months and I will mention them later in this chapter.

Broadway was a pleasant tree lined street not far from the centre of the town between the main London Road (the old A6) and a road called "The Headlands", a rather genteel upper-class road in which the wealthier citizens of Kettering resided and in which Dr Drake-Lee, our family doctor, lived and had his home surgery.

The houses on our, Southern, side of Broadway were, for the most part Victorian or Edwardian with large bay windows and ornate iron railings on the low brick walls which separated them from the pavement until, that is, Lord Beaverbrook, the Minister for Aircraft production, launched an appeal in 1940 for aluminium pots and pans, and any type of metal to boost the production of Spitfires and armaments.

In a bout of national enthusiasm and in response to his appeal, railings in front of houses all over the country were cut off at the base and taken away to storage areas. The perception was that the aluminium pots and pans would be melted down and used in aircraft production and that the iron railings would be used for munitions.

As his son, Group Captain Sir Max Aitken, a distinguished Second World War fighter ace, later admitted, the "pots-and-pans" appeal was a propaganda exercise: they and the iron railings were never and could never have been used for military purposes. Most of the iron railings will doubtless have been replaced since the Second World War but removing them in the first place was completely pointless.

On the other hand the enthusiasm and ruthless drive of Lord Beaverbrook was almost entirely responsible for the remarkable increase in the manufacture of Spitfires and Hurricanes without which we would have lost the Battle of Britain. As Air Chief Marshall, Lord Dowding, stated at the time we had the pilots, the organisation and the spirit to fight the Luftwaffe but we were losing aircraft at such a rate that, without constant replacement of them, we could not have won the battle. The resources of the Royal Air Force were being stretched to the limit. It was thanks to Lord Beaverbrook that aircraft, straight from the factories, were always available to bring fighter squadrons back up to full strength.

But I digress and must return to my description!

Number 3 Broadway was not Victorian or Edwardian. It was a modern red brick house with an integral garage, an unusual feature at the time. The front door was halfway down the right hand side of the house with an access path leading to it from the pavement. Beyond the front door was a six-foot boarded side gate. On the other side of the house there was a similar, permanently locked, side gate.

On the ground floor the house had quite a large lounge at the front, and a fair-sized kitchen and dining room at the rear. Veranda doors in the dining room opened onto a small back garden. There was a pantry in the kitchen memorable for an incident which I will relate. Upstairs it had three bedrooms, a bathroom and a landing which features later in my story.

I was put in the bedroom over the garage from which I could look out into the street and watch the traffic, such as it was, on the London Road. Immediately opposite was a large Edwardian house which, from early 1944, was to become my principal source of American comics, Hershey bars and chewing gum of many flavours but, again, more of that anon.

Beyond the back garden was an elderly, crumbling, boundary wall whose jagged appearance was improved in the summer by the profusion of Hollyhocks that grew in front of part of it. It was over this wall that I met my first "girlfriend", Gillian Blackman at the age of five!

Although our house was quite different in appearance from the other houses at the London Road end of Broadway, it was exactly the same as them in one important respect. It had no central heating. As a child I was fascinated by the "Jack Frost" patterns across my bedroom windows during the cold winters that followed our arrival in the town. They were intricate and beautiful but my bedroom was always like an icebox when "Jack Frost" appeared. I only had a sheet and a single blanket to snuggle into, with the occasional hot water bottle, to keep me warm. The only heat was from the coal fires in the dining and living rooms and the cooker in the kitchen. There were no grates in the bedrooms for coal fires and no electric heaters.

The experience of sleeping in a freezing bedroom doubtless helped to toughen me up and make me capable of enduring the cold wherever I have lived subsequently.

Further down the south side of Broadway, beyond, Mr Mobbs, the greengrocer's shop on the corner of Garfield Street which led to the Hawthorn Road Primary School, several of the houses were larger and more modern. At the end of the street were, as I have previously mentioned, the Headlands where one turned left to reach the fields, the railway bridge and the Golf Course and right to reach Sheep Street and the centre of the town.

On the north (town) side of the street was a row of terraced houses with what appeared to be a cavernous entrance for a horse drawn coach or cart beyond which I could just see a mysterious grassy area. It may originally have been part of a farmyard from an earlier century. When, as a four-year-old, I first viewed that entrance it looked somewhat sinister and, over the coming years, I never had any inclination to venture inside for fear of being harmed by whatever lurked beyond it. Such is the imagination of a small child!

Nor, in my early years, did I ever venture much beyond Mr Mobbs's shop unless in the company of my parents or, on one memorable occasion, the mother of one of my friends at Primary School. When, however, we arrived in Kettering I was clearly an unruly child and being inquisitive my first act of defiance was to attempt to climb out of the lounge window into Broadway. I wanted to explore the street outside the house rather than just look at it from behind panes of glass.

Having been thwarted by my vigilant mother I adopted another strategy. I asked to be allowed to play in the back garden and then, as related previously, stacked lumps of coal against the side gate until I could climb over it and drop onto the concrete path below. I am afraid I was the sort of four-year-old who, if older and a Prisoner of War, would have been the first to build an escape tunnel! You can imagine my mother' surprise and horror when her three-and-a-half-year-old son knocked on the front door asking to be allowed back into the house. I was scolded, the lumps of coal were broken up and that was the end of my escapade: I would henceforth have to wait until my mother was ready to take me out with her.

The first of many subsequent outings with her was a visit to Wicksteed Park about half a mile away: in retrospect taking me there was one of the principal stratagems adopted by my mother to keep me out of mischief and tire me out.

For a young child it was a magical place: it had a playground with a vast array of swings, roundabouts, slides, climbing frames, see-saws and four-seater devices with horses heads and running boards which rocked backwards and forwards as you pushed forward or pulled back. All these wonderful objects were manufactured locally on behalf of the Trustees of the Park and were sold across the country. You may well find the word "Wicksteed" embossed on roundabouts or slides in your local park if you look carefully.

The Park itself covered an area of one hundred acres: it boasted a two acre playground, a large sandpit, a twenty five acre lake, a children's bathing pool, a paddle boat pool, a boat sailing pond, an aviary, a monkey house, a banked asphalt cycle track and a cinder running track. It also had a "fountain lawn" with bandstand, beautiful formal gardens, a miniature railway and most exciting to me, a water chute.

The water chute was at the side of the paddle boat pool. One sat in what might be described as a flat-bottomed boat and hurtled from a height of about twenty feet down a ramp into the water. Everyone inevitably got wet when the boat hit the water, but it was great fun, extremely harmless and just the sort of thrill that children and young adults enjoy.

Shortly after our arrival in Kettering my parents bought me a beautiful child-size yacht and, even now, I can recall it accompanying model galleons and sailing ships as they caught the wind and moved gracefully across the boat sailing pond. Because there was a path round the pond there was no problem in retrieving the models when they reached the side of it. I sailed my yacht on the pond until I was about six by which time most of the other model owners had either been called up or had stopped visiting the Park.

Because it was, for me, such an unusual sight I can just remember a Brass Band playing in the Bandstand in late summer of 1939. The paddle boats in the paddle boat pool had stopped operating by the time I was five. My last recollection of going out in one was at Easter 1940 with my aunt Mabel when she, my grandparents and uncle Gerald visited us in Kettering.

It was the one and only occasion on which my grandparents ventured so far from their home in Becontree and was almost certainly their last opportunity to do so before the impact of what was just about to happen restricted travel by public and private transport alike.

On 10th May, not long after their visit, Hitler launched his Blitzkrieg against Belgium, Holland and Denmark all of which capitulated within days. He then turned his attention to the annihilation of the French army and the British Expeditionary Force (the BEF) which, between them, had been expected to be able to withstand a German onslaught.

Unfortunately, however, they could not and although by extreme good fortune and the incredible bravery on the part of the owners of over eight hundred "little ships", ranging from weekend pleasure boats to Thames paddle steamers it proved possible to evacuate three hundred and thirty thousand members of the BEF, the bulk of our regular army, from the beaches of Dunkirk between 27th May and 3rd June, the country was left in a state of shock by the near disaster.

Given the speed with which the German army had advanced to the Channel and the humiliating retreat of the BEF everyone feared an imminent invasion. In fact, a seaborne assault was exactly what Hitler had in mind once his formidable Luftwaffe had neutralised the Royal Air Force, the principal barrier to his achieving a successful conquest of Great Britain.

Being aware of the likelihood of invasion within weeks the Government formed the Home Guard in July 1940 under the name of Local Defence Volunteers, comprising, for the most part, men who were not fit for active service in the regular army. Signposts were immediately removed from all roads in the country in order to baffle the invaders and, needless to say, any Citizen of the Realm who did not already know his way from one location to another. The outlook for the country in July 1940 was, without doubt, pretty grim. My father joined the Home Guard immediately and also became a Fire Guard and a member of the Air Raid Precaution Service (the ARP).

All this frenetic activity and concern generated by our parlous situation passed completely over the head of four-year-old Brian Hughes. All I noticed, apart from the absence of my favourite dessert, bananas and custard, was the dwindling number of Dinky toys my father was able to buy for me. In fact, production of them dwindled in 1940 and ceased altogether in 1941.

As a somewhat irresponsible child I had a habit, when playing with them, of lining up my cars, lorries and a fire engine, rolling them along the windowsill in the lounge and letting them fall onto the parquet floor below until my father warned me that, due to the war, I had better look after them. There would not be any more for a long time. His warning "sank in" and I was much more careful with them from the point onwards.

At the age of four years and nine months my parents were undoubtedly relieved to be able to send me to Hawthorn Road Primary School. My mother was five months pregnant with my sister, Angela, who was born in January 1941. A break for a few hours from looking after an energetic and inquisitive child would have been a welcome relief for her.

Only one thing was necessary before I could attend school and that was a haircut! My mother insisted that I look neat and tidy on my first day. I can therefore recall going with her to a small, terraced house in Garfield Street, just round the corner from Mr Mobbs, the greengrocers. The front door was open and, on the right, looking out onto the street was a small room which had once been the parlour. In the centre of it was a large polished wooden chair with a low back and arm rests. There were two or three assorted chairs scattered round the room and a wooden table with ashtrays and a couple of newspapers on it.

The hairdresser, a man in his forties or fifties, pulled out a plank of wood from behind one of the chairs and laid it across the arms of the large polished chair. He got hold of me under my arms and lifted me gently onto the plank. Uttering reassuring words throughout, he snipped off my curls, which my mother immediately pocketed and put into a paper bag. She kept them for the rest of her life.

I went back to him a number of times thereafter on my own, for once I was in my second year at Primary School, I was a "big boy" according to my mother. If I remember correctly he charged me sixpence (6d) for a haircut, the amount with which I was entrusted by my cost conscious mother.

18
1940-1942

The three or four months following the declaration of War was eerily quiet as far as hostilities between Britain and Germany were concerned. In fact, for a short time, the war was called "the phoney war". But everyone knew that we would soon become deeply involved and that the civilian population of the country would be at as much risk as our Armed Forces.

Hitler had invaded Poland in September 1939 and had moved on to add Norway to his collection of subjugated states. It was when he invaded Belgium, the Netherlands and France that the British public became seriously concerned. The forced evacuation of the BEF from Dunkirk and the Blitz on London confirmed their worst fears.

One of the measures the Government activated at the time was the evacuation of young children from London and early in July 1940 two little girls appeared at 3 Broadway. They arrived with small cardboard boxes attached to string which looped round their necks. Each box must have contained a gas mask and a few clothes and probably a favourite cuddly toy. I believe they were sisters and although the eldest could not have been more than nine years old they both seemed to me, as a four-year-old, so grown up.

I regret I have not retained a mental note of their names, but they were very quiet and serious children, doubtless totally disoriented by being parted from their mother, possibly their father also if he had not already been called up. So far as I can recall they were extremely well behaved. They slept in our spare third bedroom but were found alternative accommodation not long after our local GP, Dr Drake Lee, confirmed that my mother was pregnant and would be giving birth to a second child, early in the New Year.

Once they left us, the next landmark event was my first day at School. My mother led me round to the Hawthorn Road Primary School and as I walked up the steps and through the swing doors all I could see were layers of coconut matting and a small vaulting horse on top of them.

Although I was only four years and nine months old I had already learned to read basic children's spelling books and wondered what these strange objects might have to do with education.

My mother handed me over to the Headmistress and left. From that moment I was on my own! The Headmistress put all the arriving first year children in the School Hall and allocated each one of us to a particular class. My class teacher was Miss West, a very kind and pleasant young woman, probably in her mid/late twenties who lived in a house in the London Road, virtually opposite our end of Broadway. Her house was probably less than fifty yards from ours.

We were told by the Headmistress that from that day onward we had to be at School at 9 am for assembly and prayers, that we would have lunch at School and would go home at 4 pm. Having lunch at School was important for many children because, with husbands in the Armed Forces, it had become difficult for many mothers to provide properly for them. It also gave mothers the opportunity to work during the day at one of the factories in the town without having to feed their children at lunch time. The factories in Kettering were, of course, working "full blast" turning out army boots and uniforms and needed women to operate the production lines.

We would have a sleep after lunch for thirty minutes and that if they had not already done so our mothers should make us pillows for us to rest our heads on. My mother had made me a small blue pillow out of some bedroom curtain material, padded with feathers, and according to Miss West I was the only child in the class who lay down on the floor and promptly fell asleep. I had to be woken up before we went back to our classroom whereas the other children, for the most part, had been larking about!

During my first school term raids on British cities were intensifying and I can vividly recall watching on 15 November 1940, the dogfights over Kettering as German bombers raided Coventry, only 23 miles away. My bedroom looked out on to Broadway and the main London Road and I had a grandstand view. Searchlights lit up the sky and tracked the German bombers as our fighter planes weaved in and out of them. That night the Germans destroyed much of the centre of Coventry including its magnificent Cathedral.

One or two German bombers jettisoned their bombs on their way back to Nazi-held territory but I believe the total casualty count for Kettering was a couple of unfortunate rabbits in a field on the outskirts of the town. As soon, however, as my mother found me leaning out of my bedroom window, watching the aerial battle she was absolutely horrified and promptly took me downstairs and put me in an oak Monk bench under the stairs, the safest place in the house to be, according to the Ministry of Information, during a bombing raid. The only other somewhat less safe places were a steel Morrison shelter or a sturdy table on the ground floor, usually in the kitchen.

The back of the bench folded over to become a tabletop and I was still small enough to be squeezed inside it. She only let me out when the "all clear" sounded. The air raid warning siren could not have gone off often, if at all, after that air raid because I cannot recall being put back into it again. It was, at the time, an intensely claustrophobic and unpleasant experience and I feel sure I would have remembered a second incarceration!

The one thing I still have on my conscience is that when I was five and a half and following the Battle of Britain, Jack Cansdale, the nephew of Connie Izzett, made me a beautiful replica balsa wood model of a Spitfire. He was in the RAF at the time and I just hope he was not killed during the war. As an unthinking little boy I threw it in the air, assuming that because it looked so real it would fly and land, as Spitfires did! It fell to earth and broke into pieces. Jack Cansdale was devastated by my wanton destruction of something which must have taken him hours to make and I got a good ticking off by my parents for being so incredibly silly.

My first year at Primary School was a happy one, marred by only one unfortunate incident. Throughout my entire life I have always been in a rush to get from one place to another. Instead of walking to School one morning I ran past Mr Mobbs, the greengrocers, round the corner into Garfield Street and tripped on a flagstone. I hit the bridge of my nose on the pavement and have borne the mark of that encounter to this day!

By the end of that year my ability to read books and comics had improved markedly and my father, a kind and thoughtful parent encouraged my reading habit by buying me books on a wide range of subjects including geography and science. In subsequent years he also bought me Ministry of Information publications on various branches of our armed forces, including books on the contribution of Polish and Czech pilots to our victory in the Battle of Britain, Coastal Command, the Royal Marines and Allied campaigns in North Africa.

But the most significant book he bought me was Sir Thomas Malory's "Morte D'Arthur" as retold by Waldo Cutler. Having found his poems to my mother I can now appreciate that my father had been fascinated from an early age by the concept of chivalry and tales of Knights slaying dragons or rescuing damsels in distress. I am not surprised, therefore, that he chose the book even though it was going to be difficult for a six-year-old to read it.

Fortunately, I was relieved of that particular task by my aunt Lily who arrived early in 1942 with my cousin, Jacqueline. "Jacqui", as she was known throughout her life, had been born in May 1940. Lily was married to my uncle John who had been conscripted into the Royal Artillery and who spent much of the war on the RMS Queen Mary as an anti-aircraft gunner.

The "RMS Queen Mary" being a civilian passenger liner and very fast compared with convoys of cargo carrying merchant ships made its own way back and forth across the Atlantic with minimum Royal Navy escort protection. Although it relied, essentially, on its speed to keep out of trouble and to avoid the "U" Boats that concentrated on attacking the convoys, it was equipped with a number of anti-aircraft guns, known as "heavy Ack Ack" to protect it from any enemy aircraft that might chance upon it.

Lily had become pregnant on one of his shore leaves and she had left her home in the Tilbury area of Essex for the comparative tranquillity of Northamptonshire until she gave birth to her second daughter, Jill, in May 1942. Because Morte D'Arthur was written in mediaeval English I asked her to read a chapter aloud every night when I went to bed and explain the words I could not understand. She did so until we finished it. We had both become captivated by the tales of King Arthur, the wizard Merlin, Morgan Le Fay, Queen Guinevere, Sir Galahad, Sir Lancelot, Sir Tristram and the other Knights, and the book made a lasting impression on me.

While my aunt was still with us a very unfortunate incident occurred, as far as I was concerned. Somehow my father had been able to acquire a second-hand leather football, together with its rubber "blow up" bladder. You can imagine my delight when he gave it to me. A real leather football was something that none of the other children had. I was really excited and wanted to take it straight down to Wicksteed Park and play with it. I left the house with my father who I now suspect would probably have preferred to accompany me to the park on the following weekend rather than after work, and turned into the London Road. For some inexplicable reason the ball slipped out of my hands onto the pavement and rolled slowly down the verge into the road stopping in the path of a huge tank transporter.

You can guess what happened. The lorry itself must have had six wheels and its trailer, with the tank on top of it, had wheels literally from one side to the other, front and rear. There was no escape for my precious football and to me, as a six-year-old, it was rather like watching the death of a beloved pet. The driver braked hard but, with the immense weight of the tank on the trailer behind him, he just could not pull up in time. There was a dull popping sound from the expiring football and I burst into floods of tears.

The driver stopped his vehicle, recovered the flattened lifeless object, brought it to a crying and desolated little boy and gave him a hug. He was so sorry but there was nothing he could have done to save it. I had to accept that the disaster was caused by my letting it go. Had I not dropped it and had it survived I might have become a good footballer or more popular with my friends at School but that was never to be. Resuscitation was not going to be possible. My father was equally upset because I believe he had acquired it from one of his colleagues at work.

Another disaster for which I had, once again, to accept full responsibility was the loss of my Christmas present at Christmas 1942. Unlike nowadays, there were no toys whatever in the shops and they had to be made by parents, relatives and friends. My uncle John, who was an excellent craftsman and woodworker, had already made me a realistic model of a Royal Navy Destroyer, probably an escort to "The Queen Mary", an aircraft hangar with wind vane and battery powered interior electric lighting for my model aeroplanes and was subsequently to make me an exceedingly well built crenelated castle tower and a wooden "Tommy gun". They were all prized possessions.

My father decided he would try his hand at making me a toy and warned me not to attempt to find it. I would receive the result of his efforts at Christmas. Being disobedient and ignoring what he had said, however, and in my intense desire to see what he had made as quickly as possible, I deduced that it must be at the back of the top shelf in the panty and climbed up the shelves to have a look.

And there it was, a model of a ship, an oil tanker, about fifteen inches long, its hull painted cream and its bridge and superstructure white with a plum red funnel. It looked really splendid. But as I clambered down I was caught in the act by my father. "Since you have disobeyed me, you will not receive it", he said sternly. "I will give it to another little boy". And he did. And I never saw it again. That was a salutary lesson for a wilful six-year-old. No Christmas present for me. He had meant what he said and I should have heeded his warning.

It was shortly after Lily and her two children had left us, however, that I helped save my sister's life. Angela had been born in January 1941 and by the time she was eighteen months old she was a toddler and very inquisitive, with a habit of putting objects in her mouth as children of that age are wont to do. While playing in my bedroom I heard her coughing violently in the next door bedroom and clearly in some distress. I immediately went into the bedroom and found her gasping for air. She had been playing on the bed with a green and gold tin box, a presentation box which my father had acquired from Kettering Borough Council celebrating the Coronation of King George VI in 1937 and which had probably started life with biscuits in it. But it was now full of buttons. My mother must previously have been sewing a button on some clothing and had not pressed down the lid firmly enough when she closed it.

I ran onto the landing shouting to my parents that Angela was choking. My father bounded up the stairs, realised immediately that she had swallowed something from the box, seized her by the legs, held her upside down and gave her a sharp whack on her back with his open hand. It was not the recommended Heimlich procedure but it worked. Out flew a zip fastener which had lodged in her throat. She was extremely lucky that both I and my father were nearby. I had heard her and he happened to have been at home. The tin box was promptly removed and thereafter remained in my mother's four-legged sewing table with sliding wooden doors across the top of the compartment in which she stored all her wools and coloured sewing cottons

The reason he was at home at the time and not in the Armed Forces was his poor health. It was not through any lack of patriotism. As previously mentioned, he had signed on as a Kettering Borough Council Fire Guard, had joined the A.R.P. (the volunteer Air Raid Precaution organisation) and the Home Guard at the beginning of the War. He had also signed up for military service as a member of the RAF Voluntary Reserve (the RAFVR). In connection with the latter his "call-up" papers arrived on 17th February 1941, just a month after my sister had been born.

He had to report for duty in Blackpool less than a fortnight later and it is interesting to note from his "call-up" papers that he had to report to Blackpool with his National Identity Card, Health and Pensions Insurance Card, RAFVR badge, his marriage Certificate, the birth certificates of his children and his anti-gas respirator (commonly known as a Gas Mask).

National Identity Cards were introduced, ostensibly for security purposes, within days of the outbreak of war by the National Registration Act, 1939. From September 1939 every man, woman and child had to have one and carry it on them at all times or be able to produce it at a Police Station within 48 hours. It is hardly likely that an efficient spy network would not have been able to forge realistic copies of these cards and spies were caught, in almost every instance, by betraying themselves in other ways.

The real reason for the legislation was that the Government needed to know how many people there were in the country at the end of September 1939. It was essential to have this information for wartime planning purposes. Needless to say that, as a child, I did not carry my own card at all times. It would have disintegrated within days, but the legal requirement remained on the Statute Book until February 1952. There has been a lot of debate in recent years about reintroducing them, but nothing has been done in this respect to date.

I can also remember being issued with a gas mask but apart from trying it on for a first time, I cannot recall putting it on again. They were distributed on a house-to-house basis to families in September 1939 and were intended to protect everyone from gas bombs which might be dropped during air raids. The Germans had used mustard gas a great deal during World War One and many British soldiers had been killed or injured as a result. It was odourless and its deadly effect was not felt for several hours. There was a fear that it would be used against the civilian population, men, women and children in their homes.

My gas mask had a strong rubbery smell and was very claustrophobic. One was supposed to put it on when air raid wardens sounded a wooden "gas" rattle, suck in air though the filter and blow one's breath out through the sides until the warden rang a bell. Blowing out through the sides made a sound like letting the air out of a half blown up balloon which children found amusing. Fortunately, there were never any gas bomb attacks and no one ever found out how effective they might have been.

But I digress.

My father was not a healthy man and was invalided out of the Royal Air Force about nine months after he arrived in Blackpool. He had, for some years, been prone to bouts of acute bronchitis and during those nine months in the north west of England suffered from persistent bronchitis. It may have been triggered by the wintry weather and the lack of heating in his RAF billet. I suspect that the pre-existing weakness of his chest may also have been exacerbated by the removal of his appendix in December 1939 and the development of a duodenal ulcer which led, in the later 1940s, to a colic fistula, a hole in his intestines, that nearly killed him.

It was, paradoxically the bronchitis that saved his life at the time because, while he was stationed at the air force base near Blackpool he was assigned to a fire crew. Its task was to drive out to bombers that had to make a forced landing and extinguish any existing or resultant fires.

One particular day he had severe bronchitis and reported sick. The other members of the fire crew went out to a crippled bomber which had managed to land with an engine on fire. As they got within a few feet of the plane the bomb it was carrying, which had lodged in the undercarriage, and which it had been unable to drop over Germany became dislodged, fell onto the runway and exploded, killing everyone on the plane and all his companions on the fire engine.

Such are the strange twists of fate that occur during our lives. It was not my father's time to die and he had returned to Kettering, ill but otherwise unscathed.

19
My Conversion to Being Better Behaved

There is no doubt that between the ages of eighteen months and seven I was wilful, disobedient, mischievous and, frankly, a bit of a nightmare to my poor parents. All that changed, however, when I was coming up to seven as a result of my final act of disobedience and the consequences of it. As I recall, the background to it was as follows.

I made several friends at School and during the 15-minute, mid-morning milk break we little boys would play in the School playground. Just before we went back inside we would, on occasion, go into the open air and very primitive urinal in the School yard and relieve ourselves by trying to pee over the top of its five foot wall into the adjoining neighbours garden! What the next door neighbour must have said or thought I have no idea but we all thought it was great fun.

One of my fellow miscreants asked me one autumn afternoon whether I would like to go with his mother to the Headlands, pick mushrooms and watch the trains from the railway bridge there. We might, he said even see "The Flying Scotsman". This was too good an invitation to refuse and when my friend's mother asked, at the school gate, whether I had my parent's permission to go with her to the Headlands I blithely said "yes". Off we went and had a lovely time watching the trains on the main line from London to Edinburgh and gathering whatever mushrooms we could find.

When I had not returned from School at 4 pm my mother, fearing the worst, had telephoned my father from the nearest public telephone box and had asked him to leave his office and come home to look for me. Having scoured the neighbourhood he was not at all amused when I tripped gaily though the front door two and a half hours after I had left School. I had worried the lives out of my parents who were just about to go to Kettering Police Station and report me as "missing, presumably abducted". I deserved punishment for my thoughtlessness and it was duly meted out. The few token mushrooms I had brought home were not going to mitigate it.

"Bend down" said my father and I can remember to this day looking through my legs at the four grey enamel supports of the electric cooker as he gave me three hearty whacks on my bottom. People say that corporal punishment does not work or can be counterproductive but it must have led to my "conversion" because from that moment onward I decided it would be prudent to "play by the rules", respect my parents' wishes and behave myself. My mischievous streak never left me, however, as I will relate later in the book and my independence of spirit remained undimmed. `

My remaining days at Hawthorn Road Primary School were happy ones and the only incident that caused me some apprehension during that period was a summons to a small room where a middle-aged man in a white coat told me to sit in what looked, in retrospect, like a Dentist's chair. No sooner had I done so than a nurse swiftly placed a pad full of chloroform over my nose and mouth. I can just about remember him saying, "There is nothing to worry about. We are only going to remove your tonsils." With that, I slipped into unconsciousness. When I came round, I was given a note to take to my parents explaining what had been done and what I should eat and drink until my throat was less sore. Definitely no toast!

It was thought, at the time, by the powers that be, that tonsils acted as receptors and breeding grounds for germs whereas exactly the opposite was the case. Tonsils do indeed catch the germs but, in doing so, they prevent the germs that we breath in from going further into the body. But in 1943 children had no option. If the Government said they had to come out, they came out! In point of fact, removal probably had little adverse impact on me but it is interesting to note how all Governments can make elementary miscalcuations like this at the behest of so-called medical experts. The pots-and-pans fiasco to which I have already referred is another striking example of Government ineptitude and misunderstanding of what one could actually do with them.

In terms of what I should or should not eat after the removal of my tonsils there was not a great deal of choice. Food rationing had started at the beginning of the War. The first items to be rationed were bacon, butter and sugar. These were followed by meat of all types, tea, jam and marmalade, biscuits, breakfast cereals, cheese, eggs or egg powder, lard (used in cooking) milk, canned fruit, dried fruit like sultanas and raisins, and sweets. The sausages one could buy from the Butchers had hardly any meat in them, biscuits were incredibly plain and it was extremely difficult to find canned or dried fruit. German U Boats were waiting to sink any ships bringing food into the country so we all had to do without lots of things that people nowadays regard as necessities.

At this point I can sense some readers asking, "What about coffee?" It is such a staple drink in this day and age. I am afraid there was little or no real coffee during the War. The nearest approximation was "Camp Coffee" which was not really coffee at all. It came in small square sided bottles and was, for the most part, chicory extracted from the roots of a flower. Pre-War, coffee had been an upper-class drink and shipping it into the country was not considered a priority when merchant ships were being sunk in large numbers.

Tea, on the other hand, was considered vital to the war effort. A "cuppa" kept the workers going in factories and gave comfort to a beleaguered population. It continued to be imported throughout the war. Work without a tea break was inconceivable and mugs of tea were indispensable for members of the Armed Forces.

Because Camp Coffee tasted nothing like real coffee the bottle of it that my parents had bought remained pretty well unused in the pantry for as long as I can remember.

From July 1942 children, like myself were only allowed eight ounces of sweets a month, just under two ounces (about 25 grammes) of sweets per week. With my ration book I could try to buy a few of my favourite sweets with sherbert inside, alternatively humbugs, called "gobstoppers", or boiled fruit sweets. There were other varieties but sweets generally were in short supply all over the country and when they arrived in shops, like Woolworths who were the largest retailers of confectionery in the country at the time, long queues of children, like myself, gathered at the "pick and mix" counters to seize whatever was available.

Because I do not think they were part of the sweet ration I seem to recall going into Connie Izzett's corner shop and buying sticks or rolled up coils of black liquorice, or liquorice roots themselves. One had to chew them all in order to extract any sweetness but they were better than nothing.

The only alternative was chocolate but that was equally scarce and advertisements appeared in "Picture Post", a popular photo news magazine, asking adults not to buy bars of chocolate for themselves but to allow children who needed nutrition the most to buy them. Most adults were decent enough to respond to this type of request since young children did not have much else to look forward to. Many a dad was in the armed forces and many a mum worked in a factory or an office. Sweets and chocolate were children's only indulgences. In fact sweets and chocolate were rationed until February 1953, nearly eight years after the end of the Second World War. It was like going into "Aladdin's Cave" when rationing ended and one could buy as many sweets and bars of chocolate as one's pocket money would allow

In view of the long list of everyday items that we now consume without a second thought you may be wondering what food was not rationed! Well, there were a few things, the most obvious of which was bread. You could buy as much of it as you wanted during the war years although, paradoxically, it was rationed for a couple of years after the War. The reason you could do so was that, despite it being a staple element in everyone's diet, it was "mushy" in taste and unappetising. No one wanted to eat a lot of it.

I still have a vivid memory of running (as I have always done) to the Bakers Shop in Hawthorn Road, more or less opposite the Primary School, and buying with the 4 ½ d (roughly 2p) my mother had given me, a large loaf. These large loaves were called National Loaves because they contained the same ingredients wherever in the United Kingdom one brought them. As a result of wartime shortages of white flour popular white loaves had become unavailable by 1942. Merchant ships that had previously bought white flour into the country were needed for more vital imports. The Government which wanted to ensure that no one missed out on the basics of a healthy diet therefore introduced a standard wholemeal flour loaf with added calcium and vitamins. It was not unlike the plain brown wholemeal loaf we can buy in shops nowadays but nowhere near as tasty. Given the continuation of rationing post war of many food stuffs, the National loaf, was not abolished until 1956. By this time white flour was sufficiently plentiful to provide white bread for everyone who wanted to eat it. Sliced bread was still well into the future!

Homegrown fruit and vegetables were not rationed either. Mr Mobbs, the greengrocer in Broadway, always had vegetables and fruit in season and there was nothing to stop people growing their own. My parents grew runner beans in the back garden although there was not such space for anything else. Indeed, the government encouraged people to grow their own vegetables and big posters appeared in Post Offices and Railway Stations. "Dig for Victory" they proclaimed, and people did. Lawns were ripped out and all sorts of vegetables were grown in their place by people keen to supplement their meagre rations and, of course, to save money.

My mother bought glass storage jars with rubber seals under the lid known colloquially as "Kilner jars" whether they were manufactured by Kilner or not. In them she put fruit which she had bought in the summer and had stewed for consumption during the winter, particularly at Christmas. They, like the wooden tanker I never received, were kept on the top shelf in the pantry. Fruit is available from various parts of the world all year round nowadays but that was not the case during the war and one had to stew and bottle most of it for use out of season.

Another unrationed item was fish but the chances of buying any fish, other than the occasional smoked kipper, were remote. We never had any during the war.

One of the things young children under the age of five do not normally have to endure these days is a spoonful of cod liver oil every morning but for me it was compulsory . My mother was intent on taking advantage of free cod liver oil and orange juice offered by the Government to pre-school children. The orange juice, which came in bottles and which I suspect was concentrated, did not taste too bad but, to me, cod liver oil was a medicine which one had to swallow reluctantly whether one liked it or not. Cod liver oil was also available at low cost throughout the war to primary school children as also was Virol, a sticky, brown, semi-sweet syrup, packed full of malt, sugar and vitamins, such as Riboflavin: it was a supplement intended to give children an element of immunity against coughs and colds. Now, that, I really enjoyed!

In addition to the milk ration, the government introduced free half pint bottles of milk to children at School during their morning break in an effort to assist bone growth and prevent malnutrition. The free School milk scheme was popular and continued until Margaret Thatcher (nicknamed "Milk Snatcher") restricted it to children under seven years of age in 1971. Despite, therefore, our spartan diet and the rationing of so many things we liked to eat, most of us children grew into healthy, young adults. There was no obesity and no place for fads and fancies: as a child you had to eat what was available and what you were given. I have to confess that I hated two desserts one of which, tapioca, I called "frogspawn" because it looked like frogspawn and the other was semolina. The taste of both was pretty awful, perhaps, if I am charitable, because my parents did not know the best way of cooking either.

I cannot remember the free School meals at Hawthorn Road Primary so they could not have been very interesting. Nor, sadly, were the little girls who went there. We boys regarded them as "cissies" or "cry babies" while they considered themselves so much better than us. Their often repeated taunt was "what are little girls made of?" Sugar and spice and all things nice. But what are little boys made of? Slugs and snails and puppy dogs' tails". Well, I ask you, how could a little boy respond to that inbuilt sense of female superiority!

But there was one little girl I liked a lot and she lived in the house on the London Road beyond the crumbling brick wall at the back of our garden. As previously mentioned her name was Gillian Blackman and she was the same age as myself. Her parents were Jewish and I believe her father had been in the shoe trade in Germany. As a family they had managed to flee from the country before the Nazis started to arrest their relatives and put them into concentration camps like Auschwitz and Buchenwald. I knew they were Jewish because when I went into their dark and somewhat forbidding house, albeit infrequently, I saw the gleaming silver Menorah multibranched candelabra on their sideboard in the dining room.

She would either clamber over a broken section of the wall between our two homes or walk round the corner to our house and we would play together. It was all very innocent and I remember that my parents drove down to Brighton and Hove in the early 1950s to pay a social visit on the Blackmans. By this time Gillian was a beautiful dark haired 15- or 16-year-old and I was utterly lost for words. In fact I made a complete idiot of myself. She was absolutely stunning and I did not know what to do or say. I am not sure where she went to School in Kettering but it was certainly not to the Hawthorn Road Primary School.

Following my friendship with Gillian between the ages of five and seven and from about the age of eight I met a friendly little boy who lived a few doors further up the Broadway. His name was Peter and his aunt, who was looking after him during the war, happened to work as an Usherette at the Regal Cinema in the High Street. It was her job to show people to their seats when the auditorium lights were dimmed, either just before or during the film performances.

It was one of the three cinemas in Kettering that I can recall, namely the Regal, the Odeon and the Pavilion and was probably the most popular. There was no television in those days and cinema attendances were high. Cinemas were warm and comfortable places where women, in particular, could go out for an evening with a friend, female or male. Pubs, on the other hand, were not really "their scene". As a child I can remember quite vividly two middle aged ladies standing in Broadway discussing their favourite films and one saying to the other, "Are yer go-in ter Regal?" to see whatever was showing that night. I have always had an ear for phrases and accents and enjoyed listening to the local Northamptonshire accent which my parents did not have.

Peter's aunt must have found it difficult to keep him entertained and occupied especially during the summer holidays and was pleased when we started to play together. In fact, she used to let us into the cinema by the fire exit door at the side of the cinema so that we could watch the latest films. It is partly thanks to her that I developed my great love of cinema and for a couple of years my terror of life size paintings on walls. Perhaps I should explain!

When my parents moved into Broadway they hung a large framed painting of "The Laughing Cavalier" by Frans Hals on the upstairs landing. From the time they did so I was under the impression that this splendidly dressed gentleman was watching me as I walked past him on the way to the stairs or the bathroom. His eyes seemed to follow me everywhere and in order to avoid his gaze I used to crouch beneath the painting as I passed by it.

In November 1944 his aunt let us into the cinema to watch a film "One body too many". Although it was billed as a comedy/mystery, probably the reason why my parents let me go to see it, it was about the murder of a number of obnoxious, presumptive beneficiaries of the Will of an eccentric millionaire. They had gathered at his mansion to hear the reading of the Will and ascertain the bequests they had hoped had been made in their favour.

One by one, however, they were being murdered in their beds even though their bedroom doors were locked. This was a complete mystery to the, by now, terrified guests, but the cinema audience was aware that the eyes of the life size paintings on the walls were moving. The murderer was using secret passageways within the walls. The paintings would swing out into the room giving him access and the eyes painted on the canvas would be put back in place after the dreadful deed was done. The impact of the film reinforced by the gaze of "The Laughing Cavalier" gave me nightmares until my parents took the painting down, prior to our moving from Kettering. I must have had a very vivid imagination!

As a child the one thing I noticed about adult cinema was the playing of the National Anthem at the end of each performance. Performances usually consisted of a comparatively short "B" film, British Movietone or Pathe News and the main "A", feature, film. The audience would rise and stand still until the end of the National Anthem and, only then, head towards the exits. Sometimes, however, one or two people would push their way along the rows of seats to the central aisles and start to walk out before it had finished. They were hissed at or admonished by the rest of the audience because it was considered highly unpatriotic and disrespectful to do so when so many members of the audience had husbands, family members and relatives serving in the Armed Forces and putting their lives at risk for the sake of the civilian population. Ostentatious lack of respect for the sacrifice of others was considered contemptible.

It was not as if members of the audience were unaware of what was going on. British Movietone and Pathe news reels, showing the activities of British Servicemen on many fronts in different parts of the world, were, before the introduction of television, the principal visual record of them and consequently an integral part of any cinema performance. There was the magazine, "Picture Post", if one could afford it, and news on the radio and in the newspapers was informative. But people wanted to see what was happening at home and abroad and the cinema was the only place one could actually do so.

Children's cinema, however, was very different and most Saturday mornings I would head off to "The Odeon" cinema where, at the beginning of the programme we would all sing along to popular jingles, the words of which appeared on the screen. A little dot would jump from word to word so that we could follow the tune and all join in. Children's cinema featured films like Laurel and Hardy, Charlie Chaplin, Micky Mouse, Zorro, Sabu, Sinbad the sailor, Aladdin, Robin Hood and his Merry men, Westerns, swashbuckling adventures of many kinds and Tarzan. Johnny Weismuller, an American Olympic Gold medal swimming champion was a children's favourite as Tarzan with his high pitched "yodelling" animal call, his companion, Jane, and his pet chimpanzee, Cheeta. These films were the equivalent of the family television of today but rationed, for most children, to Saturday mornings only. The Regal and the Odeon were not the only cinemas I went to as I will mention later.

By the age of eight the teachers at Hawthorn Road Primary School thought that several boys and girls stood a good chance of passing the "8 plus" entrance examination to Kettering Grammar School. In 1944 the "8 plus" was more or less the equivalent of the "11 plus" introduced by the 1944 Education Act the following year. Miss West, my form teacher was keen to see me take and pass the exam and invited me to her home for extra tuition after School. I do not know why but I can vividly recall coming out of her house on the London Road, virtually opposite Broadway, after one of these additional lessons, and looking down from the verge in front of it. It was a glorious day. The sun was sinking in the West and cast a bright light, like a searchlight, along the entire length of Broadway. It was spectacular and made a lasting impression on me.

The examination duly took place and, after a couple of weeks, a letter from Kettering Grammar School dropped through the letterbox. My mother brought it into the hall where I was sitting on the stairs and asked me whether she or I should open it. I decided to open it myself and my relief was tangible.

As one of the eight boys out of nearly thirty who had taken the entrance exam I had passed and the next chapter in my life was about to begin.

20
Kettering Grammar School

Having passed the "8" plus" entrance examination I was kitted out by my proud parents in my new School uniform. This comprised a black school blazer, with the Kettering Grammar School "rose" stitched onto the breast (chest) pocket, a black school cap similarly adorned and the other specified articles of school wear, namely a black tie, white shirt, black shoes and grey flannel trousers. In the case of youngsters like myself they were, of course, short trousers.

The school's requirements were specific but if a boy could not meet them when he first entered the School the "missing items" had to be obtained when "his next lot of clothing is bought". This is an oblique reference to clothes' rationing to which I will refer later. It is interesting to note the requirement that "all boys who cycle to school or who walk long distances must keep a pair of dry socks or stockings at school". I assume, in this context, that socks are ankle length and that stockings cover the calf. The requirement was sensible and practical and reflected the ethos of the school, as did the School Rules. I have not encountered this particular requirement at any of the other schools I and my children have attended.

On my first day I set off for the school wearing my school uniform and sporting, for the first time, a brown leather satchel with its twin buckles. I walked up the London Road to the corner of Bowling Green Road, past the small Church Hall where I attended Sunday School, the garage which never seemed to have any cars in it and the photographic studio of Helen Speight to which my mother took Angela and me on a number of occasions. She wanted portrait photos which she could display or send to close relatives separated from us by the War. My parents also had a box "Brownie" camera which they used a lot. Opposite me as I turned into Bowling Green Road was the former cattle market and almost next door to it was Kettering Grammar school.

The school had been opened in September 1913 and was an impressive building. It had absorbed the previous Kettering Grammar school, founded in the reign of Queen Elizabeth I in 1577 and the Kettering Pupil Teacher Centre instituted in 1899. It was divided into separate and distinct boys and girls schools and never the twain did meet! We junior school boys never encountered the girls even though we shared the same building. We were in the right hand part of it, the girls in the left.

The school was well organised. Lunches were provided at a cost of 6d (2 1/2p) a day and teas could be obtained after school at a cost of 4d a day (under 2p). The school fees were four pounds and five shillings per term (£4.25p) and for boys "who intended to follow a commercial career" typewriting and shorthand lessons were available at ten shillings and six pence (53p) per term. In addition to the school uniform boys had to have a gymnastic vest, white shorts, black rubber soled gym shoes and football and cricket outfits.

A copy of the school Rules was sent to me shortly before my first day at the school and although I will not quote them all some reflect the times and social attitudes very well.

"Disorderly or unmannerly conduct of any kind in the streets, in trains, buses, in bus queues or in any public place is a school offence". In other words letting down the school in public would be punished. I never encountered anyone who had been punished but it was probably the cane or, in a serious case, expulsion.

"Every boy, not riding a bicycle, must salute by raising his cap when meeting or passing any master, lady of the staff or lady accompanied by a member of the school". You had to raise your cap to the mother of one of the pupils if you passed them both in the street. Good manners and respect for those in authority and the mothers of fellow pupils were considered essential. Interestingly, you did not have to be quite so polite to the fathers!

"No boy may have his hand in his pocket when meeting or passing a master or anyone who visits the school". This was clearly regarded as slovenly and rude. I wonder what schoolboys in the twenty first century would make of these basic rules and whether any could be enforced in the same way as they were enforced in the 1940s.

Among the other rules the most notable were the following: "no climbing through school windows without permission, no drinking of alcohol or smoking during term time and no boy may have in his possession at school firearms, fireworks, explosives or chemicals"! I assume one was allowed to climb out of windows if the school was being bombed and that boys could drink alcohol and smoke during the school holidays! But would school children actually contemplate going to school with revolvers in their satchels?

They might bring fireworks, perhaps, but the rule does clearly anticipate that, in a time of war, other eventualities might occur. The school Rules ended by stating that the air raid shelters were out of bounds, as was the school basement and all other areas of the school, after school hours.

In the letter accompanying the school rules it was stated that, during term time, boys had to wear the school cap if they were in school uniform and, parents please note, "had to maintain a high standard in all matters of personal neatness". In other words, there was to be no long hair, no muddy shoes, and no dispensing with the school cap when one might be recognised as a pupil. The boys were encouraged to take pride in their appearance and to embody standards the school set for them.

My form mistress throughout my time at the school was a Miss Cottrell and I thoroughly enjoyed being taught by her. Thanks to the books my father bought me on history, geography and science which I read at home I was always near the top of the class in those subjects. I also quickly made friends with a number of boys in my class, including Peter Cotton, David Little and a boy by the name of Roger Robinson who I suspect was not quite such a friend as I originally thought.

My suspicions, in this respect, relate to the disappearance of my stamp collection but more of that anon. Prior to its disappearance we were together all the time and being nine years olds we all wanted to know what was so fascinating about cigarettes. Most men and women smoked not only in real life but on the cinema screen as well. We had to try one! So, one afternoon after school we all went round to David Little's semi-detached house, stood behind the side gate between the house and the boundary fence and had a puff. David had managed to extract a cigarette from his mother's packet of "Craven A" without her noticing! We all coughed and spluttered and one lungful was enough to put me off cigarettes for life. I did, however, try a pipe for a short time at university although this was more for effect than out of any real desire to inhale tobacco.

Our little group also descended "en masse" on Peter Cotton's parents who lived in a very handsome 1930s Art Deco style house with a green tiled roof and green tiled windowsills. Their house backed on to Wicksteed Park and we either played in their back garden or in the park itself.

The disappearance of the stamp collection was unfortunate because it deprived me of the only thing Grandfather Hughes had ever given me. One day, and much to my surprise, I had received a large brown envelope from him, full of used postage stamps he had taken off letters in his writing desk. He had presumably decided to throw the letters and envelopes away and thought I might as well have the stamps. Full of excitement at this surprise package I asked my three friends to come round to my home after school and to look at them. Most of them were British and related to the reigns of George V, Edward VIII and George VI, including his Coronation.

I proudly showed them to my friends but, once they had left our house to go to their homes, the brown envelope had mysteriously disappeared. My mother and I scoured the house but could not find it. I walked straight round to my friends' homes and asked whether one of them had accidentally put it in his satchel. Roger was the only one whose denial was unconvincing. Following that incident and thereafter throughout my life I have kept a beady eye on any possessions I show to anyone! I have also made it a principle not to lend items of value – in personal or monetary terms – to friends, having been badly let down on two subsequent occasions. Items lent to friends, I have discovered from the experiences of myself and others close to me, are rarely returned.

By and large, however, I had a really happy time at Kettering Grammar school, coming within the top five in my class each term and, on Sports Day 1945, coming 3rd in the 100-yard race for my age. Maybe it was this achievement that led to my subsequent involvement in running although I did not appreciate it at the time.

Other events at the school which, again, I remember well, were a visit by the entire school to the Odeon on Montague Street and by my class to the Municipal Baths for my first swimming lesson at which I managed to slip under the surface and swallow rather a lot of chlorinated water!

We were all taken to the Odeon to see Lawrence Olivier playing the starring role in the film adaptation of Shakespeare's "King Henry, the Fifth"

It was in glorious technicolour and had spectacular scenes of battle. Lawrence Olivier was magnificent as the King and his address to Westmoreland before the Battle of Agincourt was meant to stir the patriotic souls of everyone in the audience. I can still hear the ringing tones of his superb voice as he declaimed the famous speech, part of which I give you:

"This story shall the good man teach his son and Crispin Crispian shall ne'er go by from this day to the ending of the world but we, in it, shall be remembered. We few, we happy few, we band of brothers for he today that sheds his blood with me shall be my brother. Be he ne'er so vile this day shall gentle his condition. And gentlemen in England now abed shall think themselves accursed they were not here and hold their manhood cheap while any speaks that fought with us upon Saint Crispin's day".

We were all taken to see what was, in essence, a Government propaganda film emphasising the need for us all to support the War effort and it made a terrific impact on us youngsters. Moreover, whether true or not, we had been told at school that if Hitler won the war, he would kill all Grammar school children. They would, when adult, represent a serious threat to his control of the Country and would have to be destroyed. This certainly added to our enthusiasm in and support for the Armed Services as exemplified by "Good King Harry and his valiant fighting men".

I also went with my mother to see "The Way ahead" at the Regal. I can distinctly recall the visit because the cinema had constructed a large "desert tableau" in the Foyer which was dotted with models of British and German tanks, field guns and army lorries. I was impressed, as were the rest of the audience, by the film which celebrated the turning point of the war in North Africa. In the closing scene members of the eighth army played by David Niven and Stanley Holloway and their comrades strode in determined fashion through a smoke screen, bayonets fixed about to take on an Italian army detachment which had been lobbing mortar shells at them. Stirring stuff and part of the Government's efforts to demonstrate how the grit and determination of our troops was turning the tide of war in North Africa in our favour.

Propaganda was an essential weapon in the Governments armoury. It was used not only to mislead our enemies but also to reassure the British public that, whatever the setbacks, we would win the war. There were many similar films including "In which we serve" about the Royal Navy, sarcastically referred to in the upper echelons of the Admiralty as "In which we sink", and "Dangerous Moonlight" and "The First of the few" about the RAF.

As a child, and courtesy of Peter's aunt, I saw them all and was thoroughly caught up in the patriotic fervour of the time, reinforced, in my case, by the Ministry of Information books my father bought me. He also bought me a book on Rank and Badges in the Navy, Army and Air Force and Auxiliaries like the Royal Observer Corps, the British Red Cross Society and the National Fire service. Being a voracious reader I learned all the badges by heart, soaking up the detail in the book like a sponge.

Not that I needed accompanying to the cinema or the assistance of Peter's aunt. As a confirmed film buff by the age of nine I was quite happy to take myself off to the Pavilion Cinema where I remember seeing "Pygmalion", the film adaptation of George Bernard Shaw's play with Lesley Howard, who was tragically killed during the War, as Professor Henry Higgins, and Wendy Hiller as Eliza Doolittle. As long as I was at a cinema and they knew which one, my parents had no qualms about my going out on my own, but I was warned by them to stick to the centre of the town and not to venture into the factory area on the other side of Kettering. They would have been content to stay at home looking after my little sister, confident in my ability to look after myself.

It may be difficult for the reader of this book to understand the fascination of a young boy for films. But try to imagine life without a television set in your own home and you will better appreciate how important other forms of visual representation were during the War years. Theatres were closed and the only other sources of news and entertainment were the Home Service and the Light programme of the BBC. They were more for adults than children.

21
Clothes Rationing

I made reference in the previous chapter to the need for any boy who was unable to appear in a complete school uniform at the beginning of term to obtain any outstanding items "when his next lot of clothing is bought". What that really meant was "when he had the necessary clothing coupons to enable him to do so and the items were actually in the shops".

Clothes rationing began on 1 June 1941 when I was five and a half years old and ended on 15 March 1949 when I was just over thirteen. It extended nearly four years beyond the end of the War. Why was it introduced and why did it last so long?

Rationing was intended to limit the ability of the civilian population to buy clothes and to ensure an element of fairness. At the beginning of the War one of the first noticeable changes in the dress of people on the streets was the increasing number of men and women in uniform. One only has to watch "Dad's Army", a humorous representation of life in Britain in the early 1940s to see the number of people in "Walmington on Sea" having to wear a uniform of some sort.

The demand for uniforms put intense pressure on Britain's textile and clothing industries which could only produce limited ranges of clothes for civilian consumption. In order to ensure fairness, the answer was to limit the ability of everyone to buy them. Whether rich or poor people would only be able to purchase the same number of clothes and would have the same number of clothing coupons. The only problem with this concept was that "well off" people could afford to buy robust expensive clothes whereas the "less well off" could only afford cheaper garments that lasted half as long. But nothing could be done about that.

Everyone was therefore given a clothing book with coloured coupons in it. Each page of coupons was a different colour to stop people using up all their coupons at once. People were only allowed to use one colour at a time. The Government would tell people when they could start using a new colour – but you could use unused coupons from one year in the next year. Every item of clothing was given a value in coupons and manufacturers were told what they could and could not produce. No longer could they, for example, manufacture silk underwear, silk night clothes or wedding dresses: the silk was required for parachutes. In order to buy any item of clothing, people had to hand over their Clothing Book to the shopkeeper who would cut out with a pair of scissors the number of coupons necessary to purchase the garment in question. The purchaser would then pay for their purchase after which the shopkeeper would return the Clothing Book and hand over what had been purchased.

At first people were given a book with 60 coupons but this had been reduced to 48 coupons by the time I went to Kettering Grammar school. As a growing child I was allowed an extra 10 clothing coupons a year, sufficient for my mother to buy a school uniform for me.

By way of illustration of how the rationing system worked in my case over the twelve-month period I set out below the way in which my mother would have spent my 58 coupons in September 1944.

7 coupons for an unlined dark blue mackintosh for wear to school in the winter
8 coupons for my blazer
3 coupons for a grey woollen pullover
6 coupons for my short trousers
3 coupons for my gym shorts
6 coupons for pyjamas to keep pace with my growth in size
2 coupons for two pairs of socks
8 coupons for two white shirts
3 coupons for one pair of black shoes
4 coupons for two pairs of pants
4 coupons for two vests
2 coupons for black rubber soled gym shoes

All the clothes she bought would have been oversized to allow for my growth during the year. One pair of shoes for a small boy, however, would not have been enough had it not been for "Blakey's". The leather on the sole would have worn out. Blakeys were metal studs which one banged into the new soles so that the leather did not actually touch the ground. One could buy blakeys in any hardware store and we would all "clink" along the pavements on our way to and from school.

Kitting me out for my first year would have left 2 coupons and I suspect she used them to buy cotton handkerchiefs because, in those days, there were no such things as tissues or kitchen roll. After use, and looking pretty revolting, the hankies would have been put in a saucepan specially reserved for the purpose and boiled until they were clean. They would then be ironed by my methodical Mum and used again (and again until they were unfit for purpose).

As a small boy I quickly made holes in my socks and nearly all my socks had to be repaired at least once or twice because of the cost and scarcity of new ones and, of course, lack of additional coupons. As a result, my mother introduced me to the mushroom shaped object which one inserts into a sock in order to darn and repair it. She taught me how to sew the wool across the hole in the sock and make it wearable once again. The ability to do so came in very handy during my National Service in the Army and the "mushroom" and a ball of grey wool were essential items in my kitbag.

From well before the War my mother had become proficient at embroidery, and she spent a lot of her spare time during the War embroidering everything from tablecloths to napkins and handkerchiefs when she could obtain the right colours of cotton thread. On 16 October 1942 she took her embroidery and clothes making skills one stage further when she purchased for nine pounds one shilling and eight pence a Singer sewing machine from the Company's shop in Kettering. With that machine she intended to "repurpose" a number of old clothes by taking them apart and reconstituting or mending them. The Singer Sewing Machine Company had shops in many towns because their machines were extremely useful and popular during the War years.

She also knew how to knit, a popular outlet for creativity, and would take apart woollen garments which had holes in them, or which had outlived their purpose or the fashion of the time and would rescue the wool. With that wool she knitted a number of "Fair Isle" pullovers for me, using a knitting pattern she had acquired: she also knitted gloves for my sister and I and many of my sister's buttoned cardigans. Pattern books were available from bookshops and stationers and production of them was probably subsidised by the Government. The pullovers were called "Fair Isle" probably because they were multicoloured as a result of the use of the wool rescued from a number of different garments.

In fact, the Government exhorted women to "make do and mend" and making or repairing your own clothes became an integral part of wartime life. Clothes had to be made with whatever was available, including old curtains, or carefully preserved because it was so difficult to purchase new ones. By way of information 11 coupons were required for a woman's dress, 2 for a pair of woollen stockings, 8 for a man's shirt, 8 for a main's pair of trousers, 5 for a pair of women's shoes and 7 for a pair of men's shoes.

For the most part women's clothes on sale in the shops were drab and dull and there was a distinct shortage of civilian shoes, particularly for women. The reason for this was that manufacturers in places like Kettering had switched the bulk of their production to manufacturing boots and shoes for members of the Armed Forces. In fact, women did rather badly because, in addition to the shortage of attractive new clothes, there was no "make up" in the shops, very little lipstick and none of the beauty products that they can so easily purchase in this century. Some of the younger women resorted to using beetroot juice for lip colour, boot polish for mascara and to drawing a straight black line with a pencil up the back of their legs to make it look as if they were wearing expensive silk stockings which had, of course, completely disappeared from the shops.

One can imagine how pleased the young women in Kettering were when the "Yanks" arrived at the newly built USAAF base at Grafton Underwood. The Americans could obtain silk stockings and "make up" from the United States which added to their attraction. It would be interesting to know how many G.I. (Government Issue) brides were first drawn to their American bridegrooms by the latter's ability to provide luxuries that their British counterparts could not.

I should perhaps mention that, although I am not aware that my mother took advantage of them, the Women's Voluntary Service (W.V.S) set up "Clothes Exchanges" in most towns and cities where mums could "trade in" the clothes their children had outgrown for "points". These points could then be used to acquire clothes that better fitted their children. It was a sensible and practical scheme given the facts that the husbands of many women were in the Armed Forces, money was tight and ten extra clothing coupons per year were not necessarily going to cover the requirements of rapidly growing children over a 12-month period. In addition to its "make do and mend" poster campaign the Ministry of Information published leaflets giving information on these Clothes Exchanges and advice on such subjects as "how to prevent moth damage to woollens", "how to make sure shoes last longer" and "how to repair and renovate" one's clothes.

Why did clothes rationing continue after the end of the War? The answer is pretty straightforward. Thousands of ex-Servicemen did not have any decent clothes when they were demobilised, nor could they afford to purchase an expensive item like a suit.

The civilian clothes they had worn when attending the recruitment centre to which they had been summoned, often their best, had been unceremoniously thrown away when they were issued with a uniform. They may have worn that uniform for years and when they, at last, reached home their remaining clothes were either too big, too small or just too old. Most of my own clothes disappeared in the same way when I reported for National Service at Park Hall Camp in Oswestry.

For Servicemen, back to "Blighty" from abroad or for those fortunate to have been stationed in Britain, the priority post "demob" was to secure employment in "Civvy Street". Most needed, at minimum, some help in acquiring a suit to wear for a job interview and, afterwards, at work, once employed. The Government therefore initiated a subsidised "voucher" scheme which enabled them to go into a tailor's shop, like Burtons, and obtain an "off-the-peg" utility suit. As a result, production of clothing had to be switched to a large extent from service uniforms to utility suits and other utility garments. This meant continuing shortages for the rest of the civilian population while demand for utility wear was satisfied.

Among other utility garments were gowns for schoolteachers and Undergraduates where they were obligatory and my first gown at Cambridge had the utility "E" (for economy) label inside it. It had been bequeathed to me by a former post war member of my college and was probably made from the same cloth as black-out material used to prevent light emanating from houses during German bombing raids.

The British sense of humour emerged with the introduction of utility suits, and I quote one of the jokes about them below. It was told to me by my Godfather, Arnold Willis, in the 1950s and I have been longing to get it out of my system for ages. Perhaps, by putting it in writing and inflicting it upon yourself, the unsuspecting reader, I may be able to lay it to rest!

"A hard-up ex-Serviceman with a voucher in his hand went into a tailor's shop and asked whether the tailor had any utility suits. The tailor looked him up and down and said that he had just the suit for him.

The suit was duly produced and the ex-Serviceman tried on the trousers. Although they were a good fit the right leg was slightly longer than the left. The ex-Serviceman pointed this out and was told that the voucher did not cover alterations and that he would have to pay for them. "But", said the tailor, "All you have to do is lean slightly over to the left and the trouser bottoms will be level". The ex-Serviceman then tried on the jacket. When he leant over to the left the left shoulder of the jacket rose up slightly. "That is no problem" said the tailor. "All you have to do is lean forward with your left shoulder and it will even up the top of the jacket on each side".

Not entirely satisfied with his new utility suit but not having any money to spare for alterations the ex-Serviceman handed over his voucher and stepped out into the street. He had not gone more than a few paces when another ex-Serviceman stopped him in the Street. "Ere, Mate, who's your tailor?" he asked. "He is just a few doors down the street". "Well, I'm going there to get my suit" the other replied. "If he can make one for a cripple like you he can make one for me".

I plead, in mitigation, that this was not my joke and regret any adverse reaction on the part of the reader to it.

22
Life at Home During the War: Part One

It is easy to describe events and recite facts but it is difficult to pin down and articulate on paper the effect certain incidents and experiences can have on one's behaviour and attitude to life. I am incredibly fortunate in having a photographic memory from which I can retrieve incidents and the names and often the faces of people from as long as eighty years ago. Without it I would probably not have passed as many examinations as I have!

Not that it has had much effect on my later life but, even now, I can bring out of my "memory bank" the sight of the Walls ice cream man who used to pedal on his four-wheeler down Sheppey Road on the Becontree Estate and stop close to my grandparents' house. In front of his handlebars was a refrigerated box full of ice creams and the cheaper orange flavoured lollies for which, I seem to recall, my parents paid a penny.

This was when I was three and three quarters, at about the same time as the outbreak of the Second World War.

In terms of experiences nor do I forget being bitten much to my surprise, by a large brown spider at the age of six and a half in the summer of 1942. Whoever heard of spiders biting people but there they were, two tiny red spots on my arm where I had brushed it off. I had fallen into the long grass and weeds of my grandparents' unkempt front garden which must have harboured insects of all kinds. I can visualise the "bite marks" even now. As a result of that particular experience, I steered clear of spiders for many years!

The above are trivial recollections of no great significance but the experience of living with a sickly father was more profound and led to my adopting the lifestyle of one of my favourite comic characters "Wilson, the wonder athlete" whom I will mention later. My father, sadly, suffered from poor health throughout his life whereas my mother, until overtaken by Parkinsons Disease, was a ball of energy.

During my first few years I did not really notice that my father had health problems but by the time I was six they were becoming painfully apparent. He suffered continuously from bronchitis and his constant coughing, particularly during cold weather, led me to trying to protect and develop my own lungs in whatever way I could.

My father's resistance to coughs, colds and bronchitis was not great from the time his duodenal ulcer was diagnosed in 1942. Moreover, it was clear that, as a result of it, and as a consequence of the meagre food ration allocated to adults, he would not get any better. In fact, he appeared to be steadily losing weight from 1942 onwards. He was therefore allowed, among other items, additional rations of milk powder and egg powder both of which could be used in cooking. I am not sure whether semolina and tapioca were rationed but they both appeared on the dining table a lot from 1942 onwards. He was welcome to both as far as I was concerned! I did, however, appreciate the Victoria sponge cakes which he was occasionally able to bake, courtesy of his extra rations: they were moist and delicious and he never lost the ability to make them. My mother, on the other hand, accepted that she was not such a good cook as her husband and left much of the meal preparation to him throughout their marriage. His example has prompted me and my children to have a go at cooking and not to be afraid of creating dishes of various kinds: my daughter 'Stella', has actually achieved Cordon Bleu status and a granddaughter has baked superb cakes from the age of ten, including Victoria sponge cakes! His "cooking gene" has clearly been passed down to members of my family.

Although my father's health was poor my mother, sister and I remained in good health during the war years. My only encounter with doctors, therefore, apart from the unexpected removal of my tonsils, was the brief visit I paid to Dr Drake-Lee's surgery in the Headlands, at the age of nine, to collect a prescription for my father and pay the Doctor's fee of half a crown (two shillings and six pence). There was no National Health Service in those days and, until it was set up in 1948, Doctors would charge what they considered appropriate for the medicines they prescribed or the treatment they gave. They also took into account the means of the patient where hardship might be involved.

My parents had realised from my earliest days that I was a very independent little boy and it does not surprise me, in retrospect, that they sent me round to the surgery with the money or to the bakers to buy bread or to the greengrocers to buy vegetables. My father would have been poorly and my mother would have been looking after my sister, Angela, at the time.

My sister, to whom I have only briefly referred in previous chapters was born in January 1941. She was a sweet and good-natured little girl and, like her older brother, self-assured. By the time she was three and a half she would go into the home of our next door neighbours, sit by the bed of the eighty year old Mr Dorr and tell him how lucky he was to have her to talk to. She treated him as a Grandad in the absence of her real grandparents and there is little doubt that the bedridden Mr Dorr appreciated her company and that of the dolls which accompanied her on these visits.

In fact, by way of appreciation of her visits, the Dorrs gave her an upright four-wheel Victorian pram for her dolls which, as an eight year old, and, to my shame, I used as a sort of racing car along Broadway. They were both in their late seventies/early eighties when we arrived in Kettering and my mother was highly amused when during one of her many chats with her, Mrs Dorr remarked that she had recently visited a "little old lady in Hospital", which Mrs. Dorr was herself. My mother never forgot the conversation and mentioned it subsequently on more than one occasion. Mr Dorr, like my own grandfather, had also painted country scenes in watercolour and gave my parents a number of his paintings.

Angela was also a favourite of the American airmen whom I describe in the next Chapter. She would sit on the low red brick wall of Mr & Mrs Dorr's house which had formerly sported black railings until the pots-

and-pans fiasco and talk to the GI's opposite who thought she was a "charmer". It is so sad to contemplate how fears for a child's safety would prevent any such occurrence in this day and age, but many airmen had their own young children back in the United States and would never have thought of molesting in any way a pretty and outgoing four year old little girl.

23

The Arrival of the Americans

During the first three months of the Second World War, living conditions for the civilian population remained very much the same as before, tolerable and relatively normal. Certain items of food and clothing were beginning to disappear from the shops but that was all. From early 1940 until October 1942, however, the combined effect of the Blitz, the subsequent devastating bombing of Cities like Liverpool, Glasgow, Bristol, Exeter and Coventry and the introduction of draconian rationing was to turn the bright and sunny horizons of peace and prosperity envisaged in the 1930s into the sombre grey of deprivation and disaster.

As a Nation we were suffering during this period grievous military losses almost everywhere and there is no doubt that a sense of grim reality had seeped into households across the land. Young and old became aware of the threat. We knew we had our backs to the wall and that our Armed Forces and the workers in factories supporting them were striving to save us and our way of living. It was not, in fact, until the battle of El Alamein that we realised the Germans could actually be beaten and that we could look forward to a successful outcome to the war.

Our hopes were boosted immeasurably by the Americans entering the war and, in the case of Kettering, by the arrival of the USAAF (United States Army Air Force) at the newly constructed airfield at Grafton Underwood on the outskirts of the town. Whatever benefits they brought to the young women of Kettering they brought an almost immediate one to me which I will mention shortly.

When the Americans arrived, they were overconfident in their ability to inflict damage on German factories and military installations and embarked upon daylight bombing raids, where they could, of course, see their targets. They believed that large formations of heavily armed B17s ("Flying Fortresses", albeit in the air) would be able to defend themselves against enemy fighters and that by flying at high altitude would evade anti-aircraft fire. The only problem with this concept was that the enemy could, by the same token, see you coming and maximise its number of fighter aircraft to attack the formations. The anti-aircraft guns could also hit aircraft at an altitude greater than anticipated by the Americans.

As a consequence, I would stand in our back garden after school and at the weekends and watch badly damaged B17s, often with only two of their four engines still functioning fly over the house at probably not much more than six or seven hundred feet. Sometimes an arm would appear through one of the machine gun portals on the fuselage as a member of the crew fired a Verey rocket into the sky, a red one for "bomb on board" or a yellow one for "wounded on board". These rockets would warn the Fire and Ambulance services to be on hand as the crippled aircraft landed or tried to land and would have been used when radio contact with the airfield had been lost.

It was only when, in early 1944, P51 (Mustang) fighter planes, capable of escorting them to Germany and back, were introduced that losses of American bomber aircraft were substantially reduced. Before their introduction a massive number of B17s had been shot down. On one particular mission every aircraft had failed to return. Most of those that made it home had been hit by German fighters or flak from anti-aircraft guns and many aircrew had been badly wounded.

There could not have been enough space for all the wounded at the nearby base because the large Edwardian house in Broadway immediately opposite our own house was requisitioned in 1943 as an American Hospital/Convalescent facility. The recuperating aircrew who were sent there were very friendly and took an immediate liking to Angela and myself and, as previously mentioned, proved a rich source of chewing gum, Hershey chocolate bars and comics. They showered me, in particular, with all types of chewing gum, Wrigleys with the red, green and white wrappers, pink packets, yellow packets and packets of a variety of other colours and flavours, spearmint, regular and so on.

One American serviceman, named Ralph, became a regular visitor to our house: I think he missed his own wife and family in the United States. For the time he was "over the road" he was my prime source of chewing gum and once he realised that I was collecting the different types of chewing gum wrappers he brought as many as he could to me. I never realised there were so many different types of chewing gum although I quickly appreciated that Americans could not seem to function without it. The number I met and spoke to who were not smoking "Lucky Strike" or similar or who did not have gum in their mouths was minimal!

I was absolutely devastated when, at the end of the war and in one of her "tidying up my room" phases my mother threw all my wrappers away!

Because the Americans gave me lots of their comics, which I am afraid she also threw away, I got to know all about Superman, and Batman and Robin well before other British children. In them was another "good guy" who turned himself into a red-hot aerial missile and who powered his way through brick walls and wooden doors "in the cause of justice"! I thought he, Batman and Robin, and Superman were most impressive.

There was no one to compare with these three in British comics which I also read avidly and which I will mention in the next chapter.

24

Life at Home During the War: Part Two

Children who only had a fleeting recollection of pre-war days came to accept food and sweet rationing as the norm. We were, for the most part, healthy and happy during the 1940s and despite the shortage of toys and playthings with which later generations have been showered at Christmas and on birthdays we did not feel deprived from the point of view of material possessions. We learned to make do, to a large extent, with what we already had. We and our families used imagination and creativity to compensate for what could not be purchased. As children we also read a lot and absorbed ourselves in stories of adventure of every kind, whether in books or comics.

Because, moreover, we were all in the same boat there was no sense of jealousy or any feeling that other children were receiving more presents or were being treated better than ourselves.

Christmasses were particularly austere during the war years. It was extremely difficult to get hold of a Christmas tree and apart from whatever they had managed to save from before the war, like rolls of multicoloured crepe paper which could be attached to dado rails with drawing pins and hung below the ceiling, most families had to use their ingenuity to bring a festive atmosphere to their dining or living room.

My parents like everyone else would try to find sprigs of holly with berries on or mistletoe and, if successful would hang them on the wall or use them to adorn the dining room table.

With my mother and father, I would decorate pine cones and make paper chains with whatever pieces of coloured paper they had been able to acquire during the year.

I was lucky enough to have toys made by Uncle John but, as a general rule, mums knitted toy dolls for their daughters and dads made toys for their sons.

You will appreciate from what I have already said about food rationing that "Christmas dinner", usually at lunch time on Christmas Day, was limited in content and variety. With our homemade paper hats on our heads, we nevertheless enjoyed whatever our parents had been able to conserve in the preceding months or purchase prior to our celebratory meal.

The only thing we really did miss was the ability to visit members of our family who did not live nearby. I, for example, missed seeing my grandparents and my uncle Gerald at Sheppey Road. The war had restricted the ability of people to travel any distance by public transport and for civilians who had a car there was petrol rationing until 1942 and, thereafter, no petrol at all.

I can recall our last eventful visit to Sheppey Road before the complete ban on the civilian use of petrol came into effect. It was going to be a short visit to attend the wedding of my aunt Pat and to introduce my one-year-old "baby sister" to her grandparents. We set off from Kettering early in the morning on the A6 which ran down the London Road only a few yards away from our home. The car had not been used very much in the preceding few months and it was not until we reached the outskirts of Luton that my father realised that there was something seriously amiss. The engine was making odd noises.

He stopped the car, lifted the driver's side of the bonnet and discovered to his horror that a metal plug, the size of a 5p coin (or sixpence in those days), two thirds of the way up the engine block had disappeared. As a result, oil had been spewing out of the hole and there could not have been much oil left in the engine. Our predicament could have been disastrous, but my ingenious and highly practical mother took the cork out of a medicine bottle in her handbag and suggested that my father bang it into the hole with the starting handle. Which he did! After allowing the engine to cool down, they drove to the nearest garage where they topped up the engine with oil.

Incredibly the cork stayed in place until we returned to Kettering where my father was able to have the engine repaired. I should perhaps point out that a 1936 Morris Minor, like many other small cars, did not have an electric starter motor and that the engine had to be started, with the choke partly out, by cranking it with a starting handle which one inserted into the engine block through a hole in the front bumper. Turning over the engine in this way was hard work and could not have helped my father's chest. During the First World War many of the fighter aircraft were started in the same way by ground crew vigorously hand turning the wooden propellers until the engines came to life with a throaty roar.

While on the subject of our little car I have to say that, although it never let us down, it did have its moments, probably due to being laid up in the garage for long periods during the war. On a later occasion in 1945, when limited amounts of petrol were once again available for civilian use, it sprang a leak in the radiator on our way from Kettering to Sheppey Road. Steam appeared and my father once again stopped the car. There was a small crack in the radiator from which water was escaping. Ever the pragmatist my mother quickly went into a grocers shop nearby, bought some porridge oats and poured spoonfuls of it into the top of the radiator. The porridge expanded and blocked the crack but I seem to remember that my father had to pay for a new radiator to get us back from Sheppey Road to Kettering. A rather more expensive "temporary fix"!

But again I digress.

Deprived of newly manufactured Dinky toys, Hornby train accessories and Meccano engineering kits from 1941 onwards a young boy, like myself had to make do with what little he possessed and whatever friends and relatives could make for him. He could also collect stamps and cigarette cards which were "currency" amongst schoolboys like myself. "Swaps" were the order of the day, like the exchanging of football player cards that has been popular with subsequent generations. One can more readily understand, in the circumstances, why the loss of the precious addition to my collection of stamps upset me at the time.

Another thing I discovered one could collect was the occasional poster from the National Savings Office behind the High Street in Kettering. During the First and Second World Wars the Government of the day encouraged everyone to support the war effort by putting whatever they could afford into Post Office Savings Bank Accounts and National Savings Certificates. Interest was payable on both.

My mother had her own Post Office Savings Bank Account and encouraged me to open one as well (Kettering 30915). One could buy National Savings Stamps at the Post Office from as little as sixpence (2-1/2p) and when one had saved thirty stamps (75p) they could be converted into a 15-shilling National Savings Certificate upon which a higher rate of interest was payable, if one did not encash it early. The Certificates were stuck into a blue Government Issue Savings Certificate book and when the princely sum of £5, five pounds, had been saved one could trade in the Certificates for a "Defence Bond". Savings Certificates of numerous denominations above fifteen shillings were available if one could afford them. Six pence and fifteen shillings might now be considered derisory amounts, but fifteen shillings was quite a lot of money in those days.

My mother must have taken me into the National Savings Office possibly to buy my first 15-shilling National Savings Certificate because when I went in I saw a magnificent poster on the wall. It had flags all down one side of it, an image of Lord Nelson on the other and a representation of a destroyer just like the one my uncle John had made for me in the middle.

On the poster appeared Lord Nelson's famous message at Trafalgar, in the flags themselves and in script beneath: "England expects that every man will do his duty". They did and during the battle in 1805 our navy put the French warships to flight. It was a stirring victory and well worth emphasising during our struggle for Naval supremacy in the Atlantic in the early days of the Second World War.

In an effort to drive up savings, the Government initiated different "Savings weeks" in which they asked the public for funds for specific items like Spitfires or a particular type of warship and this poster had probably advertised a "Warship week". I loved the poster and asked if I could have it. The Manageress of the office generously gave it to me and it remained one of my proudest possessions, neatly folded and kept in pristine condition in the monk bench until, as inevitably happened, my mother had one of her regular clear-outs and threw it away!

While on the subject of savings the Government issued posters portraying the "Squanderbug" – an odious squidgy blob of a creature, adorned with swastikas which encouraged people to spend any extra cash they might have on unnecessary items. "Don't listen to him", the posters proclaimed, "contribute to the war effort through savings instead". Like Herr Hitler, it met a "sticky end".

Beside "collecting", playing with one's toys and doing jigsaw puzzles there were many other ways of passing "out of school" hours. Between the ages of eight and thirteen I became a voracious reader of books of all kinds. I devoured stories by Captain W.E. Johns (Biggles), R M Ballantyne (Coral Island), Frederick Marryat (Masterman Ready), H.C. McNeile (Jim Maitland), Edgar Wallace (Sanders of the River), Sir Walter Scott (Ivanhoe), Baroness Orczy (The Scarlet Pimpernel), Richmal Compton (Just William), Grace Richmond (Red Pepper Burns) and many others: it was so easy to absorb oneself in the stories of these great writers and in the adventures and escapades of the characters they portrayed. My father bought all these books for me as well as the Ministry of Information, science, geography and history books I have already mentioned, and I am deeply indebted to him for doing so.

There were also comics like Wizard, Rover, Hotspur, Dandy and Beano which I purchased with my pocket money, and one of the characters in Wizard affected my future from the moment I read about him. His name was William Wilson, the wonder athlete, a man whose age was indeterminate but who kept himself supremely fit. He might have been two hundred years old but he could still break World Records in running and jumping. He was depicted as an unassuming totally dedicated loner, wanting no glory or publicity and he was hailed when he appeared in 1943 as a welcome wartime morale booster.

In fact, it is fair to say that, albeit a fictional character, he was an inspiration to many British athletes in their careers. He exemplified British grit and the "stiff upper lip" and, as an eight-year-old, I wanted to be like him. It is partly thanks to him that I was still going for a five-mile run once a week, rain or shine at the age of eighty five. He motivated me to look after my chest and to try and avoid the ill health suffered by my father who died in his early fifties.

One of the competitive sports in which we could engage during the autumn was "conkers". This involved piercing a bright and shiny horse chestnut with a metal skewer and passing a piece of string about a foot long through the hole in the middle of it. The horse chestnut, called a "conker", would sit at the end of the piece of string, kept in place by a knot in the string beneath it. We youngsters, boys and very occasionally girls, would take it in turns to unleash our conker onto that of our opponent which would be hanging down, awaiting the impact. The child whose conker survived the alternate blows would be the winner. A "sixer", a conker that had survived six such contests would be hailed as a champion and retired from further combat by its exultant owner!

The desire to win was so great that some children even went to the lengths of soaking their conkers in vinegar overnight in the belief that it would give them greater durability, the equivalent, perhaps of performance enhancing drugs taken by athletes in the Olympic Games! I do not know what has happened to Horse Chestnuts (or indeed Spanish Chestnuts) over the last seventy or so years, but they no longer appear as large as those we picked up from the ground in the 1940s. Maybe it was because we were smaller, and not the chestnuts!

Another popular game among small boys was "marbles". Marbles were small round balls of toughened glass, and the object of the game was to roll your marble along a flat surface and hit your opponent's marble. It called for a keen eye and an element of skill and depending on the rules of the game you were playing you could lose quite a few of them. Many boys carried bags of marbles in their school satchels and played with them during the morning and lunch time breaks. You will doubtless have heard of elderly people "losing their marbles" when they suffer from a lack of mental capacity. The expression must relate back to this game.

One could always listen to the radio but, apart from the news which invariably told us how well Allied forces were doing, whether they were or not, the only programmes that I listened to as a child during the war years were "I.T.M.A.", "Music While You Work", "Workers Playtime" and "Children's Hour".

"Workers Playtime" was a Variety Programme that ran between 1941 and 1964. It was designed as a morale booster for industrial workers during the war and was broadcast at lunch time three times a week from different factory canteens across the country. It was so popular that it continued nine years after the war and featured an immense range of talent.

During its early years long forgotten comedians like "cheerful" Charlie Chester, "Gert and Daisy" (Elsie and Doris Walters) and singers like Anne Shelton and Dorothy Squires appeared regularly on the programme. It went on post-war to display the talents of a host of famous comedians and singers including Peter Sellers, Frankie Howerd, Tony Hancock, Terry Thomas, Julie Andrews, Morecambe and Wise, Roy Hudd, Bob Monkhouse, Janet Brown, Ken Dodd and many others. As a child I particularly liked Percy Edwards, the impersonator who could accurately imitate over six hundred different birds and many other animals. Although he never said so during his performances, he was a professional zoologist and, in later life, was awarded an MBE for his services to ornithology and to Variety.

"Music while you work" broadcast continuous live popular music twice daily, principally through the Tanoy systems in factories from June 1940 until September 1967. The idea was that "non-stop" popular / light music played at an even tempo would help factory workers become more productive. They could sing or whistle along to the tunes as they worked.

"I.T.M.A." (It's that man again) was a comedy programme. "That man" was Tommy Handley, a fast-talking comedian who was surrounded by an array of exotic characters. In-built into the programme was a fair amount of propaganda. There was Funf, the incompetent enemy agent who was designed to make the German propaganda machine a source of public ridicule, Ali Oop, the Middle Eastern hawker trying to sell dodgy worthless goods (the equivalent of the Squanderbug), Mona Lott, the mournful laundress whose favourite expression was, "Its being so cheerful as keeps me going", Colonel Chinstrap, a retired alcoholic army officer, always on the lookout for a free drink ("I don't mind if I do, Sir"), Cecil and Claude (no explanation needed!), the unfortunate one legged Diver whose catch phrase was "don't forget the diver") and my counterpart, Mrs. Mopp, the charlady, who would interrupt conversations Tommy Handley was having by bursting into the room, saying "Can I do you now, Sir?" Her other famous parting remark was T.T.F.N. ("ta ta for now") which became a national byword for saying "goodbye". Everyone used T.T.F.N. for years after the war.

I say "counterpart" because "Mrs. Mopp" was my nickname at primary school. I had a mass of brown curly hair and because no other little boy had so much I almost inevitably acquired it. My nickname at Brentwood school, when my hair was much shorter was "haggis", not because I looked like one but for a fairly obvious reason. All my life, I have, in fact, encountered adaptions, misspellings and mispronunciations of my surname from Hews, to Huges, to Hugges, to the French version Hugues with a hard "g". I don't mind that one because there was, once upon a time, a Royal family in France by that name!

"Children's Hour" was hosted by "Uncle Mac", Derek McCulloch, and he introduced us to Toytown and "Larry, the Lamb". He was head of Children's broadcasting and had strong and forthright views on its role. "Nothing but the best is good enough for children", he said. "Our wish is to stimulate their imaginations, direct their reading, encourage their various interests, widen their outlook and inculcate the Christian virtues of love of God and their neighbours". He had a very reassuring voice for children many of whom had been evacuated and were no longer living with their parents and he always closed his programme by saying "Goodnight children, everywhere".

From "D-Day" on 6 June 1944 it became clear that we were going to win the war in Europe and that it was just a matter of time before The Third Reich was battered into submission. Bombing raids on Germany were as heavy as those of the Luftwaffe on the United Kingdom but there was little sympathy for the German civilian population in view of the suffering inflicted by Hitler on millions of Europeans. There was even less sympathy when the inhumane treatment of inmates of Belsen, Auschwitz and Buchenwald was revealed in Pathe and British Movietone news reels at cinemas.

Allied armies, in tandem with the Russian army were retaking territory previously occupied by Nazi forces and confidence was high. We could all look forward to happier days although these, in truth, did not arrive until at least ten years after the war had ended.

On 8 May 1945 the fateful day arrived when the unconditional surrender of Germany was declared, and the Nation could celebrate. My parents took Angela and me up to the Market Place in Kettering, just below the parish church, where there was dancing, singing and a lot of exuberant letting down of hair: alcohol doubtless had a lot to do with that. An army sergeant came up to me and, with my parents' permission, put me on his shoulders and jigged round the Market Place to the tunes of the band that had assembled. Flags and bunting were out, and it was all immense fun.

Everyone was so happy that no more lives would be lost, in Europe at least, and that their loved ones would soon be coming home. We had yet to defeat the Japanese and many of our troops were still fighting in Burma. To most people this area of conflict was considered a "side show" to the main event, the defeat of Nazi Germany and the liberation of Europe. It was with some justification that our soldiers in the Far East called themselves "the forgotten army".

Little thought had been given during the war to the consequences of servicemen being kept away from their families for long periods, the traumas and attitudes they brought back with them and the adjustments that would have to be made in relationships once they were reunited. We were too busy fighting for our freedom and planning, behind the scenes, for a fairer society when the fighting was over. The consequences appeared in a "baby boom" and not surprisingly, in the breakdown of many marriages, where wives had learned to become independent of their men folk during their absence and men had become inured to and transformed by the hardships and atrocities of war. But on 8 May 1945 pent up relief and joy were the order of the day.

Although these adult "outcomes" had not occurred to a nine year old like myself I had, by the age of ten, come to few conclusions about marriage. If I ever married, I thought to myself, it would have to be to a girl like Janet Caswell who was, I believe, Connie Izzett's granddaughter. She was, of course, too old for me because I was ten and she was so much older, at least twelve or even thirteen! I did not see much of her because she lived in the Headlands but, to me, she was the sort of girl one could fall in love with, when one was grown up, and trust implicitly. She just had that air about her – self-possessed in a calm and dignified way, sensible and good natured. Even at my age I recognised and respected her for the qualities she displayed. I doubt whether she ever noticed me but she must have become a subconscious "reference point" in the same way as, I am told, I have become a reference point for others.

It is a pity that I did not subsequently listen to my ten year old self because, in my early twenties I met and fell deeply in love with a delightful young woman with just those qualities. But I "fluffed" my chance to marry her and she married someone else. Fortunately, all was not lost because some fifty years later and by an extraordinary coincidence she found me and love blossomed again. But that, dear reader, is another story!

After the war my father felt it was time to move on from Kettering and to progress his career in Local Government one stage further. He was only 33 but already had fifteen years' experience of working for Local Authorities. Both he and my mother preferred to return to their home in Hornchurch, if at all possible, and he was aware that efficient administrators, like himself, would be needed to put into practical effect the social reforms the new Labour Government had outlined in their election manifesto. He had been involved in Town Planning for many years and south-east Essex was familiar territory for my parents.

He was lucky enough, in the circumstances, to secure employment as Assistant Town Clerk to Billericay Urban District Council, a rapidly expanding area in terms of population in the centre of which a new town, Basildon, would subsequently be built.

The next phase in all our lives was about to begin.

25
Kettering to Ramsden Bellhouse

It is not easy to summarise in a few brief paragraphs the mood of the nation in 1945. It had proved to be a momentous year. The war in Europe had been won and a new Labour Government had been elected.

The austerity of the early war years, the mixing together during that period of people from all levels of society, including the dispersal of child evacuees from poor quality housing and living conditions in vulnerable towns and cities into middle class homes elsewhere had led to a realisation among people who were moderately well off that a great deal of squalor, deprivation and poverty still existed. This realisation gave impetus to a national aspiration that life had to be better for everyone once the war was won.

At about the time it became apparent that the war could be won, a Report on social insurance and allied services was commissioned by the National Government in 1941, and published in 1942. It was called the Beveridge Report after the name of its author, Sir (later Lord) William Beveridge, and was welcomed with almost universal approval by people of all shades of opinion and by all sections of the community

The Report set out a comprehensive blueprint for the future wellbeing of our Society and advocated, among other things a National Insurance scheme underpinning social security for all and the creation of allied services in the fields of health and medicine. New towns would replace slums and the determination that was winning the war would be harnessed to "winning the peace" once the conflict was over.

From the moment the Report was published politicians appreciated the significance of it and steps were, in fact, taken during the remainder of the war to implement aspects of it, including the Education Act, 1944 which replaced the fee paying system for County and Municipal Grammar schools and introduced the "eleven plus" examination with free secondary modern education to sixteen years of age for all and grant maintained places at fee paying independent Grammar schools. I was one of the first to benefit from this legislation.

Both Conservative, Labour and Liberal parties promoted the concept of a fairer society, as espoused in the Beveridge Report, in the lead up to the 1945 General Election but whereas the other two parties advocated a measured and phased approach to reform, given the dire state of the country's finances, the Labour Party promised to introduce and implement reform immediately and set out a raft of radical and far reaching legislative proposals.

The General Public which was only too well aware of the unfulfilled promises of Prime Minister Lloyd George at the end of the First World War some 25 years previously, opted for "certainty today" rather than "jam tomorrow". The nation had accordingly voted the wartime Prime Minister, Winston Churchill and his Conservative Party, out of office and Clement Attlee, the Deputy Prime Minister and his Labour Party into it.

The Labour Government was as good as its word insofar as it introduced the concept of the Welfare State by passing the National Insurance Acts in 1946 and 1949, the National Health Service Act in 1946, the provisions of which came into effect on 5 July 1948 and the Landlord and Tenant (Rent Control) Act in 1949 which protected Tenants from arbitrary increases in the rents they were expected to pay, and gave some security of tenure.

It also passed the Town and Country Planning Act, 1947 which set out a lasting framework for the orderly development of land for housing, commercial and community purposes and the preservation of the rural environment wherever possible. Town Planning was an area in which my father had been involved in Dagenham and Kettering as a legal assistant and in which he was subsequently to be involved at Billericay.

But, as the Labour Government and much of the population subsequently came to appreciate the economic state of the county proved a formidable barrier to further reform and to the improvement in the quality of life that had been promised. As a result, the Labour Government was voted out of office in 1951 But that is another story and I digress!

After applying, without success, for administrative posts with his former employers, Hornchurch Urban District Council and, strangely, Bexley Heath Council during the latter part of 1945, my father attended a job interview at the offices of Billericay Urban District Council in January 1946, only a couple of weeks after my tenth birthday. As previously mentioned, he was fortunate enough to be offered the post of Assistant Town Clerk and accepted it on 5 February. However, the Council wanted him to start work on 11 March, some five weeks later. He had just enough time to give his employers, Kettering Borough Council, the necessary four weeks' notice.

This left him with a number of logistical and financial problems. The Steadmans were still living in our house in Hornchurch and refusing to move out despite the fact that they had not paid any rent for nearly two years and I was in "midterm" at Kettering Grammar school. He had to find the family alternative accommodation while he regained possession of our home and an alternative Grammar school that would take me from the beginning of the Summer term if that was humanly possible.

In view of the fact that I had done so well at Kettering Grammar school he was very reluctant to send me to a local Junior school just after my tenth birthday and then, immediately prior to my taking the eleven plus examinations, to a Secondary Modern school. Neither would have any great academic pretensions.

The moves from school to school, moreover, would seriously impact on my chances of passing the examinations and getting into an Essex Grammar school. I would probably finish up in Billericay school, built in 1937, which provided an education for local children who had not passed the "eleven plus" and which concentrated on technical achievement and basic learning to "O" Level only.

But he only had approximately six weeks in which to obtain a place for me at one or other of the two fee paying Grammar schools in the area and find a convenient home from which I could travel to it at the beginning of the Summer term. As a family we all had to be back together as quickly as possible, given the need to relocate permanently from Northamptonshire to Essex.

In desperation he asked Mr Scott, the Headmaster of Kettering Grammar school to write a letter of recommendation to the Headmaster of Brentwood (Grammar) school, a Headmaster's Conference school. I had come first in four subjects in the Michaelmas term and my father hoped that this achievement and the support of Mr Scott would influence the headmaster into accepting me. The new Headmaster of Brentwood school, Charles Ralph Allison, was favourably disposed to do so and offered me a place in the Preparatory school for the Summer term.

The fee, however, was a "whopping" 19 guineas a term (19 pounds 19 shillings or a shade under £20 in modern parlance). Compared with the £4 a term fee at Kettering Grammar school this must have been a lot of money for my father to find out of his salary or to borrow, and he told me at the time that he could only afford two term's fees. I would have to leave the school if I did not pass the "eleven plus" examination – no pressure then!

Billericay Urban District Council also came to his aid by offering a temporary home for our family in a war-requisitioned bungalow, known as "St. Olaves" in Homestead Road, Ramsden Bellhouse, within the Urban District but some four miles from the centre of town. During the war houses could be requisitioned, where unoccupied, to accommodate families whose own homes had been damaged or destroyed by enemy bombs or rockets, and this was presumably the basis upon which my father and our family were allocated the property for a brief period.

The property was a 1920s timber framed and timber floored bungalow on an unmade road which it shared with a number of similar properties: the original attraction to the owners of them must doubtless have been the size and cheapness of the plots upon which they could build properties of whatever shape or size they wanted or could afford. The bungalow had a large and well-ventilated cavity under the floorboards, three usable bedrooms and somewhat antiquated kitchen and bathroom facilities. Behind the locked door of what may have been a dining room or fourth bedroom were, I understand, the furniture and other household possessions of Mr Brown, the owner. My father was told the property would be available for occupation on 3 April.

The first logistical problem was immediately apparent. My father's employment with Kettering Borough Council would end on 3 March and he was due to start work with Billericay Urban District Council on 11 March just over a week later. I would be leaving Kettering Grammar school on 12 March and would have to take up my place at Brentwood school (as it preferred to be called) in early April within days of my mother, sister and I arriving at St. Olaves. He would have to find lodgings in Billericay between 4 March and 3 April.

In the event he quickly found accommodation in the Rayleigh Road, Billericay with the "Lowe family". Mr Lowe was a local builder and the name of his wife was Grace. They had a son, Gerald, whose name Mrs. Lowe insisted on pronouncing with a hard "G". My father never found out why. Since I had an uncle with the same name I found the guttural version of it eccentric, to say the least. They looked after my father well and it was with great joy and relief that we all joined up as a family again at St. Olaves on 3 April and settled into our temporary home.

Organising our arrival there on the same day must have been quite an intricate operation because we had no telephone at our home in Kettering and communication between my parents had to be by letter or by the occasional brief telephone call by my mother from a telephone box near our home to my father's new office. Moreover, petrol rationing restricted his ability to drive back from Billericay to see us during the time he was lodging with Mr & Mrs Lowe.

The garden, orchard and large area of land on the east side of St. Olaves had been left untended for years and was completely overgrown with hillocks of matted grass and large blackberry bushes scattered about it. We quickly discovered that, hidden in the undergrowth, were a large number of adders, snakes with a poisonous bite that can cause severe harm to a young child.

The first incident involving them was when I ran round a blackberry bush on a hot summer's afternoon and was confronted by a very large adder, coiled up and sunning itself on a mound of grass. Going too fast to stop and with my heart in my mouth I jumped over it, probably higher than I had ever jumped before, and was relieved to see that I had not disturbed it. Shortly afterwards, however, I noticed another large adder slithering through the long grass under the swing my father had attached to the bough of one of the apple trees and upon which my five-year-old sister happened to be sitting at the time. I warned her not to move until the snake had disappeared and reported both incidents to my parents.

That was not the end of incidents with snakes. Angela commented on rustling noises under her bedroom floor and my father prised up one of the floorboards. There, in the under-floor cavity was a nest of them. He immediately called the Council's Pest Control Officer from the nearest public telephone box in the main road and they were quickly despatched. There must have been a lot of them about at the time, because, shortly thereafter, the milk float that made its way down Homestead Road every morning ran over a very large adder whose zig zagged blue/black and grey body was still lying in the road as I ran to the bus stop at 8 am.

Fortunately, the bus stop for Brentwood was just round the corner in Church Road which ran from Ramsden Heath in the north to Ramsden Crays in the south. Ramsden Crays is on the London Road, between Billericay and Wickford, part of the old stagecoach route between Whitechapel in London and Rochford, the most important town in southeast Essex in the 18th century. I will refer to this in a later chapter.

When we arrived in April 1946 most of the properties in the area were modest bungalows that appeared to have been built between the early 1900s and the beginning of the Second World War. Like "St. Olaves" they were somewhat "down at heel" and to me "the Bellhouse", as it was called, was the back of beyond and in the middle of nowhere. It was just so quiet.

I had been used to living in a bustling south Midlands town where there were so many things for a 10-year-old to do when not at school. It was therefore with some relief that I was able to board a "City" bus and travel via Ramsden Heath and Billericay to Brentwood Preparatory school only a week or so after we moved in. At least I would meet some young boys like myself at school.

Church Road was a prime example of ribbon development that was prevalent before and prevented subsequently, apart from infilling and the replacement of existing properties, by the Town and Country Planning Act, 1947. Ribbon development was, in essence, the unrestricted and unregulated building of houses on land fronting roads whether made up or not, wherever the opportunity presented itself and whenever the demand existed for it. Most of this type of development resulted to a certain extent from the lean times Essex farmers were going through from the 1880s and their consequent willingness to sell off fields which had access to roads.

By late 1888 the Great Eastern Railway had extended its newly constructed line to Wickford and the intention of the Railway company was that the line would ultimately provide a service between London, Liverpool Street and Southend on Sea, Victoria stations, as indeed it does today. In pursuit of profitability the Railway Company wanted to encourage as many people as possible to use its trains during the day in addition to the transportation of farm produce and freight, principally to London, at night.

The line crossed the northern end of Church Road, at a point approximately halfway between Billericay and Wickford and with additional passengers in mind I understand that the Railway Company provided or considered providing platforms there so that people interested in buying a plot or a property in the Village could alight and view whatever was on sale. A well-known property company by the name of Homestead Estates, calculating that there might at some point be a railway station for the village if there was sufficient demand for one, bought up a number of fields adjoining Church Road from impecunious farmers and started to build low-cost bungalows upon them. The Railway Station never materialised but many of the people who had bought these bungalows as "weekend retreats" occupied them permanently after the first World War, having been forced to sell their more substantial properties in the east of London during the economic depression and hard times of the 1920s and early 1930s.

In the 75 years since I lived there Ramsden Bellhouse has changed out of all recognition. The original nondescript bungalows have disappeared, the four side roads, including Homestead Road, named, presumably, by the property company, have been surfaced and extended and wealth exudes from the well built and desirable properties that have replaced them. Indeed, a Railway Station might well now be justified, given the extensive development that has taken place since the Second World War.

Apart from the Church of St. Mary the Virgin halfway down Church Road and the Manor House close to it there is little sign of the original village or hamlet. Any permanent record of its history commenced after William the Conqueror arrived in 1066 and defeated the Anglo Saxons who had farmed land in the area. In the Domesday Book, for example, the area was called Ramesdana which, in Anglo Saxon meant "the valley of wild garlic". It was in the Hundred of Barstable, created by the Anglo Saxons and effectively abolished in 1886, over a thousand years later.

We tend to regard the Norman Conquest as a starting point for our history because we have so little by way of written record of life before the Normans arrived but there is little doubt that the Anglo Saxons, the resident population, cultivated a lot of land in southeast Essex and that farming communities existed at the time. These communities were enslaved by the Normans and hamlets developed: strict religious observance was demanded leading to the construction of churches in the hamlets of Ramsden Bellhouse and Ramsden Crays.

The first reference to a church in the "Bellhouse" occurs in 1281 when the Church of St. Mary the Virgin with the land around it is recorded as being owned by the Bishop of London from 1066. It is more than likely, however, that, in the first flush of success, William granted the land to his half brother, Odo, the Bishop of Bayeux along with vast tracks of land in Kent and the rest of Essex and that the Bishop of London acquired it after Odo "blotted his copy book" in 1076 a few years later. I make this observation because, in the Domesday Book of 1086, the hundred of Barstable belonged to the Bishop of London with two men-at-arms from Bayeux. Odo had been disfranchised but his two lieutenants clearly had not.

That particular 13th-century church has long since vanished, and the current church is a mixture of mediaeval and nineteenth century construction. The Chancel collapsed in the 18th-century because burials within the church itself had undermined the foundations, necessitating a rebuild of the Chancel in the nineteenth century.

Apart from the church the life of the village, in 1946, centred round the village store and Post Office opposite Homestead Road and the Community Hall close by. On the other side of the railway line at the Ramsden Heath end of the village was the "Fox and Hounds" Public House which, being far too young, I never visited but which, I understand, replaced the original "Fox and Hounds" some distance away on the Heath road to Billericay and made inaccessible to the villagers when the railway tracks were laid.

Although Ramsden Bellhouse was virtually unrecognisable as a village, stretched out as it was along Church Road from the railway bridge at one end to the sinister Black Barn on the corner of the London Road at the other, and had hardly any of the features you might expect to find in one it did at least have a regular and reliable bus service.

The City Coach Company whose original function was to transport day trippers from the Wood Green area of North London to Southend on Sea in the late 1920s operated a fleet of chocolate brown and cream-coloured coaches from its depot in the Ongar Road, Brentwood. One of its routes was between Brentwood and Shotgate on the outskirts of Wickford via Church Road, Ramsden Heath and Billericay.

The terminus at Brentwood was only a short distance from Brentwood Preparatory school which I will refer to from now on as "the Prep" and the bus which stopped close to the end of Homestead Road at ten minutes past eight every morning got me to the school with a few minutes to spare. I was equally fortunate that, on my homeward journey a City bus left Brentwood High school at about 4.20 pm every afternoon and stopped outside the Village Stores equally close to home.

I have previously mentioned running to catch the bus to school because, despite my parents' prompting, I invariably left home two or three minutes before it was due to arrive. However, the driver would always stop and wait if he was early and could see me attempting to reach the bus stop in time. Such consideration is rare these days.

As all who know me well will confirm I have had a tendency throughout my life to put off anything onerous or unpleasant, like homework, until I have little option but to do so. That is why my father constantly reminded me that "procrastination is the thief of time". I suspect, however, that I am not alone in this respect. Fortunately, I have usually allowed myself just enough time to do whatever is necessary or have been allowed it by others.

Travelling by bus, on the other hand, has never been an onerous experience for me, from the moment Grannie Somers brought me back from Oldchurch Hospital to her home in Sheppey Road in a couple of "big red buses" after my recovery from Scarlet Fever at the age of five and, as I will relate later, I became an inveterate collector of London Transport bus numbers and frequent visitor to their garages from the age of eleven.

The City bus that fascinated me at the time was number "G1," a highly distinctive Leyland coach, one of only three ever built in 1938, with four front wheels instead of the usual two. As a ten-year-old I wondered how on earth a bus could turn four front wheels in the same direction at the same time, but it did. The fact that it was sold off by the Company in 1948 confirmed my reservations about its practicality and I cannot recall having seen a bus or coach like it since.

Our five-and-a-half-month sojourn in the depths of the Billericay Urban District but not my association with the City Coach Company came to an end on 17 September 1946 when we returned to our vacant and recently repaired home in Hornchurch. Unbeknown, however, to me our brief stay in Ramsden Bellhouse determined where my parents would live for much of the rest of their lives and where my sister and I would have our home until we married our respective partners in the mid-1960s.

Every morning my father and the City bus followed the same route to Billericay. It led from Ramsden Heath, on the north side of the railway bridge, along Heath Road, through open countryside, to the outskirts of Billericay where it became Norsey Road. Norsey Road ran alongside Norsey Wood, an ancient area of woodland, and through John Strong, an architect with a growing practice close to the Council Offices who had already purchased a plot, he discovered that the owner of the Wood was contemplating the sale of more plots along the northern, Norsey Road frontage of them before the forthcoming Town and Country Planning

Act put an end to ribbon development.

My father must have felt that if Planning consent had been obtained before the legislation was enacted it would be possible to build on woodland bordering Norsey Road because he applied for and obtained permission for the erection of a dwelling house in Norsey Road on 21 September 1946 while we were still living at St Olaves in Ramsden Bellhouse and some two months before he signed a contract for the purchase of a plot.

A newly built home in a woodland setting on the City bus route to Brentwood, if I passed the eleven plus, or Billericay Secondary Modern school if I did not, would solve my transport to school problem and would be preferable in every way to our both having to travel from Hornchurch to our respective destinations and back again. We would have a detached property instead of a pre-war semi, a much larger garden and, as a family, access to an attractive town with many amenities and community activities.

Having obtained the planning consent and being able to assure the owner of the Woods that he could build a residential property on it my father negotiated the purchase of a plot. On 14th November 1946, therefore, some eight weeks after we moved back to Hornchurch he paid a ten percent deposit of £24 to buy one for £240. It had a 40-foot frontage, a depth of four hundred feet and a width at the rear of sixty feet.

Having committed himself, undoubtedly with the whole hearted support of my mother, to the purchase of the plot so soon after our return to Hornchurch, he now had to work out how to synchronise the sale of our semi-detached property with the date of completion of our new home and, what is more, how to find a contractor who would be able to build it.

My own future would depend on my performance in the prep and in my first term in the Upper school. Would I pass the eleven plus and be able to stay at Brentwood school or go to secondary-modern schools in Hornchurch and Billericay? That was the question to which no one knew the answer at the time.

26
Brentwood Preparatory School 1946

Having been taken out of a midland's grammar school at the age of ten years and two months I was now about to experience a completely different type of school in southeast Essex one month later. Nor was there any certainty that I would stay there. That would depend on my passing the eleven plus examination in less than a year's time.

It was therefore with some anxiety that I arrived in Brentwood on the City bus on my first day in the prep. I was excited but apprehensive. All the boys in my class relied on wealthy parents or grandparents to pay the substantial fees for their education. My father, on the other hand, had had to borrow enough to pay them or use whatever savings he had to cover two terms' fees. They were clearly more privileged financially than someone like me who had relied on a Local Authority Scholarship and the modest fees charged by Kettering Grammar school.

Nevertheless, I settled in quickly. The education I had previously received had been so good that I was ahead in virtually every subject and had no difficulty in coming second in my class of 21 boys, being beaten only by a boy whose name was David Tench, whom I will mention later.

I sat near the front of a class whose form teacher was a Miss Haynes, an elderly spinster. I marvelled at her ability to swivel round and throw a wooden board rubber unerringly at any boy who was misbehaving, while she was rubbing chalk off the blackboard and hit him squarely in the chest from a range of up to twenty feet! If there had been a category for throwing board rubbers at unruly children in the 1948 Olympics, she would have been in the medal category. After a term with her, and subsequently a year with Mr Kershaw, whose method of keeping order

I will describe later, I came to the conclusion that my former school in Northamptonshire was far more enlightened in its approach to discipline.

I quickly made friends with John Farrant and Michael Welsford. John lived in a very nice, detached house in the main road at Gidea Park and claimed a similar connection to the Williams Wynne family as myself, albeit on the right side of the sheets. Michael's parents had a shop with a flat over it in a parade of shops in Lodge Avenue, Becontree. I visited him and played in the flat on more than one occasion on a Saturday afternoon before walking back to my grandparents' house in Sheppey Road, a few streets away.

In fact, we three decided to have a common nickname and the most memorable incident was when we went for school lunch one day. The prep was located in a Georgian building called "The Old House" in the Shenfield Road while on the opposite, south side of the road and part of the school was, and still is, "Mitre House", a beautiful black and white Tudor House.

In the summer of 1946, before it became the home of "Daddy" Brooks, one of our English masters, his wife and daughters, we had our school lunches for the first two or three weeks of term in Mitre House. Mr Cockell "Cockles", a French teacher who later became my Junior Housemaster presided over us and John, Michael and I sat next to him at table. "And what is your name, boy?" he asked me. "Ernest, Sir". "Oh, that is a very traditional name", he replied "and what is your name?" he asked John Farrant, "Ernest, Sir". "Oh, and what is your name?", he asked Michael Welsford" Ernest, Sir,", at which point I piped up and said, "Yes, Sir, I am Ernie One, he is Ernie Two and he is Ernie Three". It was at this point that we were rumbled. But he took our replies in good part, and we were not chastised for this bit of fun.

My summer term in the prep turned out to be more enjoyable than I had expected and passed all too quickly. Achieving good marks in the subjects on the curriculum had not been difficult. I had found new friends and had got used to travelling to school by bus. The following term would, however, be decisive and would determine whether or not I would be able to stay at the school.

27

Hornchurch 1946

As soon as my father arrived back in Essex in March 1946 he had, as previously mentioned, visited the Steadmans who told him that they were unable to pay the two years' arrears of rent and that they would oppose any effort he made to evict them. He would have to take them to Court if he wanted to regain possession. "We are in the house and possession is nine parts of the law", they declared, an attitude with which, during my professional career, I am only too familiar.

Having obtained, courtesy of his new employers, a temporary home for us in Ramsden Bellhouse, my father had no option but to commence proceedings at the Romford County Court. The Order for possession and payment of rent arrears appears to have been made in July 1946, but when my father drove over to 46 Alma Avenue to serve it on them the Steadmans had already disappeared. He never found out where they had gone and never recovered what was due from them.

Since, however, the house was unoccupied he immediately applied for the Grant which the Government had made available to enable house owners to carry out remedial work to their war damaged homes. The blast damage was repaired by L.W. Butcher, a local builder and contractor to Essex County Council at a cost of 56 pounds 17 shillings and nine pence.

When, therefore, we moved back into the house it was in relatively good condition and a much more agreeable place to live in than "St. Olaves". The only major drawback was that it was far less accessible to Brentwood and Billericay. That fact had doubtless prompted my father to snap up the plot in Norsey Road two months later and to decide to move out of Hornchurch as soon as a new home could be built on it.

Pending the move to Billericay and provided I passed the eleven plus it looked as if I would have to catch the number 66 London Transport bus from its terminus at Hornchurch Station, part of the London Underground system, about a quarter of a mile away to Romford and from Romford the number 86 or Green Line, 721, service to Brentwood. This would, however, mean my leaving home very early in order to get to school on time.

Being the considerate parent he was, my father decided to drive me to school every morning from 1 September 1946, including Saturdays, until we moved back to Billericay on 14 January 1948. I could either return home by public transport or, on Saturday, stay on the number 86 to Chadwell Heath and catch the number 62 from there to Sheppey Road. We travelled to Brentwood in his trusty Morris Minor via Upminster, the "Southend Arterial" road, and Warley. From Brentwood he would drive on to work in Billericay. It was not much of a detour for him, and it was enormously helpful to me.

The "Southend Arterial" as it is now known has an interesting history. During the decade following the First World War times were hard, as I have already mentioned, and people had little spare money for luxuries like holidays. They could no longer afford to travel with their young families to a resort by train and spend a week by the seaside as they had during the pre-War, Edwardian era.

On the other hand, the First World War had brought about a revolution in the development and design of reliable mechanised vehicles of all kinds, including open topped charabancs and enclosed coaches. Moreover, Southend still possessed a lot of attractions. It boasted the longest pier in the world, a massive amusement arcade called the Kursaal and, for children, a number of delights including sweet, sticky and chewy "Southend Rock", "Rossi's" ice cream and the prospect, though not necessarily the reality, of being able to play in the sunshine on the beach in front of the esplanade which stretched along the Thames Estuary from Southend to Westcliff.

The decline in boarding house bookings in the 1920s spelt disaster for the proprietors of them, including Grandfather Hughes who had invested his remaining wealth in one, following the collapse of the

Anglo Baku Oilfield Corporation. Nevertheless, Londoners still wanted a weekend excursion of some sort and charabancs and coaches provided the necessary means. The only problem was the antediluvian road system linking the towns and villages between London and Southend which would not be able to cope with the increase in traffic that was likely to occur.

The Lloyd George government could not honour its promises to improve living conditions for the "heroes" who had fought for their country during the war, but it could, at least, promote the construction of a road to take Londoners directly to Southend for an enjoyable "day out" by the seaside. As part, therefore, of a road building programme, announced in 1920 and designed principally to create jobs for ex-soldiers, works began a year later on what was said, rather grandly, to be England's longest new road since Roman times!

It opened as the A127 on 25 March 1925 to great fanfare, but it was only a single lane highway in each direction and you can doubtless guess what happened. By the summer of 1935 it had become so congested that motorists, including the many middle class people who had been able to acquire a car, avoided it. It should be borne in mind that anyone could get behind the wheel of a car and drive without having to pass a test until 1934. Motoring for the masses was a novel concept until the Ford Motor Company opened its huge factory in Dagenham in 1931 at which point highway authorities realised, belatedly, that adequate provision would have to be made for the increasing number of cars on the roads.

"Watering holes" along the length of the Arterial Road had already been created for the relief and refreshment of the "day trippers", the best known of which was probably "The Half Way House" at Brentwood with its ample parking spaces for coaches and charabancs. But little serious thought had previously been given to private cars taking families to the Southend area.

In order to relieve the congestion, it was decided, in 1935, to make it a dual carriageway in both directions and the duplication process started a year later. Construction continued and, in 1940, some nineteen years after it was first conceived the dual carriageway throughout was finally completed. As someone sagely observed, the Romans would have built it quicker!

But I digress once again.

During our drive to school and to work each morning my father and I always had plenty to talk about. He was wise, kind and amusing and I loved being with him. I could not help noticing, however that despite his cheerfulness and optimism he was not healthy. He had a bad cough most of the time and he was very thin. I did not appreciate that, by mid 1948, he would reach a point at which his life hung in the balance and that it would only be saved by the newly created National Health Service. But more of that anon.

As previously mentioned, I had to travel home or to my grandparents house in Sheppey Road on London Transport buses which I quickly noticed all had different numbers. Some little boys collected train numbers and were known as "train spotters". I decided, however, to become a "bus spotter" and bought, for the sum of two shillings Ian Allan's ABC book, listing the number and types of every London Transport bus and coach that existed at the time. If I was going to travel on their buses, I might as well collect the numbers. This hobby turned into a passion and, over a period of three years, gave me an encyclopaedic knowledge of London and the Home Counties as I will explain later.

Reverting to the drive to Brentwood my father constantly emphasised during the journey how important it was that I continued to work hard and pass the eleven plus. He was confident that I had the ability to pass the examinations, but it was up to me to do so on the day. He need not have worried in that respect. Failing them and going to a secondary modern school was not a welcome prospect to me either. In fact, it was not until the results of the examinations were announced in early 1947 confirming that I had passed that I felt secure at Brentwood and could look forward to being there on a permanent basis. My father's gamble on my future education had paid off and one of his principal concerns had been resolved.

My father, age 19

My mother, age 18

My parents playing leading roles
in St Martin's Church pageant, 1935

Lyons Corner House 'Nippies'

My father's Scout troop, early 1920s

Dudley Moore,
aged 15, with female friend

A teenage Dudley Moore,
with his mother, Ada, and our
cousin, Richard

My grandfather, John Somers (centre)
with his brothers, c.1905

My grandmother, Gertrude Evelyn Somers, c.1910

My maternal grandparents, 1940

Uncle Gerald and myself, 1939

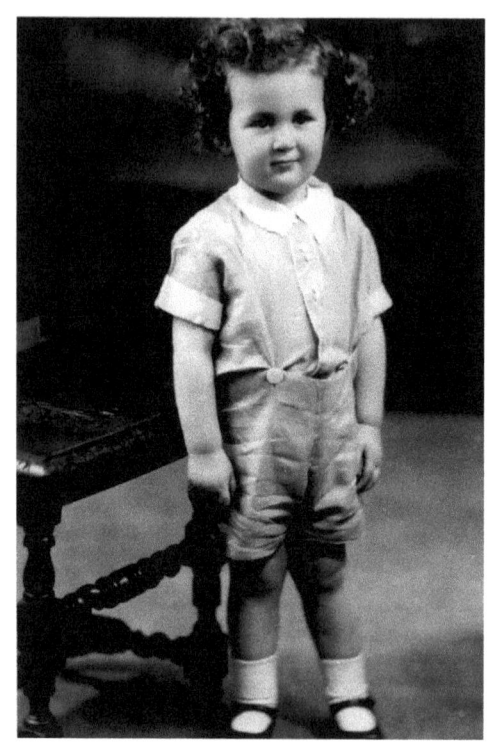

Myself, aged 3

Myself, aged 7

3 Broadway, Kettering

Myself and Gillian Chapman, age 8, and Angela

Ralph the GI with mum and Angela, 1944

G.I.s with father, Angela and me, 1944

8th June, 1946

TO-DAY, AS WE CELEBRATE VICTORY, I send this personal message to you and all other boys and girls at school. For you have shared in the hardships and dangers of a total war and you have shared no less in the triumph of the Allied Nations.

I know you will always feel proud to belong to a country which was capable of such supreme effort; proud, too, of parents and elder brothers and sisters who by their courage, endurance and enterprise brought victory. May these qualities be yours as you grow up and join in the common effort to establish among the nations of the world unity and peace.

George R.I.

Message from King George VI to boys and girls, 8 June 1946

Myself in Kettering Grammar School uniform

Romford Market, 1950

Pink Cottage, Billericay; our former family home

Brentwood Old Big School, much as it was in my time

Charles Allison MA, Headmaster

Myself in Scout uniform, 1954

Billericay High Street, early 1950s

On holiday with KV 8557 and the caravan at Corton, 1950

The Skylon at the Festival of Britain, 1951

I WISH TO MARK, BY THIS PERSONAL MESSAGE, my appreciation of the service you have rendered to your Country in 1939.

In the early days of the War you opened your door to strangers who were in need of shelter, & offered to share your home with them.

I know that to this unselfish task you have sacrificed much of your own comfort, & that it could not have been achieved without the loyal co-operation of all in your household.

By your sympathy you have earned the gratitude of those to whom you have shown hospitality, & by your readiness to serve you have helped the State in a work of great value.

Elizabeth R

Mrs. Hughes.

Message from Queen Elizabeth II to takers of evacuees

Mr Rennie

Mr Nicholls

Mr Higgs

Mr Hodgson

Peter Preston with his father's Jaguar

Mosaics at Lullingtone Roman Villa, 1953

London Transport Coach TF7c

Boys queuing for milk outside the Tuck Shop, 1950

Brian in Scout uniform, aged 12, with Angela, 1948

Messrs Benson, Cluer, Rowswell and Barron,
Greece, 1954

Dignitaries at Scout camp, Vouliagmeni, 1954

School production of *1066 and All That*.
I'm second from the right, in CCF uniform.

Angela and I, Summer term, 1954

28
Brentwood Upper School 1946

Having successfully completed a term in the Prep, and having moved from Ramsden Bellhouse to Hornchurch, the time had come in September 1946 to enter the main school. Brentwood was not, however, one large self- contained building, like Kettering Grammar school, but a cluster of them acquired or "purpose built" over a period of four hundred years from the date of its foundation by Letters Patent on 5 July 1558.

Queen Mary, who died in November 1558 only four months after the Letters Patent had been sealed, had given Antony Browne, Serjeant at Law, licence to found a free grammar school in Brentwood, but he died, a Knight of the Realm and former Chief Justice of Common Pleas, nine years later, without having actually built one.

We tend to think of a grammar school, in this day and age, as a fairly substantial establishment but, in the sixteenth century it was not necessarily more than a single storey schoolhouse with a paid schoolmaster who had been provided with somewhere modest to live. The wealthier the founder the more he was inclined to display his munificence in the size of school he built.

Although he had no schoolhouse in mind, Antony Browne nevertheless appointed a priest and Master of Arts by the name of George Otway as first schoolmaster on 28 July 1558 only three weeks after the licence was given. Since one cannot have a schoolmaster without a school or a school without a building to put it in, Antony Browne, as a temporary measure put George Otway into a house on his large estate.

The name of the house was "Redcross" and it had a family chapel attached to it. It was located on Brook Street Hill, well to the west of the populous market town of Brentwood on the site of what is now Honeypot Lane. Antony Browne, clearly felt that since the house was of reasonable size and the chapel was twenty eight feet long and twelve and a half feet wide the two buildings would suffice as a schoolmaster's home and schoolroom respectively until he could erect a proper school house.

Antony Browne who was described by Edmund Plowden, a famous lawyer and commentator, as a man of "profound ingenuity and grand eloquence" and who had made a great deal of money buying and selling estates, following the dissolution of the monasteries between 1536 and 1541, doubtless had plans, at the time, for something rather impressive. Until, however, he could acquire more land closer to the centre of the town the schoolmaster would have to make do with "Redcross" and the young boys with the chapel. He must have thought that a couple of benches on each side of a long table in the chapel would resolve, for the time being, the accommodation requirement as far as teaching the children was concerned. All he had to do was take the necessary items of furniture out of Weald Hall, his very substantial principal residence, not very far away.

In fact, in his Will dated 20 December 1565, over seven years after the licence had been given, he left "Redcross" to the foundation he had created "because as yet there is no convenient place appointed to keep the said school in nor apt place for the habitation of the schoolmaster that shall there be and remain". One is tempted to ask, in the circumstances, what serious efforts he had made to find a suitable alternative location for his proposed grammar school and schoolmaster's house during that period.

At this point I can hear former pupils of Brentwood school asking why the year 1557 features so prominently in its literature and history and the answer would appear to be as follows.

In 1557, a year before the foundation of the school, Antony Browne had purchased a house, farmyard, cottage and orchard from a Robert Nightingale. The property was adjacent to the horse and cart track which led to the hamlet of Ingrave, close to the eastern end of Brentwood's main thoroughfare and close also to the spot upon which William Hunter had been burned at the stake in 1555.

On 31 July 1558, three days after appointing George Otway, he endowed the foundation with the property together with the Manor of Chigwell Grange, and may well have intended to use the land upon which the farmyard, orchard and cottage stood as part of the site for a school. If so, it is more than likely that, as a man of wealth and a former Chief Justice, he wanted to purchase more land at the rear of it and endow the foundation with sufficient to build a schoolhouse that reflected his status.

I make this observation because, in 1564, only a year before Antony Browne made his Will, Richard Rich, 1st Baron Rich, a former Lord Chancellor from whom he had purchased Weald Hall in 1548, founded Felsted Grammar school, less than twenty miles away, with what could well have been more land in its endowment than in his own.

Richard Rich had also made a considerable fortune out of the dissolution of the monasteries and, if one is to judge by the statement in his Will, Antony Browne felt that Robert Nightingale's former property was of insufficient size for a school and a schoolmaster's house that would bear comparison with Felsted.

The content of a Will is intended to be disclosed to the beneficiaries of it upon the death of the Testator, the person who made it. Executors appointed by the Testator are intended to execute (carry out) the wishes of the deceased person. Antony Browne made his Will on 20 December 1565 and died unexpectedly and after a short sudden illness some sixteen months later. His was no "death-bed" Will.

A reasonable inference from the statement in his Will that there was "no convenient place appointed to keep the said school in nor apt place for the habitation of the schoolmaster" would be that he had no real intention of purchasing an alternative piece of land for his grammar school between the date of making his Will and the disclosure of its content on his death. Why otherwise make the statement in December 1565 in anticipation of his death and the reading of the Will at some indeterminate date in the future? The only alternative inference is that he intended to make another Will once he had completed the necessary purchase.

One also has to consider the basic bodily functions of any schoolchild, namely "to eat, to wee and to poo"! The fact that "Redcross might not have adequate toilet facilities did not matter too much. It is more than likely that there was a large wooden bucket outside the chapel door which was emptied into the nearest ditch at the end of each school day by one of the pupils and that George Otway had a chamber pot or privy of some kind within Redcross. The house had a four-acre field attached, the chapel was some way from the town and no-one would really notice how the children relieved themselves or how the result of their doing so was disposed of.

But a grammar school closer to the centre of Brentwood would require adequate sanitation and Antony Browne would have appreciated that. There was no schoolmaster's house in Ingrave Road. A much larger bucket would have been needed for the increased number of boys being taught in the newly built school room, as well as somewhere to dispose of its contents. In this context the words "a convenient place appointed" in his Will acquire additional significance. We still use the word "conveniences" to describe public toilets and there may be a subtle subtext to Antony Browne's statement that has slipped by unnoticed.

In the circumstances, his desire for a fitting epitaph in the shape of a bigger and better grammar school was never realised. The recently knighted Antony Browne died on 6 May 1567. He had left "Redcross" to the foundation but there were to be no more endowments of any kind to add to it. His stepdaughter, Dorothy, and her husband, Edmund Huddleston would have to use whatever land in Brentwood was within the endowment of the foundation to build a school room, if not a grammar school, with accommodation for a schoolmaster.

They wasted no time. They had no pretensions of grandeur and appreciated the immediate need. Whether it was likely to be smelly or less than ideal from the point of view of bodily functions, a school room would, at minimum, have to be built on the site of Robert Nightingale's former property before any beneficiaries of Sir Antony's Estate could object legally to the unfulfilled purposes of the foundation and its unfinished statutes. He had never got round to finalising them either.

It is clear that however ingenious or eloquent he might have been, he was not very good at carrying what he initiated through to a satisfactory conclusion. He appears to have been far too busy in his role as a Judge in London while, at the same time, currying favour with the Court of Queen Elizabeth in pursuit of a knighthood.

Well before the date of his death, as Dorothy and Edmund were aware, the citizens of Brentwood had been complaining about the inadequacy of "Redcross" and its distance from the centre of the town. Less than one year later, therefore, the foundation stone of the "Old Big school" was laid on 10th May 1568. Construction of the school room above it was completed without delay.

The threat to the foundation was very real. Wystan Browne, the nephew to whom Sir Antony had left his land and property "in tail" (for inheritance through the male line) was intent on seizing whatever he could and failed, as Executor, to carry out the terms of his late uncle's Will. In fact, he almost acquired the foundation's endowments, but that is another story.

I was actually taught in that first school room as a member of Classical Four in 1949/1950. The wooden desks at which we sat, inscribed with the initials of former pupils, reflected an earlier era, probably the late 1890s, with their ink wells and sloping tops. The rear wall of the partly wood panelled room was obscured by the massive painting of Weald Hall which now hangs in the school's dining hall. The room reeked of age and reminded us constantly of the conditions in which young boys had been obliged to study during previous centuries. We felt a direct link with them.

Should the reader wonder why wealthy men like Antony Browne and Richard Rich would want or be encouraged to found free grammar schools, the explanation is quite simple.

Due to the cost of his Court, his civil service and his various abortive involvements in European "power politics", Henry VIII ran very short of money in the 1530s. He looked at the well-endowed Monasteries and Abbeys which were not at all happy with his break from Rome and thought "they are sitting on vast wealth. I will help myself to it and thereby shore up my finances". Which, of course, he did. In the process a lot of men, including Antony Browne and Richard Rich made a great deal of money, a bit like the oligarchs who made fortunes out of the collapse of Communist Party rule in Russia during the 1990s.

Before Henry launched his assault on it and had initiated the Reformation the monastic system, with the many facilities it offered, had been an integral element in the lives of most people. It was, moreover, part of a powerful church structure that could offer "heavenly favours", at a price, and that controlled, through its teaching, what one was allowed to think and do. No one had previously dared to fall out with the church. Rich men had consequently bequeathed wealth to both institutions and both had become immensely wealthy.

Priests, moreover, were usually the only people in villages and small towns who could read and write and had become a kind of "civil service" as clerks and advisers of local, county and manorial courts while monks in monasteries had acted as teachers of young boys many of whom, like George Otway, went on to become priests and graduates of universities.

What Henry and his "scavengers", whether they were members of the aristocracy, opportunistic lawyers or merchant adventurers, overlooked at the time was the effect their actions had on the education of the sons of tenant farmers, artisans, and traders in villages and small towns across the land. The livelihoods of their parents had depended on the dismantled monastic structures, and they had been taught by and had relied upon the free "song and grammar" schools operated by the various religious orders. In fact, many of them who had gone on to become monks or priests found themselves literally "thrown out on to the street" when their religious establishments were closed down by order of the King.

The Chantry school in Chelmsford, for example, which had ceased to function as such on the dissolution of the monasteries, was only rescued from oblivion by local citizens who paid for its continuation until its revival and refoundation on 24 March 1551, under Edward VI, as a free grammar school. Few schools had survived the dissolution and free education of the poor had effectively come to a grinding halt. Those that had been lost had to be replaced and the most obvious people to pay for new free grammar schools were the men who had made the most money out of the dissolution.

Henry VIII had also cast an eye over the universities and their substantial wealth but had been deterred from swooping on them. A determined rear guard action had been mounted by academics, including Lord Somerset, the Chancellor of Cambridge University, who is known to have written to the King as follows:

"If learning decay, which of wild men maketh civil, of blockish and rash persons wise and godly counsellors, and of evil men good and godly Christians, what shall we look for else but barbarism and tumult? For when the lands of the Colleges be gone it shall be hard to say whose staff shall stand next the door".

Without learning "the staff standing next the door" might, in other words, be brandished by an uneducated ruffian who would use it, not to protect but to terrorise those "behind the door". The "ungodly" would pose a threat to the peace and stability of the realm. The King and his successors should expect anarchy if the assets of the universities were also seized.

The message was not lost on Henry. He was so impressed by the representations of Lord Somerset, in particular, that, rather than seizing the university's assets he founded Trinity College, Cambridge in 1546 and wrote back to him as follows:

"I tell you, sirs, that I judge no land in England better bestowed than that which is given to our Universities for, by their maintenance, our realm shall be well governed when we be dead and rotten". Henry had realised, belatedly, that the future stability of the country could only be assured by educating bright young men to succeed those they replaced in government and in the civil service generally.

In terms of realisation of the importance of teaching those who could not afford education a corner may have been turned, but could the King and his successors extract the necessary finance for free grammar schools from the oligarchs of the time? The next twenty years, within the life expectancy of most of them, would prove crucial.

In this respect it must have been apparent to the Lord Protectors of King Edward VI, to Queen Mary and subsequently to Queen Elizabeth who, by repute, was never "very keen on putting her hand into her royal pocket" that, despite their religious differences, the "educational deficit" had to be remedied quickly and that men of recently acquired wealth had to be encouraged to found and endow free grammar schools, thereby reinstating, by other means, the teaching of reading, writing and arithmetic that had previously been available to those who could not afford to pay for it through Monastic schools.

Although I am not a historian, but merely an inquisitive lawyer, I hope, nevertheless, that the reader will be able to glean from my narrative some idea of the state of education and the efforts made to revive it between 1545 and 1570.

As previously indicated Antony Browne had drawn up statutes for the school, but, here again, he never had them legally executed and they had to be drawn up afresh in 1622, some 54 years after the schoolhouse had been erected. I refer to them in the following chapter.

29

School Rules

Having obtained the necessary Letters Patent from Queen Mary in July 1558, Antony Browne would undoubtedly have delegated the task of drafting the provisions in the statutes of the foundation that related to his new grammar school (the school rules) to the well-educated George Otway. As schoolmaster George Otway would have wanted to have a say in the content of them.

Antony Browne, on the other hand, as a busy Serjeant at Law and Justice of the Peace, would have regarded the provisions merely as regulations, the preparation of which should be best left in the hands of those who would have to apply them.

Although the provisions in the draft statutes were undoubtedly approved by him, Antony Browne failed to have them legally executed, notwithstanding the fact that he was a lawyer. Was he too engrossed in other matters to have them legally executed? That seems to be the most likely explanation. He could see, moreover, that George Otway was performing his role of schoolmaster effectively. In his view there would probably have been no pressing need to have them executed immediately.

Alternatively, did he intend to expand the draft statutes to include some other worthy endowment? We shall never know. All we do know is that he was not very good at finalising projects he had initiated, and that he must have put them on one side for the time-being with the intention of returning to them later. As a lawyer myself, I am well aware of the temptation to defer consideration of matters that are less pressing, and less demanding of one's immediate attention!

Notwithstanding an Order by the Court of Chancery in 1570, some three years after the death of Sir Antony Browne, that the constitutions of the school should be drawn up properly, the draft statutes languished, gathering dust on a shelf, or in a cupboard, for the next 50 years. In fact, it was not until Sir Antony Browne's cousin took a decisive hand in matters that they were finally sent to the Bishop of London and the Dean of St. Pauls in accordance with the Court Order.

George Montague, the Bishop of London and John Donne, the eminent poet, lawyer and Dean of St. Pauls, were tasked with review and revision of the statutes as they deemed appropriate. They were drawn up afresh and constitutions that reflected the 1620s rather than the 1550's were duly approved and legally executed on 18 July 1622.

The 64 years between 1558 and 1622 had seen some fundamental changes in society. When Roman Catholic Mary died unexpectedly 3 months after the foundation of the school at the age of 42, she was succeeded by her 25-year-old Protestant, half-sister, Elizabeth. Because the majority of the population had remained deeply catholic in its outlook during her reign, Mary had tried "to turn the clock back" on her father's decision to break with Rome and had sought to re-establish the position of the Pope within the English church. In the brutal process introduced by her Statute of Heretics many people, including 19-year-old William Hunter who lived in Brentwood, were burned at the stake. Antony Browne, as her commissioner, was responsible for ordering his death and ensuring that the sentence was carried out.

As school librarian for two years, I was the only "day boy" in the school to have my own private study. It was the small storeroom within the library in which the school kept its most valuable books. Among them was a massive leatherbound edition of Foxe's Book of Martyrs which listed in detail people, many of whom, like William Hunter, had been influenced by the teaching of Martin Luther, and had stood out against her. I was able to read the chilling accounts of the torture and death of these brave souls, and of Mary's brutality towards them. She was not known by protestants as "Bloody Mary" for nothing!

When Elizabeth I became Queen the country had been in a state of religious ferment for 11 years. They must have been difficult and dangerous times for people like Antony Browne and Richard Rich, having to stay in favour with those on opposing sides of the religious divide, particularly so in their case, since they had made so much money out of selling the assets of monasteries and abbeys. They had had to be enthusiastically pro Reformation during the reigns of Henry VIII and Edward VI and avowedly anti Reformation during the reign of Henry's daughter, Mary. But they both managed to live through that tumultuous period with their fortunes intact.

The first thing Elizabeth did on her accession was to pass the Act of Supremacy which re-established the independence of the Anglo Catholic Church in England from papal authority. However, she tolerated Roman Catholics, like Antony Browne and George Otway, worshipping in private, if they wished to do so. Being aware of the growth of a Protestant middle-class she also wisely fused the Anglo Catholic and Protestant versions of the prayer book used in her churches, removing one major source of religious controversy and division. Antony Browne and George Otway would have breathed a sigh of relief when she did this because the school could use the new prayer book without offending any of the Protestant parents of children from the market town of Brentwood.

She went one step further when she published the Thirty-Nine Articles in 1563 which set out the duties owed by Anglo Catholics, whether priests or lay persons, to the state and to society. The Articles which, in effect, established the Anglican church stated that although Anglo Catholic views were being challenged by Lutherans, traditional rather than Protestant practices would nevertheless be followed. They also emphasised, however, that her church would remain firm in its refusal to accept the disciplines and primacy of Rome.

Sir Antony Browne, as he had become, died in 1567 and had been able to worship in private as a Roman Catholic until his death. However, the "crunch point" for priests like George Otway came in 1570, when, after years of dithering about how to react to the Act of Supremacy and the Thirty-Nine Articles, Pope Pius V issued a Papal Bull which excommunicated Queen Elizabeth, purportedly deprived her of her right to rule and released her subjects from obedience to her, even if they had previously sworn allegiance to her. Moreover, anyone who obeyed her orders after the issue of the Papal Bull would also be excommunicated.

This missive, perhaps better described as a missile, from the Pope was swiftly countered on the part of Queen Elizabeth by the Treason Act, 1570, which made it treason for anyone to say or write that Elizabeth was not the true Queen of England and Wales. People who wanted to remain Roman Catholics, and whose private beliefs had previously been tolerated, consequently found themselves caught in the withering crossfire between the Queen and the Pope.

What was George Otway to do? He would almost certainly have spent the early years of his education in a monastic school before he went to Cambridge University and would, like Sir Antony, have been baptised as a Roman Catholic. He probably felt that he had compromised his basic beliefs to a certain extent by becoming the schoolmaster of a free grammar school. On the other hand, he could see the need for teaching young boys whose parents could not afford to pay for their education. Now that a schoolhouse had been built in Ingrave Road, it was increasingly likely that he would have to teach Protestant, as well as Anglo Catholic, children and, as a consequence, abandon or conceal his Roman Catholic faith and outlook. He must also have been apprehensive that the application to the Court of Chancery would result in the statutes and ethos of the school becoming more Protestant. In the event, and being staunchly Roman Catholic, he resigned in 1570.

It is always possible that religious conviction was not the only reason for his resignation. Once the new schoolhouse had been built in a less than sanitary location on the road to Ingrave, George Otway and his successors would have to walk (if he did not have the luxury of a horse) well over a mile in the early hours of the morning from Redcross to the schoolhouse, and then walk back again later in the afternoon, whatever the weather. He is unlikely to have felt inclined to walk home during the late morning break between lessons, referred to below, and I doubt whether he had anywhere else to spend it apart, perhaps, from the St Thomas a Becket chapel in the main thoroughfare of the town, There could also have been antagonism towards him from the Protestant families in the town as a result of the cruel death of William Hunter, whether or not he had stated that he had converted to the Anglo-Catholic Church.

Despite the fact that the original provisions in the statutes relating to the school were never formalised, George Otway and his successors would have felt bound to observe them until, that is, the constitutions for the school were made legally effective in 1622. By today's standards the provisions were extremely onerous, and I set out below extracts from them which will give you an idea of what was expected of the schoolmaster and of the boys whom he taught. I have paraphrased them, but in using the word "scholar" for "schooler" I do not imply that the boys being taught had passed any form of entrance examination.

First of all, who did George Otway have to teach?

"The schoolmaster shall receive any scholar that shall be offered to him out of the Parish of South Weald or out of any Parish within three miles of the schoolhouse, and shall teach and instruct him in virtue, learning and manners".

You will note that no specific subjects are mentioned, but George Otway would have done his best to make the boys proficient in reading, writing and arithmetic before possibly introducing them to the rudiments of Latin. The study of Latin and Greek became "de rigueur" for Grammar school boys in the seventeenth century since the classics were felt to instil mental discipline, and expand and improve the intellect. But George Otway had to start with boys of whose intelligence and ability he was completely unaware when the school opened in the small chapel at Redcross in 1558.

A three-mile radius was obviously intended to cover the whole of Brentwood and to cater for the sons of its Protestant traders, as well as members of the largely Anglo Catholic farming community.

Virtue, learning and manners had to be taught as well as academic subjects and these core precepts remain integral to the culture of the school to the present day.

What were the school hours for the boys?

"The schoolmaster shall cause his scholars to be at school upon school days by 7 am in the morning in the winter, and stay until 11 am, then go to eat, be back by 1 pm and stay there until 5 pm and then to supper. In the summertime, begin at 6 am and leave at 6 pm keeping the other hours as before".

Boys and girls at Brentwood in the 21st century can have little conception of the length of a grammar school boy's day in Elizabethan times. They were, however, spared school on Saturday and homework during the week. Some only had to write up notes on the Sunday morning sermon and present them to the schoolmaster on Monday morning! But more of that anon.

Who was to monitor the behaviour of the boys?

"The schoolmaster shall appoint monitors to observe the devotion, manners, behaviour, conditions and diligence of the scholars in school and other places, and those who are found to offend shall be corrected by the schoolmaster at his discretion".

Correction presumably included the cane and, for monitors, read modern day praeposters or prefects.

As for the behaviour of the boys at the school the relevant provision reads as follows:

"Scholars shall revere their patron (Antony Browne), their schoolmaster and their guardians at all times and places with cap courtesy and other civil behaviour and shall conduct themselves civilly, decently and courteously towards all other persons".

I assume that guardians would, broadly speaking, be the equivalent of school governors today and echoes of "cap courtesy" can be found in the rules of Kettering Grammar school nearly four hundred years later. We at Brentwood school, were similarly expected to raise our caps to adults and to give up our seats on the bus to ladies. We were taught that "manners maketh man" in very much the same way as our forebears and other grammar school boys across the country.

The behaviour of the schoolmaster was similarly circumscribed:

"The schoolmaster shall neither be a common gamester or haunter of taverns nor by extravagant and unnecessarily expensive clothes or otherwise bring the school into disrepute and set a bad example to the scholars"

The words actually used in the provisions were "evil example" and although one can accept gambling and drinking in Tudor times as damnable and devilish one does not nowadays associate what one wears with good or evil. In a roundabout way this provision is saying that although we, your superiors, can dress as we like, you as a schoolmaster must dress soberly and piously.

Puritan sobriety in dress gradually became more and more marked from 1558 onward, as did the regulation of what one could say and do, and it is little wonder that people living in small towns and villages, particularly in the south-east of England considered emigration to the New World, as did the passengers on the Mayflower in 1620 in order to avoid the restrictions placed upon them by the Anglo Catholic Church.

Although few schoolmasters in my days at Brentwood were what one might describe as "haunters of taverns" those who had to find somewhere for lunch, because they had no homes to go to nearby, tended to gravitate towards "The Artichoke", a public house close to the new gymnasium at the rear of the school. More than one came into afternoon lessons, therefore, a little bit the worse for drink!

In this respect I can recall Mr Chisnall who taught English and who "lunched" at The Artichoke, coming into Classical Four one afternoon and telling us to get on with an essay while he stood at the back of the class.

After a few minutes there was a tremendous crash. We all turned round and found him lying flat on his back. For some unexplained reason he had been trying to kick high enough with his right leg to reach the lower mount of the painting of Weald Hall on the rear wall. He had caught his foot on the ledge below the painting, lost his balance and had toppled over. It was as embarrassing for him as it was amusing to us.

Mr Chisnall, whose nickname was "cheesenose", lost respect among the pupils as a result of his extracurricular activities. He had a 1936 Austin Seven and, on another occasion, after what must have been a bibulous evening at The Artichoke, sensibly decided not to drive home, but to leave his car parked by the side of the Fives Court. A fives court, incidentally, is a brick built structure in which a game similar to pelota is played.

The game of fives is believed to have originated in medieval times when young yeoman would throw a ball of some kind at the exterior wall of their local church or chapel, presumably before or after attending a service and see who could bounce it back from the wall to the other with a bare or gloved hand. This spontaneous and popular pastime was adopted by Eton College who, as was their wont, turned it into a proper sport. The college had buttresses on its chapel which gave the players three walls to hit the ball against and in 1840 a senior master, probably The Headmaster, devised a set of rules for it and had a fourth, rear wall, constructed to stop the ball from disappearing into the grass behind the players. Hence the birth of "Eton Fives". The name "fives" which has been used since the 1600s is believed to refer to the fingers on a hand as a "bunch of fives".

Once Eton had "regulated" it all the other top schools in the country wanted a fives court. Harrow and Winchester followed suit, and, between 1890 and 1900, any school with pretensions built one. It was about the size of a modern squash court and had no roof. All I can remember is boys, in my day, hitting tennis balls around the walls as if they were playing squash. The structure was demolished sometime after I left the school in 1954.

But once again, I digress!

Mr Chisnall returned to school next morning, sober, and discovered to his surprise that his little car had somehow taken residence in the fives court. The door into the court was less than three feet wide and the rear wall was a least five feet high. Although no-one ever "owned up" suspicion fell on the boarders in Otway, the boarding house closest to the court. They must have taken the wheels off, hoisted it over the rear wall and put the wheels back on again. A group of the younger and more muscular masters had to remove it.

The last of the provisions I will mention relates to church attendance.

"The schoolmaster shall cause all his scholars resident or staying within the parish of South Weald to be at prayers and at the sermons given by the vicar every Sunday morning in South Weald Parish Church (Saint Peters) and shall make them sit together in the seats provided for them. Monitors are to take the names of absentees and note the misbehaviour of those present.

Those scholars not within the parish shall be examined as to their diligence and those who are able to do so shall take notes of the sermons at their respective parish churches in writing and deliver them in a fair hand to the schoolmaster the next, Monday, morning."

There was no getting away with it.

If you did not have to be in South Weald Parish Church. George Otway and his successors wanted a neatly written account of the sermon at the parish church you attended, or you would be in trouble!

Looking back at the history of the period, Britain's decision to exit the European Union in the 21st century is as nothing when compared with the break from Rome and the disruption to people's lives in the 16th century. Nevertheless one cannot help reflecting on the apparently innate and long-standing instinct of the English to be closely involved in Europe but not be part of it.

30

My First Year in the Main School

When I arrived at the main school for my second, and possibly last term, I knew that I had to work hard and pass the "eleven plus". I felt that, having passed the "eight plus" it was a bit unfair to have to jump another academic hurdle. But there was no option. I had to take the recently introduced examination if I was to be awarded an Essex County Scholarship and stay at Brentwood.

The 1944 Education Act had completely overhauled the educational system. No longer would bright, young boys and girls have to try and win scholarships to grammar schools at the age of 8 and pay, admittedly nominal, fees. Those who were able to pass the academically oriented "eleven plus" examination would be offered free state, or county funded, places at Local Educational Authority (L.E.A) grammar or county high schools, alternatively at independent grammar or public schools which had agreed to open their doors to direct grant pupils.

In the case of Brentwood this meant that the fees of a substantial proportion of the 11-year-olds in my class who had, like myself, managed to pass the examination, were directly funded by central government or by Essex County Council. The fees of the other boys who entered the school at this age, either directly or from the prep, were paid, for the most part, by parents who could afford to do so. It is said that, on average, independent schools, like Brentwood, received well over half their income from the state or from LEAs as a result of the direct grant scheme.

When the direct grant scheme ended in the 1960s independent grammar schools had to decide whether to be absorbed into the state sector of secondary education or to rely on fee paying pupils for their survival. The King Edward VI Grammar School in Chelmsford was one of the many that joined the state sector, whereas Brentwood chose to remain independent and emphasise its public school status. In this respect Brentwood had always been referred to locally as a grammar school rather than a public school because of its foundation as such in 1558. It was nevertheless a member of the HMC (the Headmasters' Conference), a body which represented fee paying public and grammar schools.

The privately funded pupils were either day boys like us or boarders.

Boarders lived in boarding houses within or adjacent to the grounds of the school and were provided with dormitory accommodation and all meals during term time. One of the boarding houses was School House, located next to the original 16th-century schoolroom in which I was taught for a year and, another was "Otway", named after the first schoolmaster who, ironically, had to live at Redcross, some distance away, during his period as a schoolmaster.

The senior boarders had their own studies in a corridor close to the old schoolroom and, very much to my surprise, "fags", junior boarders, who cleaned their shoes and cadet corps boots and kept their studies tidy. The name "fag" has, in recent years acquired an unfortunate connotation, but the boarding school concept, as far as School House was concerned, did not appear to me to have changed very much since "Tom Brown's School Days", when I first walked down that corridor in September 1946.

The immediate post war era and the 1944 Education Act did, however, usher in a complete change in the attitudes previously prevalent in the school, and its Governors, at the time, were fortunate enough to acquire, in 1945, a young and far-sighted Headmaster, Charles Ralph Allison ("Chas", to the boys) who helped transform it and lay the foundations of its subsequent massive expansion.

From my perspective entering the main school was merely a matter of crossing from one side of Shenfield Road to the other. Between 1946 and 1949 the prep, and a number of junior boarders, were located in a Georgian building known as "The Old House" on the north side of the road. Having been used thereafter by the school for other purposes until 1965, it was sold to Brentwood Council which converted it into a Community and Arts Centre.

On the opposite side of the road and not far from the Memorial to William Hunter, who was burned at the stake in 1555, was, and still is, Roden House, a fine red brick Queen Anne house, which had been acquired on behalf of the school in 1917. In my day it had a spacious garden with extensive lawns and a large brick-faced ornamental pond at the rear to which I will refer later.

It was on the ground floor of Roden House that we, Form Lower One, the lowest of the low in the hierarchy of the school, were accommodated with our form master, Mr Kershaw (who so far as I am aware never acquired a nickname!). I got the strong impression that the house had been used as private accommodation for the previous headmaster for reasons I will give later. Immediately next door to it, only a few feet distant, was Mitre House in which John Farrant, Michael Welsford and I had our first school lunches until lunches were relocated to The Ivy Restaurant, opposite The Artichoke. This relocation did not last very long. Once in the main school we had our lunches in St. Thomas's Hall just off Queens Road, before the school built its own dining hall.

There were 40 boys in Lower One and we might have represented a challenge to anyone else, but Mr Kershaw ruled with a rod of iron. He had arrived at the school in September 1940 and told us that he had previously taught at a school in China. He had returned to England when, as a result of the Japanese invasion of the country it was no longer safe for him to stay there. We had no reason to disbelieve him. He had, he told us, bought back from China a pair of very thick plimsolls which he wore out there and which he would inflict on the backside of any boy who misbehaved. He only had to see you out of the corner of his eye talking to another boy in class, or not paying attention, and you would be summoned to the front for a hefty whack on the bottom from his heavy-duty footwear. The plimsolls really hurt and there was one poor boy in the class by the name of Girdwood, uncharitably nicknamed "Fatty", who started to cry before he actually received his punishment. The rest of us tried to look brave. I was a regular offender and, like my fellow miscreants, knew exactly what to expect. There was nothing unusual about this sort of behaviour on the part of schoolmasters at the time. It was the norm as far as we were concerned. I will refer to their various types of chastisement in a later chapter.

Notwithstanding Miss Haynes's somewhat Victorian method of controlling the behaviour of her 10-year-old pupils, she had been a capable and experienced teacher. I, moreover, had had the benefit of an excellent preparation for the "eleven plus" during my two years at Kettering Grammar school. It put me ahead of all, but one, of the boys in her class.

When, therefore, we moved up from the prep into the main school most of us passed the examination. In fact, I seem to recall that 31 out of our class of 40 obtained Essex County Scholarships thereby relieving our parents of the need to pay fees, apart, of course, from the comparatively low number of parents who still had to meet their sons' boarding costs.

Because we came into the school through its main entrance in Ingrave Road and made our way to Roden House from there, our classroom appeared to be at the rear of the building. Light came into it through large French windows which looked out over the lawns behind it. When I say "appeared to be at the rear", the room, which extended from the back to the front of the building, would also have looked out over the Shenfield Road had not the front windows been bricked up in the 18th century in order to avoid or reduce payment of window tax.

It is an unfortunate fact of life that Governments, of whatever nature or persuasion, have a penchant for imposing taxes on the owners or occupiers of domestic property. Charles II started off the whole sorry business of taxing people's homes by imposing a Hearth Tax in 1662 when he returned to England from exile. He needed the money to help fund the public, or, in his case, the royal, purse and his ongoing military engagements with the Dutch which, incidentally, deprived the sheep farmers of East Anglia of their principal outlet for the sale of wool. It was a "double whammy" as far as they were concerned. They had to pay this new tax when their main source of income had disappeared, thanks to the ongoing trade wars with the States General (the Netherlands), but that is another story!

The rationale behind the tax was quite simple. Over the preceding decades more and more people had added external chimneys or built chimneys into their homes. It enabled them to have hearths in ground floor and, in some cases, upper floor rooms, and to retain the heat generated by fires within the brickwork. Adding an external chimney to a Tudor house was very much akin to adding a conservatory in the twentieth century. Before that heat and smoke just went out through a hole in the roof of most houses.

Hearths were an additional luxury as far as Charles was concerned. "Why not impose a tax of two shillings a year on every 'firehearth or stone' in all dwellings", thought he. "What a splendid and 'surefire'(!) way of raising a bit more money for the State". Except that it wasn't, and after his own tax commissioners had been chased out of most people's homes or assaulted in the street, he put collection of the tax out to tender. A number of city merchants undertook to collect it in return for a share of the proceeds, but they did not fare much better. He persisted, nevertheless, with the tax until the end of his reign. It was not until William and Mary came to the throne that this incredibly unpopular tax was repealed in 1689.

But it was not long before William and Mary also realised that they needed to raise money, principally for military purposes, and in 1696 they were obliged to introduce a Window Tax. Houses with less than 10 windows only had to pay a House Tax of 2 shillings a year, but houses with more had to pay Window Tax. Roden House, which appears on the 1717 map of Brentwood, was built in "Queen Anne style" between 1702 and 1714 when only House Tax would have been payable on it.

Along comes George III, however, and his government decides in 1766 to reduce the threshold for Window Tax from 10 to 7 or more windows. The tax increased the more windows one had. The lowering of the threshold led to a massive number of owners bricking up the windows of their properties, including the owners of Roden House at the time. Like the Hearth Tax it was extremely unpopular but was not repealed until 1851, but again, I digress!!

Being young boys, we naturally wanted to explore our new surroundings and found a rusty Bren gun in the shrubbery between

Roden House and Mitre House. We reported our find to Mr Kershaw and the army came to retrieve it. It may well have been issued to the local Home Guard who had just abandoned it at the end of the war in Europe in May 1945.

Although we were warned by Mr Kershaw that we should, under no circumstances, go up to the top floor of the house I, as is my wont, ignored his "out of bounds" injunction and decided to explore it. Most of the rooms were locked, but one was not and it was like an Aladdin's cave. The room was full of Zulu shields and assegais and tables upon which stood domed glass cases containing stuffed birds and animals. It was quite spectacular.

I concluded that an occupier of the house before Lower One moved into it had been to South Africa and that he had also been an avid collector of what I can only describe as Victoriana. I crept downstairs and told no-one what I had seen. My guess was that the previous Headmaster, Mr Hough, had lived at some time, in Roden House and that he had stored many of his possessions on the top floor until he was able to find suitable accommodation for them elsewhere.

I previously mentioned the ornamental pond behind the lawns because I was caught playing "Scott of the Antarctic" on the ice that covered it during the ferocious winter of 1946/1947. With my friend, John Farrant, I had decided to venture onto it, contrary to strict instructions from Mr Kershaw not to do so. As we moved across the ice, which had previously been very thick, but which was beginning to look suspect, we were spotted by Mr Burrell the school bursar who told us to get off it immediately and report to Mr Kershaw. Since he had not taken our names and since Mr Burrell was clearly going home to lunch at Mitre House we thought we might get away with not doing so, but we were wrong!

Mr Kershaw came into the classroom at 2 pm and asked "which of you boys were on the pond at lunch time? Raise your hands". We kept ours down. "In that case", said Mr Kershaw", every boy will remain here in the classroom after school until I find out". Since this would have been a bit hard on everyone else in the class John Farrant and I put our hands up. "Follow me into my study", he said, and after lecturing us on the risk of drowning if the ice had given way, he got out his cane. "Bend over" was the terse command and we each received three of the best. However, to our surprise and great relief the cane was nowhere near as painful as his massive plimsolls. We both felt that we had got away lightly.

Mr Kershaw was, in fact, a decent man. He never mentioned a wife and we did not know whether he was married. However, he was a stern disciplinarian, and we got the impression that he would have treated any sons in the same way as he treated us.

My next escapade with John Farrant was to go into the school swimming pool in April before we were officially allowed to do so. We chose a moment when no one else was about and opened the unlocked door. We changed into our swimming trunks, which we had surreptitiously brought to school with us, in the cubicles at the side of the pool, and gently lowered ourselves into the water at the shallow end, gasping a little as we immersed our bodies to waist level.

At this point, doubtless fortuitously, the door giving access to the pool swung open and there stood John Seabright, the head boy of Otway. He must have heard us splashing about. "What on earth are you boys doing in the water?" he shouted and walked across to the pool thermometer encased in a white foam wrapping, attached to a piece of cord. "Don't you realise it is only 42 degrees Fahrenheit. Get out at once". I had to admit that ten degrees above freezing was pretty chilly. We were shepherded by him out of the swimming pool and that was the end of that particular adventure.

I have previously mentioned David Tench who came first in my class in the Prep. He was very bright academically but not such a good businessman. Early in the summer term of 1947, as Dinky toys came back onto market I decided to buy and sell them for a bit of extra pocket money. In his case I can recall swapping a pristine green and black London taxi which I had purchased for about 2 shilling and 3 pence and which he desperately wanted to acquire, for a box full of cigarette cards, a very nice genuine leather wallet and a rather battered pre-war sports model. I took the items home, sold the wallet to my father for a pound and found, among the cigarette cards, a complete set of "John Player" Scott of the Antarctic cards which, even then, were quite valuable and which I have kept to this day!

The other cigarette cards were traded where necessary in exchange for other Dinky toys as cost-balancing items where the purchase and sale values I attributed to the various model cars, lorries and planes were different. I was fortunate, in this respect, that toy shops could not afford to stock the entire Dinky range, nor did they sell "second hand" models.

The only other memorable events during my first year were accidents. As previously mentioned, I ran, and until advanced old age, have always run everywhere and, one morning, as I raced to the Tuck Shop in the Lawrence building to collect the half pint bottle of milk provided free of charge and courtesy of His Majesty's Government to all young children, I tripped and crashed headfirst at speed into the paving. Although Dandy and Beano, two of my favourite comics, portrayed characters seeing stars and planets when "biffed", I never, until that moment, thought it true in real life. But I was badly concussed and did literally see stars and planets floating across my eyes. It was so very strange. I was taken to the school sanatorium and kept in bed by the school nurse until my father collected me on his way home from work.

The second accident occurred when I ran down the cobbled passageway, that led from the main school to Roden House, so fast that I could not turn right into the garden in time and hit the brick wall of the building. I had to assure my mother that my black eye was not acquired as a result of fighting.

Most of the boys I had been with in the Prep and who had joined me in Lower One were allocated to different classes at the beginning of my second year (1947/1948) but John Farrant and I stayed together in our new form, Upper Two. Michael Welsford, who had not unfortunately passed the eleven plus, went into a less academic class and I consequently saw less and less of him. Although my commercial activities had not materially affected my position in class during my year in Lower One, thanks largely to the head start Kettering grammar school had given me, the reckoning was to come in Upper Two.

31

Wearing the School Uniform

When I arrived at the Prep in 1946 the regulation school uniform for the summer term was a plain, dark-blue blazer, white shirt, black tie, short grey trousers, grey socks, black shoes and a plum-coloured cap that bore, embroidered in gold above the peak, the insignia of the school, namely an eagle's wing on top of a lions paw. It was a modest but distinctive uniform and, apart from the blazer and the badge, which one had to sew on its breast pocket, not too costly for parents to provide.

The badge representing the coat of arms of Sir Antony Browne is still worn on the school's blazers to this day and the insignia also appear regularly, albeit not in gold, above the word "Incipe". This is Latin for "begin" or, as I interpreted it in my time, "get cracking"! Below the coat of arms are often inscribed the words "Virtue, Learning and Manners", taken from the original statutes of 1558.

Since my economical mother considered that my black, Kettering Grammar school (K.G.S.), blazer had another year of life in it and looked close enough to dark blue for anyone to really notice the difference, she simply took off the KGS badge and replaced it with the Brentwood school coat of arms.

In fact, no one was expected to be able to afford or even obtain very much in the way of new clothing in the immediate aftermath of the Second World War and there was no comment from the school on any such deviation from its prescribed dress code. As an alternative, moreover, to wearing the blazer in the summer term, younger boys could continue to wear the grey jacket and short grey trousers they wore during the winter and spring terms. Only the cap was obligatory at all times.

Bearing in mind the substantial influx of Essex County scholars from 1947 onwards, it was not long before Charles Allison, (Chas) the new headmaster, decided that, in the interests of economy, a new school uniform should be introduced. It was made of a hardwearing, interwoven black and white tweed like material, which gave the overall appearance of grey, and which was promptly nicknamed "Allison serge".

Chas, an inspirational and far-sighted person, had appreciated that many parents of scholarship boys were not at all well off and that standardisation of dress was essential. He did, however, encourage the wearing of blazers and flannels during the summer term, with boaters for sixth formers, and introduced flowing, royal blue, gowns for "head of house praeposters" (prefects), similar to the black gowns worn by form masters. Being made of straw some of the more irreverent boarders in schoolhouse grew cress on their boaters, but I never actually saw any of these green topped aberrations being worn by them.

In terms of "houses" all boys were allocated to a boarding or a day house on arrival. I was put into North Junior which seemed to contain a number of boys from Billericay, to the east of Brentwood. I could never quite work that one out, but there must have been some sort of logical process in allocating boys to North, South, East, West and Weald houses. It obviously had little to do with where one actually lived.

In order to emphasise our links to our houses, Chas also introduced dark blue ties with different coloured stripes representing each house and, paradoxically, it is doubtless true to say that he liked to create "traditions" where none had previously existed. It was all part of his giving the school and each house within it a distinct identity.

Our school "ensemble" was completed in my case by a somewhat battered leather satchel containing a bag of marbles, some rather unwelcome exercise books for homework, my Ian Allan bus spotters' book, the usual array of HB pencils, rubber, ruler, pen and pen knibs (Biros had not yet been invented) and a bottle of Parkers black ink (Quink). I later moved on to a refillable Parker pen, which was much less messy and much easier to write with.

We did rather stand out from the other passengers on the red, number 86, and the green, number 721, London Transport buses which we boarded in Ingrave Road after school, and we stood out even more when we alighted in the middle of Romford market in order to proceed to our ultimate home destinations.

In the late 1940s Romford market was huge. It was on both sides of the main road, bustling with activity and much larger than the market in Kettering which I used to frequent on Saturday mornings on my way home from children's cinema at the Odeon.

I was fascinated by the vast array of goods in the market and the "patter" of the sales people, invariably male, which would normally commence with shouts along the lines of "gather round ladies, I have the most amazing bargains for you today, and for today only", whether it be sheets, blankets, tea towels, bath towels, woolly looking bath mats, dishcloths, crockery, pots and pans, cleaning and beauty products or a host of other items.

The trader would then go on to announce that he only had a limited stock of whatever bargain he was selling that day and that he was only able to offer the items in question at knockdown prices, through having previously bought them in bulk from some low-cost source or another. He was, he said, down to the last few items (whether he was or not) and wanted to pass on the benefit of the reduced price of them to those gathered round. Having gauged the level of interest in his audience he would give a prospective sale price and, if there was little immediate reaction would go on to include another item in the price or offer to sell two of the same items at about fifty per cent more than the price for one. He had to find an acceptable figure without being too generous about it. It was virtually the same as the "three for the price of two" technique that one finds in supermarkets nowadays. But, of course, there were no supermarkets in the 1940s and there was very little, if any, discounting in retail shops and department stores.

I had to admire the battle of wits between the East End traders and the "savvy" bargain hunting housewives who were listening to these exhortations to snap up such incredible offers while they could. Even I was nearly tempted to buy a solution which turned copper coins a silver colour. I do not know what the chemical was but the idea of making a brass half penny look like a silver shilling was certainly an attractive alchemy for a ten-year-old whose pocket money and earning prospects were strictly limited.

There were, of course, all sorts of other stalls selling just about everything including carpet slippers, plimsolls, scarves and gloves for men and women, leather and wooden goods of all kinds, cheap costume jewellery, handbags, wicker shopping baskets and children's items from dolls and dolls clothes, unpainted metallic, die cast model cars, and army vehicles, to cheap colouring books and large stiff cards on which had been printed "cut out" sections of models. One could, by cutting out with a pair of scissors the constituent parts and gluing them together, create anything from dolls houses and castles to steam trains, ships and cars.

After a wander round the market I would head off to an equally interesting store, Woolworths, just beyond the traffic lights in the centre of the town with its extraordinary range of goods from, would you believe, fishing rods and tackle and feathery imitation flies for anglers to attach to their hooks and lines, to all the items one would need at home like balls of grey and black wool for darning socks, reels of sewing cotton which my mother would sometimes ask me to buy for her, boot and shoe laces, shoe polish, cutlery, coat and picture rail hangers, screws and nails of all kinds, sweets, packets of flower and vegetable seeds for the garden and so on. The number of different items seemed limitless but only a few of them caught my eye during my visits to the store.

The sale of fishing tackle in Woolworths intrigued me particularly because I could not really visualise how many anglers there might be in such a built-up town as Romford. Where, on earth, could they fish? The oily smell of the coiled fishing lines has stayed with me to this day.

I never had money for the items on sale in the market or in Woolworths, apart, occasionally, from the "cut out model" cards. My pocket money until I was thirteen was one shilling (twelve old pence) a week (5p in modern currency) rising over the years to three shillings and six pence (17-1/2p) a week when I was eighteen. The cost of a Mars bar in 1947 (still on ration) was three old pence and one bar would have taken a quarter of my weekly income, had it not been for my generous

Uncle Gerald. These amounts may appear ludicrously small now, but I had to get by on them except when, during my eleventh and twelfth years, I took up "second hand car dealing".

Before catching the number 66 bus to Hornchurch from Romford High Street , I would stand at the junction of the High Street and the main road and indulge in a bit of bus spotting, marking off the numbers of the buses listed in my "Ian Allan, ABC of London Transport" book.

Once on the bus to Hornchurch I felt very much on my own, travelling into "unknown territory" apart from the roads between Hornchurch Underground Station, the terminus of the bus route, and my home in Alma Avenue. I had no friends there: they were all at school, the centre of my social activities. There was little opportunity to get to know the area, in any event, because I was not there very much during the week apart from Sundays.

We had lessons from 9.15 am on Monday morning to 12.30 pm on Saturday with sport on Wednesday and Saturday afternoons. On Sundays I read adventure stories, did jigsaw puzzles, made models out of the sheets of card I had purchased in the market and played with coloured pieces of wood of different sizes, retained from my earlier years, my Dinky toys and some pieces of Meccano. There was none of the electronic and plastic gadgetry that children have today and nothing with an audio-visual content. There was no television. The only visual entertainment was the cinema. At home, one had to amuse oneself.

Although family life was stable and happy my mother was preoccupied with looking after our home and my six-year-old sister. My father who was looking more and more gaunt every day was engrossed with his new job, completing the purchase of the plot in Norsey Road and negotiating the details of the construction of our new home upon it. The one really bright spot in the week for me was travelling to my grandparents after sport on Saturday afternoons.

Because grammar schoolboys wore caps and looked a bit smarter than the usual secondary school boy there was a general perception that we considered ourselves superior and that we were not as tough or as brave as our secondary school counterparts. This was brought home to me very forcibly by a bruising encounter in Hornchurch on my way home from school one summer's day in 1947 when I was eleven and a half years old.

I had to get a haircut and there were Hairdressers in the parade of shops opposite Hornchurch Underground Station. I was wearing my plum red school cap, and dark blazer and the rest of our regulation school uniform when I walked across from the bus terminus and went into the hairdressers.

While I was having my hair cut, the boy sitting in the chair next to me laughed at my appearance and said that any kid dressed as I was must be a cissy and deserved to be given a beating. I must be gutless. I took exception to his remark and told him I was no such thing. He smirked and said, "Then meet me outside after you have had your haircut and prove it."

As a matter of honour I accepted the challenge but he was clearly a couple of years older than me, and much bigger and stronger. As I stepped outside the hairdressers there he was, ready to give battle. I could not let the school down or appear weak or frightened, so I took off my cap, put down my satchel and prepared to defend myself. But it was, to my mind, like a light cruiser or destroyer defending itself against a battleship, similar to being the "Ajax" or the "Achilles" when, with HMS Exeter, they took on the German pocket battleship, the "Graf Spee" at the battle of the River Plate.

I knew I was going to get hammered, but my principal concern was what my mother would say if I came home with one or two black eyes. I would then have been in real trouble! She was always so concerned about my looks that I feared her anger more than the fact I was being severely beaten.

As the blows rained down on me rescue arrived, to my immense relief, in the unlikely shape of the hairdresser who, witnessing the uneven contest from his shop window, came out, gave the other boy a clip round the ear and told him, in no uncertain terms to clear off.

He then, to my surprise, proceeded to tell me how to protect myself on any future occasion by putting both forearms in front of my face, tucking my head in, chin close to my chest and jabbing the nose of my opponent with my right fist. It was excellent advice, which I employed to good effect, when an equally aggressive boy had a go at me at school a couple of years later.

It was only a couple of weeks after this incident that I was walking back from the bus stop into Alma Avenue when I spotted the boy, whose name turned out to be Ron, with a couple of his friends on the opposite side of the road. My heart sank as they crossed the road and came towards me. To my amazement, however Ron said, "Would you like to come and play with us?" I had clearly passed the valour test. Grammar school boys who stood up to him were not "cissies" after all.

I agreed to do so and went with him and his two friends down to a stream at the bottom of Alma Avenue, long since built over or diverted. We dammed up the stream and made a small pond upon which we sailed twigs converted into boats with paper sails from one of my exercise books.

I never had an opportunity to play with him again and often wondered what happened to him. He would have done National Service, like me, and that experience would hopefully have channelled his aggressive instincts in the right direction.

Apart from that incident there is not much more to say about Hornchurch. It was as quiet as Ramsden Bellhouse and nowhere near as lively as Kettering where we lived so close to the centre of the town. My parents appreciated that I needed to get out and about and expend some of my restless energy and, on 30 August 1947, after our camping holiday in Wollacombe and Mortenhoe, took me to Sissleys in Hornchurch and bought me an Elswick bicycle for twelve pounds three shillings and ten pence, and a chrome plated bell for two shillings.

Because I wanted to ride it after dark, I used what pocket money I had saved to purchase a dynamo which operated off the tyre on the back wheel, and which powered lights at front and rear. The bike became my most prized possession and proved incredibly useful once we moved to Billericay where my home lifestyle changed out of all recognition.

32
The Move to Billericay

My parents put 46 Alma Avenue up for sale in the autumn of 1947 and, on 14 January 1948, eight days after my twelfth birthday and four days after the Surveyor to Billericay Urban District Council had issued his certificate of satisfactory completion of the structure, we moved into our new bungalow.

Because of the shortage in the post War years of building materials and Government regulations limiting the use of them for private purposes the bungalow was not as large as my parents would have liked it to be but it was, nevertheless, as large as our three-bedroomed semi-detached house in Hornchurch.

It was a priority of the government at the time to rehouse as many families whose homes had been destroyed by German air raids as possible and this led to a diversion of building materials into the construction of pre-fabricated houses, known as "prefabs", in London and in other blitzed urban areas.

The layout and design of our new home was based on that of "Bowburn Cottage", the home of John Strong, a Billericay Architect, who had only a year or so previously purchased a plot less than fifty yards from our own. In fact, John Strong was supervising architect for our bungalow for which the total cost of construction amounted to £1420 (one thousand four hundred and twenty pounds).

The cost of clearing the building site by W. Wood of Rayleigh, "an experienced and recommended Land Clearing Contractor by explosives, etc." was £10 (ten pounds), and I wonder how much explosive, if any, was used to uproot the oak and Spanish chestnut trees that proliferated where our new home now stood.

It had been built during the autumn of 1947 and had not had an opportunity to dry out when we took occupation. The weather in January, moreover, was awful and about to become a great deal worse. The snow on the ground when we arrived gradually got deeper and deeper. In fact the winter was so severe that we subsequently had eighteen inches of snow across our plot for many weeks.

My bedroom was like an ice box and heated by one remarkably ineffective single bar electric fire built into the wall with a cream tiled surround upon which my father had placed a wooden plaque. It read, *"One inch of joy surmounts of grief a span because to laugh is proper to the man."* The message on the plaque, the warmth from the electric fire which could not have projected its heat more than three feet into the room and a couple of blankets were intended to keep me warm and sanguine. But I was, of course, used to the cold, having slept in an unheated bedroom in Kettering for several years with only the occasional hot water bottle for company.

I subsequently discovered that the message on the plaque was a translation of one of the quotations of Michel de Montaigne, the French Renaissance philosopher. Other "bon mots" of his were, *"Even on the most exalted throne in the world we are only sitting on our own bottom."* And, more profoundly, *"The most certain sign of wisdom is cheerfulness."* I suspect my father was an admirer of the wit and stoicism of Montaigne because he exhibited cheerfulness, fortitude and wisdom throughout his life, despite his bad health.

The bungalow was in a woodland clearing surrounded by the snow-covered stumps of the trees that had been felled and presumably blown up by Mr Wood prior to the construction of it. Some of them had been overturned in the process of being uprooted and lay with their roots pointing to the sky like stricken creatures from a past age. They would have to be removed somehow.

There was no vehicular access to the plot from the road because the four-foot-high mediaeval deer bank between the bungalow and the road had not been removed. There was a gap in it sufficiently wide for a gate and a narrow footpath. Vehicular access was gained from "the Ride", immediately adjacent to our plot, an unmade cart track that led from Norsey Road right up to the centre of Norsey Woods and that linked with the principal cart track through them.

During and subsequent to the construction of our new home Robert Jasper William Leyland, known by everyone in Billericay at the time as "Jasper Leyland", had given my parents and the building contractors verbal permission to use "The Ride" for vehicular access to our plot until my father was certain he could remove the entire deerbank and create our own drive.

The deerbank which must originally have run from Deerbank Road on the south-east side of the Woods was very old indeed. It probably existed at the time of the Peasants' Revolt in 1381 when, following the brutal and unprovoked killing of Wat Tyler by the Lord Mayor of London, the peasants from Kent and Essex realised, on their peaceful return to their Counties, that the promises of King Richard II to redress their grievances "were nought" and that he intended to suppress their revolt by arresting and hanging their leaders.

According to historians the disillusioned "men of Essex", after their initial march to Smithfield in London, reluctantly mustered in Billericay on their return and "took up their position in woods to the north of Billericay, their flanks protected by ditches and with a barricade of farm carts to protect their front".

In order to build a deerbank one has to create a ditch from which to take the soil and clay to do so and this would rather imply that the deerbank and the ditch in front of it existed at the time and was used as a defensive barrier by them. The only surviving part of the deerbank is at the front of Number 180 Norsey Road. All other traces of it have disappeared in the last seventy-five years, within my lifetime, following extensive residential development of the plots fronting Norsey Woods.

There followed what is known at the "Battle of Billericay". But it was hardly a battle. Thomas of Woodstock who lived in Pleshey Castle, to the north of Chelmsford, gathered an army for the King, including a group of heavily armed knights who charged on horseback through and over the defences and put the peasants to flight. It is said that over five hundred peasants were killed on the battlefield while the scattered remnants went into hiding. Many of the slain were buried in the churchyard at Great Burstead, probably including their principal leader, the priest Jack Straw, from Fobbing.

The Ride not being much more than a cart track was very muddy in the winter and I can recall dashing down the footpath and through the garden gate in the deerbank onto the road when catching the City bus, instead of going through the double wooden gates which opened from our plot onto it.

While The Ride still existed, we went for walks to the centre of the Woods and, on one particular occasion at Christmas 1948, my father and I and members of our extended family decided to go for a breather after lunch. Uncle Gerald was with us and, as our shoes crunched the snow in the winter half light, he suddenly stopped. We wanted to know why.

He blurted out, "we are being watched". "Don't be ridiculous, Gerald, who on earth would be watching us?" We resumed our walk and then simultaneously came to a halt after a few paces. We saw it! There, in a tall Spanish chestnut tree about forty feet away and just to the left of the path, sitting serenely and almost invisible on one of the snow-covered branches was a massive barn owl. We crept by this white breasted and ghostly looking bird as it watched us with its beady yellow and luminous eyes. Gerald was right but I am not sure to this day how he sensed its presence.

As for the name of the Wood no one can be precise as to its origin but it appears to have derived from its earliest recorded name, Nosseheye. A "hey" in Anglo Saxon is an enclosure. Nosseheye must therefore have passed down the generations by word of mouth for many centuries until Messrs. Chapman and Andre surveyed the Billericay area in 1777 and described it in their well-known map as "Norsy Wood", a slight variation on the current spelling.

My parents full of enthusiasm for our new home initially called it "Woodlands" until the owners of a pre-existing house in Norsey Road with the same name quite reasonably objected. In an attempt to circumvent their objection my father decided that we should call our bungalow "Woodlands, the Ride, Norsey Road" but this proved unsatisfactory and unacceptable to the owners of "Woodlands".

As an alternative my parents considered calling it "Rowan Cottage" because there was a Mountain Ash in the rear garden area. In a flash of inspiration, however, my mother who had a passion for painting just about anything, whether inside or out, decided to have the nondescript white snowcem exterior walls painted a soft pink and to call the bungalow "Pink Cottage". The colour would go well with the russet roof tiles. And that name continued until the bungalow was demolished in 2018 to make way for the massive and uninspiring red brick edifice with "Essex style" Grecian columns that replaced it.

Not long after my father had received clearance to demolish the deerbank in its entirety and had installed a drive on our plot, Jasper Leyland sold the Woods to Albert Butt, the owner of A C Butt Builders, who promptly obtained Planning Consent for the construction of a house on the site of "The Ride" and to turn the first four hundred feet of it into a building plot. Albert had purchased the Woods with a view to continuing the sale of plots around the entire perimeter of them, but the Local Authority objected and the Planning Inspectorate upheld their objection on appeal. Development was to be limited to the frontage of the Woods on Norsey Road alone. The Woods were later acquired by the Local Authority from a "thwarted" Albert Butt and are owned by it to this day. The remainder of "The Ride" has long since disappeared as trees and undergrowth have obliterated all traces of it.

Moving to Billericay meant another change in my "travel to school" routine. I could now leave home a few minutes later for my journey to Brentwood, albeit on the same brown and cream City bus. The bus stop, only a stone's throw from our garden gate, was opposite Jubilee Cottages, a red brick terrace built by George Sainer to house his family and the labourers who must have worked on his then substantial Norsey Farm. A plaque on the only double fronted cottage in the terrace is dated 15 June 1897 and commemorates completion of construction five days before the sixtieth anniversary of the accession of Queen Victoria to the throne on 20th June 1837.

At the time the cottages were built they were well over a mile from a small sleepy town, down a little used country road with woods in front of them and extensive farmland at their rear. The sale of woodland plots by the Layland family and the contemporaneous selling of building plots in Norsey and Stock Roads and the fields in between during the 1920s and 1930s brought about a profound change. It transformed what had been farmland into the residential area that it is today.

I had reason to be grateful to Olive Hunt, the daughter of the owners or tenants of one of the cottages. She lived with her parents, her brothers Brian and Colin, and her sisters, Myrtle and Hazel, and went to Brentwood County High school. She would kindly hold up the bus for me when she heard our front door slam, knowing that I would be racing down the garden path to catch it!

Immediately opposite our garden gate was the entrance to Norsey Farm, the entirety of which was purchased by Moody Estates, a well known firm of Property Developers. They were more successful than Albert Butt and obtained planning permission to build a very large housing estate on the former farm comprising, for the most part, three and four-bedroom detached houses for the more "well to do" members of the Billericay community.

There was a large black barn just inside and to the left of the farm entrance and, doubtless for a bit of extra "non-taxable pocket money", Mr Attridge, the owner of the farm and his younger "close companion", Mrs. Dennison, would sell vegetables from it on Saturday mornings.

On his first visit to the barn in the summer of 1948 my father crossed the road to buy some potatoes, carrots and onions. As he was leaving Mr Attridge said "Ere, and tell yer Mum we have some lovely cabbages". At the time my father was very thin, boyish in appearance and not at all well, but he nevertheless came home chuckling at the farmer's comment.

My mother, however, who had gone completely grey in her early thirties, shortly after she gave birth to my sister, Angela, was not, like Queen Victoria, at all amused! There had been no question of her being able to dye her hair brown during the War and she could not afford to do so after it. Why she went grey so young I cannot say, but it made her look old before her time and Mr Attridge had clearly jumped to the wrong conclusion.

As previously mentioned, my father who was not a healthy man and who had steadily been losing weight, was not really up to the task of clearing our plot of its surplus trees and extensive undergrowth. Many of the Silver Birches which proliferated on it would have to be removed since they were blocking the light to the bungalow and the massive tree stumps and roots left by Mr Wood had to be dug out or chopped up and disposed of somehow.

In the circumstances my grandfather, John Somers, who always enjoyed a day out in the fresh air, generously offered to lend a helping hand. As previously mentioned, between the spring of 1948 and his seventy fifth birthday in 1956 he cleared over half of our 400-foot plot, creating in the process an attractive garden with a rear lawn and flower beds, leaving only the larger oak and Spanish Chestnut trees on the boundaries of it. The rest of the plot remained woodland through which my sister, Angela and I gained access to the woods themselves.

As a 12-year-old I wanted to contribute to his efforts and felt that our new garden would benefit from some of the wild primroses that grew on the sides of the trenches that lay on the east side of the Woods. The trenches that had partially collapsed over the years had been dug during the First World War and had been used for training purposes by the regiments of soldiers, stationed in and around Billericay, who would subsequently go out and fight on the Western Front.

As I was proudly bringing a dozen or so home along Norsey Road on my toboggan I was stopped in my tracks by a furious Jasper Leyland. He regarded my taking the primroses as theft which, technically, it probably was. When I explained, somewhat nervously, that I was replanting them in a flower bed in our garden he calmed down but insisted, nevertheless, on speaking to my father and obtaining my promise that I would not take any more. It seemed to me, as a child, that they would be far more attractive and more appreciated in a flower bed than attached to the sides of waterlogged trenches, but I determined thereafter not to remove anything from the Woods.

This did not, of course, stop me from joining Brian and Colin Hunt and a number of other children, and from building a den in the woods with chestnut palings conveniently left in large quantities by the side of the main track through them. We dug out a six foot by four-foot hole, about four feet deep and placed the palings over the top as a roof. We covered them with some of the clay we had excavated and with plentiful quantities of dead bracken. The camouflage was effective and all one could see was the entrance. We used it as our hideaway for some weeks until Jasper Leyland found it and retrieved his palings!

The Woods were, of course, a wonderful playground for my sister, myself, Roger, Douglas and Howard Quirk, our nearest childhood neighbours and their friends and we had great fun in them, playing "hide and seek" and having mock battles of various kinds.

In early 1948 while exploring the Woods on my own I came across an underground brick built storeroom close to the main track through them and the remains of metal framework embedded into the ground on a hillock upon which an anti-aircraft gun would have been mounted. The underground room hidden by trees, but not far from the gun emplacement, was probably the ammunition store for it. The Army must have returned shortly after I found the room and filled it in because on my next visit to the room the entrance to it had been covered over and concealed and no-one would have known it was there. The metal framework was removed a few months later.

There were numerous other fascinating features of Norsey Woods. There was a bronze age burial mound (thought to be about 4000 years old) on the south side of them which had a Ministry of Works sign on it when we first moved into our new home, and which, I believe, is now a designated monument. There was also a burial mound on the north side of the Woods at what now is 158 Norsey Road. It was excavated in the 1880s and sadly no longer exists. I will mention it again later.

The town's stocks or a very realistic replica of them, had been placed on a piece of greensward just within the entrance to Deerbank Road. I was never sure whether they were originals or a later copy, but they looked convincing to me!

As a child three other features of the Woods stood out for me — the chestnuts, the bluebells and the wood ants.

In the late 1940s and early 1950s the Spanish chestnuts were plump and shiny when prised from their prickly outer casings but, as I have previously mentioned, appear to have become smaller and smaller over the years and consequently much less edible. My sister and I would collect handfuls of them from under the trees bordering The Ride and bring them home where they were roasted in the embers of an open fire and eaten with great relish. But, nowadays, collecting them seems hardly worth the effort.

The bluebells on the other hand have proliferated and appear to have extended in some profusion from what was originally a relatively small area known as "Bluebell Wood" on the south side of the main track to most of the Woods. In the spring they give the area where they are most dense a light blue haze at ground level and, when viewed through the trees, delight the eye in very much the same way as daffodils must have done for William Wordsworth.

The wood ants were and, hopefully, still are denizens of the Woods. They are at least twice the size of ordinary ants and aggressive when aroused. To our shame, as children we would poke an ants' nest, which was usually over a foot high and built of a myriad of small twigs, with a stick, and then dangle a couple of bluebells immediately above it. The furious ants would swarm over the surface of the nest, regard the bluebells as invaders and spit acid at the flowers, turning them from blue to pink.

The ants tend to use fissures in rotting tree stumps as the lower floors of their nests in which they store the little white sacs which presumably contain their offspring. My sister was fascinated, albeit somewhat terrified by them when they tried to climb onto her shoes and up her bare legs and, in order to put them in a better light, I would tell her bedtime stories which I made up in my head, before she went to sleep, about "Annie the ant, and her friend". I thought at one stage of putting these stories into a book but never got round to doing so although I mentioned the possibility to Archie and Moira Thomson during my National Service days in Edinburgh.

But, as always in life, there seemed to be better or more pressing things to do at the time and, as they say, the road to Hell is paved with good intentions! Whether the stories would have been worth publishing and whether any child would have read them I cannot say but, I, for one, was extremely impressed by the industry of these little creatures as they scurried along their own barely discernible tracks, carrying or pulling twigs or prey back to their "ant castles" which must have contained a myriad of passageways and storage areas.

The woods were not only a wonderful playground for me in my childhood years. They have been a constant source of pleasure throughout my whole life. Although I only had immediate access to them during my days in Pink Cottage I have revisited them on countless occasions since and have run or walked every track and winding path through them.

When running through them early in the morning I have felt completely at one with nature and have been able to enjoy their ever-changing face whether there be snow underfoot or summer sunlight glinting through the gold tinged leaves above and whether the Spanish Chestnut trees have been coppiced or stand luxuriantly tall. While doing so I have often thought about those who, in previous centuries tended them, and on one unexpected occasion, in particular, sensed the presence of a long-departed woodman standing by the main track as I ran by.

My walks through the Woods have also been memorable occasions when I have been able to share the many facets of them with loved ones. They are, in fact, a very special place and have given me unforgettable experiences and treasured memories. I am so lucky to have them ingrained in me.

33

The Journey to School from Billericay

So far as I can recall the return fare in 1948 from the bus stop opposite Jubilee Cottages to Brentwood High Street for a twelve year old school boy like myself was "thruppence". I would therefore climb aboard the City bus or coach, often at the very last moment, clutching three old pennies in one hand and my satchel in the other.

At the time our plot was the last one in Norsey Road to have a house or bungalow upon it. Other plots fronting the woods had undoubtedly been sold by Jasper Leyland, but nothing had been built upon them. One can therefore visualise the dense woodland on the left and the large farm fields behind Woodside Cottages, built at approximately the same time as Jubilee Cottages, similarly to house farm workers, on the right as the bus driver approached the first stop within the residential "envelope" of Billericay.

Ahead of him were plots on either side of the road, most of which had been laid out and built upon since the early 1920s, many retaining their original small bungalows with more substantial mid/late 1930s houses interspersed between them. The side roads on the right with similar developments lining them were still unmade and, in the winter, very muddy. We had yet to witness the massive growth in housebuilding and traffic that occurred from 1953 onwards.

At the end of the road, past Norsey Manor, a large Victorian house, set in spacious grounds on the left, and St. Andrews Hospital, part of which was originally the Union Workhouse on the right, lay Billericay, like a spider at the centre of a web of country roads and lanes that radiated out from it in all directions.

These roads would take one in many directions, namely, to the "Fortune of War" roundabout on the Southend Arterial Road and beyond that to Laindon, to South Green, Crays Hill and Wickford, to Stock and Chelmsford, to Ramsden Heath, Downham and the Hanningfields, to Mountnessing and the old A12 between London and Colchester or to Hutton, Shenfield and Brentwood. One only has to look at "Bacons" half inch Cycling Map of Essex published in the mid-1920s to appreciate how much our road system has been improved since then to cope with the massive increase in vehicular traffic.

The transformation that has similarly taken place in Norsey Road and in Billericay generally over the past seventy years is remarkable. All the side roads in the town have been made up and many are lined with expensive properties. The houses and bungalows built in the 1920s and 1930s have given way to larger and more impressive counterparts, the more pretentious among them resembling stately homes. Norsey Manor has been demolished and its grounds converted into a private residential housing development and the red brick Victorian Hospital buildings have been converted into flats.

Once in the High Street I would be joined by my Brentwood school "fellow travellers", Bill Arthy, Roy Welham and Michael Copeland. Bill Arthy's mother, a bespectacled and kindhearted lady, had a little sweet shop in the centre of the High Street. It was a favourite place for me to visit, as was the second-hand book shop, immediately adjacent, where one could buy a book, fact or fiction, for as little as thruppence. The studious looking proprietor, probably in his fifties, was lean in appearance, with thinning hair. His principal facial feature, however, was his nose which always had a drip on the end of it. He could easily have been the person from whom Ronald Searle, the famous cartoonist, drew inspiration for one of his most memorable characters.

Roy Welham lived in a house on the corner of Smallgains Lane in Stock Road, opposite "The Old Kings Head" Public House, the name of which was "Roywell". He must have had proud parents! Michael Copeland lived in a Victorian terraced house in Chapel Street, behind the High Street and no great distance from the bus stop.

At the Southern end of the High Street the bus would turn right at the Police Station, built shortly before the Second World War, and travel down the London Road with green fields on either side. On the right was a particularly large field with a ditch down the centre of it and a small cottage tucked into an overgrown corner plot at the junction with Western Road, which had, in Victorian times been called "Back Lane". The cottage, as one will readily appreciate, has been demolished and replaced by a parade of shops with flats over them. Upon the fields there are now housing estates.

Beyond the junction the bus would enter a narrow meandering road between the outskirts of Billericay and Hutton Village, a road that bore only a passing resemblance to the straighter and much improved version that replaced it. Turning sharp right after about two hundred yards into what was the junction with Mountnessing Road it would then almost immediately turn left and pass in front of the houses that now lie behind the green upon which the Billericay Town sign stands.

Descending initially and then with a series of uphill and downhill gradients over a mile or so it would come to the bend that now lies at the back of a grassed area with a white fence along the boundary of it and a detailed and attractive sign bearing the words "Havering Groves". One can still just see the old road upon which cars are regularly parked.

The old road would then cross under the line of the present road and bend at right angles behind the rear of the Hutton Plough Public House on the Brentwood side and pass in front of a row of 1920s and 1930s bungalows, before bending once again and passing what must originally have been a Georgian farmhouse, opposite a white weather-boarded cottage with a bus stop immediately outside. This small section of the old road still exists, albeit that it is only used for access to the properties on either side of it.

Needless to say, the bus stop has long since disappeared as also has the bus service between the High Streets of Billericay and Brentwood! From what remains, however, of the old road an experienced eye can deduce how narrow and meandering the whole of it must have been in the 1940s.

All the right angle bends I have described feature on the Chapman and Andre map of 1777 and very little, if anything, changed in the line of the road in the following one hundred and seventy years until it was straightened and widened in the late 1940s.

The Hutton Plough has experienced a number of metamorphoses since those post war days, having been renamed "The Winston Churchill" for some years before reverting for a short time to its original name. It is currently a Turkish Restaurant by the name of "The Mesken Bar and Grill". It will doubtless have other names in the future.

Not far beyond the redundant section of the old road the bus would skirt another, but more imposing, red brick Georgian mansion, now a private school, before passing through an avenue of fir trees into Hutton Village. Immediately past the fir trees there was an incongruous little shop in the middle of the terrace of white washed houses that still stand on the triangle formed by the junction of the main road and the lane that leads to Hutton Hall and Hutton Church. It was only from this point onward that urban residential development began once again.

The bus stop on our arrival in Brentwood was at the Ingrave Road end of the High Street, just past the water trough for horses and opposite a Dairy shop at which one could purchase white, unflavoured, yoghurt. It was considered a very unusual and "up market" product at the time. Nowadays supermarkets have every colour and flavour of it.

On my homeward journey the City bus would arrive from the western, Romford, end of the High Street and pick up passengers on the Shenfield side of the public conveniences, just outside Burgess's Bookshop and "Campbell's the "Communist Chemists" as we boys knew it. To this day I have no idea how Mr Campbell acquired this sobriquet, but it certainly stuck to him!

If ever I was early for the bus, which left at about twenty minutes past the hour I would go into the bookshop for a browse. I could never afford to buy a new book but I did, in the sixth form, receive books purchased from the shop as Classical Society prizes and I did, of course, become school Librarian. Any book shop or library has always been a magnet to me.

Once aboard the bus school rules prevailed. As previously mentioned, it was a requirement that any Brentwood school boy give up his seat to a lady or an elderly gentleman and, as a result, I often had to stand in the aisle between the rows of seats all the way to Billericay. A short "seated" ride thereafter brought me from the High Street to the bus stop immediately outside Jubilee Cottages, the total journey lasting little more than thirty minutes.

People living in Norsey Road nowadays have no bus service and are expected to have cars to transport themselves and their families to wherever they might wish to go. In this respect Brentwood High Street is no longer as attractive a shopping centre as it once was. It is now a matter of parents, who can afford the Brentwood school fees, driving their children to and from Brentwood or depositing them at Billericay Station for the somewhat long-winded train journey, via Shenfield, to Brentwood Station, some half a mile from the school.

If ever I missed the bus and my kind-hearted father was unavailable to take me to Sun Corner at the far end of Billericay High Street, opposite the Police Station, I had to run the one and a half miles to catch a bus there at about 8.40 am, just in time to arrive at school before 9 am. That is why I rarely missed it and how grateful I was to Olive Hunt for helping me to catch it!

34

Billericay: Centre of the Web

With a name like Billericay one might expect the town to be in Ireland!

In fact no one knows the derivation of the town's name. It is a complete mystery.

Local Freemasons attribute it to the Roman house or villa which must have been built on heathland that later became the site of the town. The latin word for "heather" is "erica" and so a house on a heath might conceivably be a "Villa erica". Their Lodge is therefore "Villerica Lodge". Although there are many signs of Roman occupation in the locality I do not "buy into" this suggested derivation. It is at the remote end of the spectrum of possibilities!

My own suggestion, for what it is worth, is that the name derives from "Vil" or "Bil" de Crais, the hamlet of the Crais family, Normans who administered the area on behalf of the Cistercian monks of Stratford Langthorne Abbey. In Norman French "B" and "V" were interchangeable and a Bil or Vil is a diminutive "Ville, or town. My suggestion is based on two current reminders of the Crais family, in the shape of Ramsden Crays and Crays Hill, both between Billericay and Wickford.

The first official reference is to "Byllyrica" in 1291 and there are many different spellings of the name on County maps from Christopher Saxton's map of Essex, produced in 1583, onward. All one can say is that until about 1860 Billericay was in a more important location than one might appreciate at first sight and in order to substantiate that observation, I set out a brief, potted and, hopefully, not too boring history of the town and of the ground upon which it stands.

With its elevated position of over three hundred feet above sea level and its commanding views over countryside to the south, almost as far as the Thames estuary, it is not surprising that the ground upon which the town now stands became a vantage point for the Romans when they decided to subjugate the south of what is now the County of Essex.

As they pushed further into East Anglia and established Caesaromagus (Chelmsford) and Camulodunum (Colchester), the first capital of Roman Britain, the ground assumed a different significance. For Roman Legionaries, who marched between twenty and thirty miles a day, it made an ideal place to stop and rest overnight whether they be "en route" to Colchester or returning from it to embark at the harbour for Londinium (London) close to modern day Tilbury, or to cross the Thames into Kent.

In fact, it became such an established route for Roman soldiers and officials that a four-acre military installation was built at Blunts Wall, about half a mile to the west of the modern town to accommodate them. A permanent civilian presence was also established, signs of which have been discovered in Norsey Woods and in land close to the town centre. Once the Roman Legions left Britain the then existing civilian settlement was abandoned and the military installation merged over the years into farmland around it.

The Saxons, who followed, preferred the land immediately to the south of the former Roman Settlement, as the names Great and Little Burstead bear witness. "Burstead" means "a fortified place" in Saxon. Earl Godwin, the father of King Harold who lost his life in the battle of Hastings in 1066, owned land at Little Burstead and although the Bursteads did not form part of a north / south travel route in Saxon times they were approximately halfway between Saxon London and Prittlewell, the south end of which is now known as Southend on Sea. It was the home of Saebert, King of the east Saxons whose burial site was located close to the centre of Southend on Sea in 2003.

The north / south travel route re-emerged during Norman times, almost exclusively as a result of pilgrimages to Canterbury. I will explain.

When in 1253 Henry III granted the Abbott of Stratford Langthorne Abbey permission to hold a market and fair in Great Burstead he did so for a practical reason. Pilgrims had been making their way from all over

East Anglia to Canterbury to venerate the shrine of Thomas a Becket who had been assassinated in 1170, some eighty years previously.

They needed food and lodging "en route" and Billericay, at the northern end of Great Burstead, was well placed to accommodate and feed them before they, like the Romans before them, made the day long walk to Tilbury. Its main thoroughfare was broad with plenty of space for vendors of local produce.

We tend to forget that pilgrims, unless they were wealthy and could afford a horse, had to walk to revered religious sites. Sleeping out in fields and woods was not particularly safe or healthy and they needed somewhere relatively secure to rest their weary limbs for the night and to purchase something to eat before they set off once again.

The relatively lucrative business of feeding and accommodating pilgrims lasted until Henry VIII decided to break with Rome and forced the dissolution of Monasteries and Abbeys in the 1540s. He thereby dramatically reduced the power and influence of the Roman Catholic Church and put an end to their various and highly dubious money-making schemes. At this point pilgrimages to Canterbury, Walsingham and elsewhere, promoted heavily by the Church as good sources of revenue for it, effectively came to an end.

The loss of pilgrims in the 1540s did not affect the town greatly. From the time that farmers in the southeast of England turned their pasture land over to sheep farming until the outbreak of the Anglo Dutch wars, at the end of the Seventeenth century, the production of wool for export to the Low Countries had made local wool merchants wealthy and the town prosperous.

It was not long after the Reformation and as a result of the consequent increase in travel and trade between towns and cities that entrepreneurial Lords of the Manor and private citizens decided to take advantage of the lack of accommodation and brewing facilities once offered by the Abbeys and Monasteries, by converting private houses on High Streets into Inns and building breweries. There were, of course, pre-existing Alehouses but most did not offer accommodation.

In 1593, or thereabouts, a private house in Billericay High Street became "The Red Lion Inn" and the meeting place for the Manorial

Court of Lord Petre while, on the opposite side of the street, another private house became "The Crown Inn". It took the Government at the time almost thirty years to appreciate that an opportunity existed to tax them! Licencing of Inns was introduced in 1621. It may have been irksome for the proprietors of inns at the time to have to pay a fee to operate them, but the licensees benefited them greatly over the longer term, as we will see.

The town also prospered thereafter from the production of silk and from its tannery which, records tell us, existed between 1593 and 1803. It produced malleable hides for leather goods of all kinds. Tanfield Drive to the north west of the High Street marks its approximate position.

The emergence of Colchester as a garrison town also brought substantial benefits to Billericay and in particular to the inns and alehouses. Soldiers from the 44th Regiment of Foot, the precursors of the Essex Regiment, had to march from Colchester to Tilbury and be transported by sea to whatever part of Europe or the rest of the world we happened to be fighting in at the time. They needed overnight accommodation in dormitories and stabling for the officers' horses somewhere between Colchester and Tilbury and Billericay was, once again, an obvious choice.

They also needed beer and food leading to an explosion in the number of alehouses and to the expansion of brewing facilities within the town. The town's main brewery was located in Crown Yard, part of the inn, and at the rear of the yard was the "tap room", an alehouse now known as "The Coach and Horses" where the soldiers who were in the dormitory accommodation above the stables flanking the yard could eat and drink.

Across the street in the fields opposite were springs that provided fresh water for brewing, so much water in fact that the Crown Inn was able to expand its beer production and supply it to a number of "tied" alehouses in the locality. Barrels were stored in cellars under the yard. Townsfolk could also visit the tap room and fill the jugs they brought into it with cheap beer.

In the same way as it had been on the route, whether on foot or horseback, from London to Prittlewell in Anglo Saxon times Billericay was also on the stagecoach route from London to Rochford, the principal town in southeast Essex from the sixteenth to the nineteenth centuries, resulting in additional custom for the inns and alehouses in the town.

Wealthy people had been using private horse drawn carriages to convey themselves around the country from the 1300s but, by 1750, the concept of travel between towns and cities for anyone who could pay the fare and the delivery of mail and small packets by stagecoaches on set dates and at set times had become popular and lucrative. Well-to-do merchants, attorneys, members of families and the clergy, traders in portable items of all kinds, and individual travellers from all walks of life used them. The government ever ready, not surprisingly, to exploit a potentially steady source of revenue introduced a coach tax on 25 March 1747! Nothing ever changes where governments and taxes are concerned!!

By way of information the average daily mileage of a stagecoach in the 1750s was between sixty and seventy miles, with horses being changed every ten to fifteen miles. When roads improved as a result of tolls having to be paid to travel on them, speeds increased from five miles an hour to between eight and ten miles an hour, a very welcome increase. When, by 1815, macadam roads were being laid across the length and breadth of the United Kingdom the journey from Cambridge to London, for example, took only seven hours, nearly halving the time taken some 65 years previously. With an armed guard sitting alongside the driver stagecoaches provided an element of safety from highwaymen as well as relative comfort in getting from one place to another.

Indeed, by 1777, there was a regular, three times a week, stagecoach service from "The Three Nuns Inn" at Whitechapel on Tuesday, Thursday and Saturday mornings to Rochford leaving at 8 am. Three years later and, as a result of road improvements, the stagecoach left "The Bear Public House" in Whitechapel at 2 pm, six hours later, in the summer on the same days of the week as before, but at 10 am in the winter. Billericay had become a staging point on that particular route where "spent" horses were changed for fresh ones and passengers could either disembark or resume their seats, after a short stopover, for the rest of their journey.

The Red Lion and the Crown had by this time become the principal coaching inns in the town where a modest amount of hay was stored for the horses and where the passengers could relieve themselves and have a meal and a drink before they travelled on towards Rochford or in the opposite direction towards London.

Not only were the local tenant farmers doing well out of providing farm produce and hay to the Inns they were also able to provide hay to the burgeoning horse population of London. During the summer and autumn horses and carts would line Billericay's long high street in the early hours of the morning before setting off for London with loads of hay.

Their drivers would have had a beer (or perhaps two) at one of the many alehouses, subsequently called Public Houses, before they set off. Some of them, having started out from their farms, in the small hours, would decide to have a nap on the hay and trust their horse to follow the cart in front on the long journey to London. The decision to do so could prove expensive if, for whatever reason, their horse decided to stray off route. There are Magistrate's Court records of drivers who had fallen asleep on the hay, in such circumstances, being fined a shilling, quite a substantial sum in those days, for being "drunk in charge of a horse and cart"!

In the century prior to 1860 Billericay had prospered. The High Street had been macadamised and gas lighting had been installed in the centre of the town from as early as 1842. Innkeepers, publicans, tradespeople and farmers had all benefitted from its unique position at the junction of roads from Colchester to Tilbury and from London to Rochford. But by 1860 it was becoming painfully obvious that the good times were going to come to a dramatic end.

From the moment railway lines started to be laid between London, Liverpool Street and Colchester and between London, Fenchurch Street and Tilbury it was clear that soldiers would in future be able to travel between the two points in less than a day. They would not need overnight accommodation. The alehouses and the Crown Inn, in particular would be hit hard by the loss of custom.

Worse was in store for local farmers as the newly built railway lines snaked out from London across the Home Counties. They suffered a serious decline in income as a result of farmers in areas previously without access to London using goods trains to flood the fruit, vegetable and meat markets with their products and to import into the city hay and oats at prices against which they could not compete.

On top of this disastrous turn of events the entire stagecoach industry collapsed because it could not compete with passenger travel by train. Inns which had previously relied on travellers staying overnight lost them and were forced to close. The rapid and inevitable advance of the Great Eastern Railway towards Southend on Sea meant that when the line from Liverpool Street Station, operational from November 1875, reached Shenfield in 1878, three years later, all a traveller to or from Billericay had to do was to get on board a "growler", a four wheel carriage, equivalent to a modern day taxi, for the short distance between the station and the town.

The writing was clearly on the wall for any surviving inns in the town when, in 1884, some six years later, work commenced on laying the track between Shenfield and Billericay. It was at this point that The Crown, by now a hotel and public house, decided to relocate, and built premises close to the railway line and to Billericay Station. It would, in this way, be able to sell beer and spirits to travellers by train and, hopefully, retain some of its regular customers.

One can appreciate the consternation of the residents of Billericay and of the farmers in the locality when, in 1885, an army of workmen turned up to dig a 54-foot deep cutting on the north side of the town to enable the rail line to be extended to Wickford and beyond. The cutting would prevent, at least for some months, travel by horse drawn cart and passenger carriage between Billericay and Chelmsford, the county town and principal market for corn, cattle and farm produce, as also would the rail tracks laid immediately to the east and west of the town.

Not only was this lack of access going to be very inconvenient for the residents of the town who wanted to visit Chelmsford, it was also going to deal a damaging blow to the prospects of the farmers to the south of the railway line who wanted to buy or sell produce in Chelmsford.

The "Dog and Partridge" Beer House on the Stock Road, just below the High Street, which, with its outbuildings and orchard, stood on land at the top of the gently rising slope, with views over the brickfields and sand pits at Charity Farm and the countryside to the west of the town, would have to be demolished, and the field between Stock Road and Norsey Road, known as Gentry's Meadow, which had been used in the summer as a cricket pitch would also disappear forever.

In the event the owners of the "Dog and Partridge" were compensated and a brand-new public house, the Railway Tavern, was built in 1885 to replace it. A suitable piece of land for a proper cricket ground was located to the west of the town at approximately the same time. The first goods train arrived in Billericay on 19 November 1888 and the first passenger train on 1 January 1889, less than 50 years before I was born. The new "Crown" Hotel and public house opened only a few months later.

The passenger service did not bring any immediate benefit to the residents of Billericay but the goods service did at least enable the many manufacturers of bricks in the locality to distribute them more widely. It also enabled the extractors of fine sand from the sandpits at Charity Farm to send it to iron works in the Midlands. It just so happened that the clay under Billericay had proved suitable for making good quality red bricks and that a seam of fine sand existed in an area to the northwest of the town. Brickmaking was the town's only surviving industry from 1889 onward until the brickworks closed in the late 1950s.

Insufficient numbers, at the time, wanted to travel to London to make the passenger service viable and the Great Eastern Railway stood little chance of recouping its massive investment in rolling stock until it could generate enough passenger traffic from the towns between London and Southend on Sea. I will describe how it did so later in this chapter. One might reasonably say that from 1889 until, probably, the 1950s, Billericay was "in the doldrums" as a result of the expansion of the railway system. Suddenly bereft of its traditional sources of revenue the town had reached a low point in its history when the first passenger train arrived there.

In fact, the only place that was really busy was the new Workhouse! It had been built in 1840 in more prosperous times and designed in the Elizabethan style by George Gilbert Scott who was also the architect for St. Pancras Hotel and Station and the Albert Memorial. It was intended to cater for the poor of twenty-six local parishes, but it soon found itself inundated with applicants for admission from the immediate locality. So many labourers had lost what they had hoped were jobs for life and could not find alternative employment elsewhere.

This parlous economic period lasted for more than five years until the Government, and some entrepreneurial Estate Agents, came to the aid of farmers, residents and railways alike. By 1899, some ten years later the town was in a better financial state and not quite, so poverty stricken.

So how did the Government help?

For farmers stripped of their previous sources of income the outlook was bleak until the Government, in 1894, came to the aid of those who had managed to hang on to their farms, by passing the Copyhold Act. This now, almost unheard of, Act of Parliament accelerated the move from Manorial tenancies, called copyholds, to freeholds. From the 1840s onwards farmers throughout the country had been able to apply to their Lord of the Manor and negotiate the enfranchisement of their land and the conversion of their copyhold tenancies into freeholds. The Act gave tenant farmers a statutory right to convert, irrespective of the wishes of their Lord of the Manor.

Did the Lord of the Manor lose complete control of the land enfranchised by the Act? Not entirely. He retained rights to mine under the surface of the land for minerals. In the case of Billericay, Brentwood and Ingatestone, Lord Petre who owned substantial areas of farmland in the area and whose title as "Lord of the Manor" was hereditary, was not slow to insert a reservation of these rights in the Deeds of any land he enfranchised.

This is why the freehold titles of so many properties built on land that was formerly copyhold have a reservation of these rights in them. Hypothetically Lord Petre could enter these properties and commence mining operations in the back garden! However, it would not be of advantage for him to do so. The subsoil of Billericay is, for the most part, clay with occasional seams of sand and gravel left behind in the Ice Age. Planning legislation would override manorial rights where residential development had taken place and these retained rights might only be relevant to Lords of the Manor in the case of farmland under which minerals worth mining might exist.

What was the benefit to farmers? Owning their farms outright meant that they could sell fields adjoining roads and relieve the financial pressures on them and this is where the entrepreneurial Estate Agents come into the picture.

Living in London in the 1880s and 1890s was very unhealthy for all but the wealthiest. The overcrowded streets were smelly, and disease ridden. Horse manure and urine and uncollected rubbish littered them and attracted rats and flies. The noise of the wheels of horse drawn carriages, cabs, horse buses and goods wagons on the cobbles drowned out speech. Why, in the circumstances, would the inhabitants of the city and its crowded suburbs not want a weekend retreat where they might, if they could afford it, get away from all this and enjoy the fresh air and beauty of the countryside so graphically described by the writers of the day? The answer was obvious to the Estate Agents.

They therefore approached the Great Eastern Railway with a novel solution that would satisfy everyone. The railway would lay on excursion trains at the weekends to each station as it was built. The fare for an entire family would be one shilling. The Estate Agents would already have purchased fields adjoining roads nearby from the impoverished farmers and would have laid them out in plots. London breweries would provide free beer on the train journey in return for a free building plot for a public house on any new Estate created by the Estate Agents. Once inebriated, the passengers would more easily be persuaded to commit themselves to the purchase of a little piece of the countryside they could visit at the weekend.

The families would be met at the station in question and driven by horse drawn carriage to the fields where, doubtless affected by the beer, the peace and tranquillity of their surroundings and, of course, the blandishments of the Estate Agents, they would be induced to purchase a plot, the cost of which would usually have been in the region of £5. They would be told that they could put whatever type of sleeping accommodation on it they wished, whether that be a caravan, an old railway carriage or a bungalow. All they would be obliged to do is fence the plot. I deal with this novel arrangement and the unforeseen consequences of it in greater details in my book, "A Law unto Myself".

Suffice it to say the arrangement was a great success all round until blighted by the First World War. The farmers received a lifesaving boost to their finances, the Estate Agents received from their sale of the plots substantially more than they had paid for the farmers' fields, the brewery gained the ability to put a public house on a conveniently located plot and prevent anyone else from doing so, and the railway company, the G.E.R., received a welcome boost to its passenger numbers from every station it built.

You may be wondering what happened to the farms which could not weather the bleak 1890s. Lord Petre, as Lord of the Manor, realised that the farmers who could not afford to enfranchise their land or pay the rent would have to give up their farms. He therefore started to advertise in Scotland for hardy and resilient highland farmers who would be better able to eke out a living on the rich pastureland in Essex and pay the rent until they themselves could enfranchise their land. That is why a number of Scottish names feature among the 1115 names in the population census for the area in 1901.

Although Lord Petre must have expected some financial gain from enfranchising his copyhold tenant farmers, those who remained copyholders until 1926 did not have to pay him anything. Copyhold tenure was abolished by the Law of Property Act, 1925. They were enfranchised automatically and became freeholders, thus ending a system of Manorial land holding that had existed from Norman times.

From the beginning of the First World War, Billericay fell into what one could only describe as a state of torpor. Most able-bodied men had been conscripted into the Armed Forces and money was very tight for those who remained in the town. So many men who had purchased holiday plots before the War were killed in it that plots lay untended or were, alternatively, occupied by the families who could not afford to live in London. They had been forced to sell and move out of whatever property they owned there in order to survive the economic hardships of the post war era.

As I have mentioned in earlier chapters the economic hardships were very real during the 1920s and early 1930s and although the population of Billericay grew steadily between 1918 and 1945 the increase was, to a large extent, accounted for by families who had had to move out of the East end of London or retire from other parts of metropolitan Essex to somewhere with relatively easy access to London in the west, Southend in the east and to the towns in between.

The passenger train service, particularly during the First and Second World Wars, did not attract as many customers as the Great Eastern Railway and its successor, the London and North-Eastern Railway might have wished. The service was consequently infrequent, until the electrification of the line in the early 1950s, and the journey from Billericay to London, Liverpool Street, took nearly an hour. I can recall travelling on the steam trains with their cramped individual eight seat compartments during the pre-electrification era.

As previously indicated brickmaking and the extraction of sand, Billericay's only surviving industrial enterprise, had ceased by the late 1950s. Farmers and land owners in the area had continued to make a reasonable living by growing cereal crops and vegetables or by selling land for residential development, but it was not until the children of former East Londoners started to grow up during the late 1930s and 1940s that the fortunes of the town began to look up once again.

During the early 1930s, for example, the attendance officer for the only school in Billericay, built in Victorian times, in the Laindon Road, had to visit farms during term time to collect children whose parents preferred them to work in the fields rather than attend lessons. It was only in the mid/late 1930s that there was need for a new secondary modern school, Billericay school, that a new Post Office and Police Station were built and that the seeds of the town's rebirth and subsequent expansion were sown.

Certain shopping facilities had developed for the residents of the town and for the surrounding area from the mid 1930s onward since it was the only urban centre within a rural area, but the town remained virtually undeveloped from beginning of the First World War when we arrived in Ramsden Bellhouse in 1946.

35
Billericay Urban District

Of course, my father had little knowledge of the history of Billericay or of its link with the sailing of the Mayflower to America in 1620 when he took up his post of Assistant Town Clerk in March 1946. All he knew was that Billericay was about halfway between Wanstead where he was born and Leigh on Sea where he grew up. With a land area of over 27,000 acres the Urban District was, in fact, one of the largest in the country encompassing the long-established towns of Billericay and Wickford in the north and the townships of Laindon and Pitsea in the south, with a great deal of agricultural land and the Southend Arterial Road in between.

Before the London, Tilbury and Southend Railway Company, whose London terminus was Fenchurch Street, built stations there Laindon and Pitsea had only been villages. But it was the same story as on the London, Liverpool Street, line to Southend. By building stations along the line and encouraging Londoners to buy cheap plots in the countryside in order to generate passenger traffic the Railway Company knew that the population in these two villages, whether temporary during the summer or permanent, would be bound to increase. The consequence was that Laindon and Pitsea developed into sprawling residential townships. They lost their identities as cohesive rural communities.

The two villages and the agricultural land around them disappeared as "hard up" farmers from the 1890s until the early 1900s sold land to Estate Agents and property speculators who grandly described the fields they had purchased as Estates and divided them into plots. One company selling plots at Pitsea and neighbouring Vange between 1901 and 1906 even gave away free champagne lunches and free railway tickets in its efforts to sell them. In the early days of plot selling, whether for weekend, holiday or permanent occupation, there were few restrictions on what one could put on them. Purchasers could put an old railway carriage, a caravan, a wooden hut or a bungalow of whatever size or construction upon them. Development was uncontrolled.

As mentioned previously many of the often-ramshackle properties on unmade roads, with no public sewers, water or electricity, originally intended as temporary homes, became the permanent residences of the widows and families of servicemen who had lost their lives during the First World War. Living conditions were primitive for all who had been forced to leave their former homes in London for whatever reason, until piped water and electricity became available during the early 1930s. There would originally have been a "standpipe" for water in each field that had been converted into plots, but that would have been all when the plots were sold.

I can vividly recall my father taking me to one of these "so called" Estates near Laindon when I was about thirteen. We had to park on the nearest tarmacadam road and make our way carefully along wooden duck boards at the sides of deep, muddy tracks until we reached the bungalow he had to visit. Duck boards were a type of slatted wooden planking used during the First World War and laid at the bottom of trenches to enable soldiers to move without their boots sinking into the mud beneath them.

The elderly widow resident had complained to the council that planes flying over her bungalow were directing beams or rays of some sort into it and that this was causing her great concern. My father, with a straight face, assured her that he would write to the Ministry of Aviation and ensure that they were directed elsewhere! She was completely satisfied that her Local Authority was addressing the issue and my father told me that no subsequent complaints were received from her!

It was obvious to me, however, even as a young teenager, that the muddy tracks between the rows of plots would have been virtually impassable in the winter for any type of vehicle and that something would have to be done to rehouse the unfortunate residents of these substandard Estates.

It had also been obvious to Alma Hatt, the town clerk of Billericay Urban District Council and to Essex County Council for a very long time. The lack of basic amenities and the haphazard nature of the Estates had already led the two Councils to petition the war time government for the creation of a completely new town within the district to resolve matters, once the war was over.

Put simply, the total number of people in the district, if one excluded Billericay and Wickford, was about 25,000. Most were located in Laindon, Pitsea, and Vange, which is between the two, and the hamlet of Basildon. They lived in about 8,500 homes of which about 6,000 were connected to mains drainage. That left about 2,500 homes which had no drainage or sewerage facilities at all, unless they had cesspits or septic tanks in their gardens. This was a situation that could not be allowed to continue.

As a result of similar representations from other local authorities an Inquiry was set up by the newly elected Labour Government shortly after the war, not only to deal with the resolution of this type of housing problem but also the acute shortage post war of housing in London and other inner cities. Alma Hatt was definitely not alone in appreciating the need to create a better future for his District and to improve sanitation, housing and communications within it.

The outcome of the Inquiry was the designation by Clement Attlee's government of eight areas between twenty and thirty miles from London as sites for new towns. Stevenage was one, Billericay was another. The idea was to make these new towns self-supporting and self-sufficient. Employment for those living within them would be primarily of an industrial nature. There would be no major office developments. They were not going to be "overspill dormitories" with employment still concentrated on London. Without further ado a New Towns Act was passed in 1946 and a New Towns Commission established. The Commission would acquire the necessary land for the new towns and Development Corporations for each town would oversee their construction.

Just over a quarter of the land in the Billericay Urban District, some 7834 acres, the bulk of it comprising poor quality agricultural land and the "plot lands" around and between Laindon and Pitsea would be allocated to a new town. It had to have a non-contentious name and since, right in the centre of it, was the hamlet of Basildon that was the name chosen for it. In fact the hamlet had been around for a very long time. It had even been mentioned in the Domesday book as "Balesdunum". In 1869 it had a population of 157 people. By 1931 it had risen to 1159 and it was still small when the New Towns Act was passed in 1946, a far cry from the current population of the new town of over 107,000!

The area designated was, in fact, an ideal location for a new town because it adjoined the Southend Arterial Road to the north with links to the A12, also the A13 with its direct access to Tilbury and the docklands, and its rail links to Fenchurch Street to the south.

In an effort to promote the proposed new town of Basildon the Rt. Hon. Lewis Silkin, Minister for Town and Country Planning, visited Laindon Secondary school on 30 September 1948 and addressed a packed public meeting extolling the virtues of it. Basildon, he said, "will become a City which people from all the world will want to visit. It will be a place where all classes of community can meet freely together on equal terms and enjoy common cultural recreational facilities". I am not sure whether current residents of Basildon would share his Utopian vision, and the chances of it becoming a City are remote. But that was the glittering prospect held out by Lewis Silkin at the time.

The idea of having a new town was not welcomed initially by some local people who could see their traditional way of life and such communities as existed coming to an end, but it was clear to the majority attending the meeting and to the authorities involved that the benefits of creating a new town and providing decent housing far outweighed any reservations local residents may have had. Just three months later, on 4 January 1949, a Designation Order was signed. A month later, in February 1949, a development corporation was appointed to coordinate the development of the new town of Basildon.

Before Basildon could be built, however, the acreage had to be acquired, principally from farmers and plot owners whether by compulsory purchase or by negotiation. This was easier said than done. Many plot owners had lost their Deeds and there were substantial areas within the "plotlands" where no one knew who owned vacant plots. Many local landowners also proved difficult about selling land at what they considered was an undervalue. But that is another story, and I will not dwell on it here.

Once the process of acquisition of land had been initiated by the New Towns Commission and a management team to run the Development Corporation had been appointed, town planners, architects and experts in all types of construction had to be brought together under one roof in order to turn a novel and ambitious concept into a reality. The task of the Basildon Development Corporation was formidable. It had to plan the layout and infrastructure of a new town on land acquired on its behalf by the New Towns Commission and, having done so, design and build accommodation for approximately eighty thousand people.

It also had to oversee the construction of two hundred and thirty industrial units of various sizes, four hundred shops and all the civic and public amenities one would expect to find in a town of this size including schools, parks, health facilities, religious and community centres and last, but not least, public houses! The resettled Londoners and plot owners who had previously been living in slum like conditions in substandard properties would be accommodated in solidly built Council Houses with kitchens, bathrooms and toilets, on mains drainage in "neighbourhood estates" which had broad well-lit interconnecting streets and easy access to regular bus services. The streets within the neighbourhoods were not so broad and this caused problems which I will mention below.

Citizens of working age would have the choice of employment in the factories, shops, offices, schools, commercial and professional undertakings, doctors' surgeries and complementary medical health facilities within the town, also the opportunity to travel up to Fenchurch Street from Laindon, Pitsea or from a new station in the town centre, close to the bus terminus, and work anywhere in London.

The first Council houses were completed in Vange in 1951 and from that point onward rapid progress was made. Basildon, like Topsy in the novel, Uncle Tom's Cabin "just growed."

The only serious mistake the Corporation made in laying out the town and in particular the roads on the neighbourhood Council estates, was to underestimate the growth of car ownership among what were considered at the time to be the lower or working classes. In 1949 people living in private houses in Billericay and Wickford might be expected to have space in their front garden or a garage in which to park a car if they could afford one. Council house tenants, on the other hand, whether in Basildon or elsewhere in the district were not considered able to afford anything more than a bus fare. It was not until the 1960s that this mistake became apparent and, by then, it was too late to correct it.

Given that the remit of the Corporation was to design and build the town and not provide any ongoing services and that of the New Town's Commission was to retain ownership of the land it had acquired until it could dispose of it, the question, like the proverbial "elephant in the room" was this. "Who exactly was going to administer Basildon while it was still under construction and before it had its own Local Authority?"

Alma Hatt, an astute Barrister, had correctly surmised that there would be an administrative void if his Council did not fill it. Realising, also, that the towns of Billericay and Wickford with a combined population of less than 40,000 could not survive on their own and would doubtless be absorbed in the long term into Basildon, he put it to his officers that they assume responsibility for providing the usual local authority services from the moment the construction of every street and every building had been completed by the Corporation, including, for example, refuse collection, street cleaning, maintenance of parks and open spaces, etc.

After all, every development, of whatever nature, was still within the district even though it was obvious that Basildon, when completed, would need its own local authority. Moreover, the salaries of Local Government Officers were predicated on the size of the population they administered and theirs might well decline if Billericay and Wickford finished up on their own. On the other hand, they would increase if they seized the initiative proposed by him. Naturally, none of his officers objected. They, like him, could see that the days of Billericay Urban District Council were numbered and that this bold move offered the prospect of secure employment and higher salaries. Elected Councillors and representatives of all political parties were equally enthusiastic. This seamless transfer of power and influence must have appealed to them. To some, the newly constructed town, at the time a planner's dream, must have been like having a new toy to play with.

As soon, therefore, as the first Council houses had been built Billericay Urban District Council stepped in and provided local authority services for them.

The Ministry for Town and Country Planning did not object: in fact, it was probably quite relieved that it did not have to create another Local Authority. It was not long before the Corporation built a spacious and impressive town square with shops and offices and a spectacular tower block of flats at one end of it. As soon as the offices were ready for occupation Alma Hatt rented offices in Keay House in the Town Square and moved all his officers and staff into them. He had previously changed the name of Billericay Urban District Council to Basildon Urban District Council and the change of identity and location was complete. Sadly, he saw little benefit from this bold move for himself. He died suddenly and unexpectedly, and a Town Manager was appointed in his stead.

In political terms the district had been staunchly Conservative before the arrival of rehoused Londoners but the steady increase in the number of council house tenants in Basildon changed the political complexion of the constituency of which it formed part. It led to a Labour Party majority on the Council which could have been foreseen.

It was not until Margaret Thatcher introduced the "right to buy" one's council house many years later that Basildon swung from Labour to Conservative. It is, at the time of writing this book, a political bell weather and, for journalists and the media, the home of "white van man". The nation now tends to vote the way Basildon votes.

Boundary changes and the substantial increase in the populations of Billericay and Wickford have subsequently separated the two original towns in the constituency from Basildon and each now has its own representation in Parliament. Quite why Billericay, Wickford, Laindon and Pitsea were lumped together in the first place I have no idea. All I can tell the reader is that all four communities were within the same Parliamentary Polling District in 1832 and that when district councils came into being in 1894, they were included in Billericay Rural District.

As a result of the increase in population brought about, to a substantial extent, by the railways and by property developers building houses and bungalows in the district and Estate Agents selling plots to Londoners before the First World War, Billericay became an Urban District in 1934. But I digress and must return to 1946 and my recollection of the town in those early post war years, and to my time at Brentwood school.

36

Upper Two: Dinky Toy Dealer

Having successfully navigated my way through my first year in the main school from September 1946 to July 1947 and, having passed the all important "11 plus" scholarship examination, I was allocated in my second year to Upper Two, a class which contained boys whose academic potential might well enable them to progress to a place at University at the end of their school careers.

Whereas Lower One had been located in Roden House, a large red brick Jacobean building and we had been taught in comparative comfort, Upper Two was put into one of a number of temporary single storey concrete huts hastily erected post war in an area behind the main school and close to the rear of the Bean Library.

There could not have been enough classrooms at the time to accommodate the influx of Direct Grant entrants. Something had to be done to house them. These concrete post-war structures, called "The Powlies", after a venerable Headmaster in the Eighteenth century, were incredibly cold in the winter and oppressively hot in the summer. I cannot recall that they had any form of heating. We were expected to put up with the cold or the heat, and that was that. They were painted a shade of military green, the same colour as army lorries, and being unaware of the Reverend John Powley we thought they must have been based on the type of hut in which German prisoners of war (POW's) had been housed!

The Powlies were not the best environment for serious study and, feeling secure after passing the scholarship I have to confess that my mind turned from academic subjects to my existing Dinky toy "dealership" and to my latest passion, collecting the numbers on the sides of London Transport buses. How could I possibly indulge the latter without earning enough from the former to buy the "red rover" bus tickets which would enable me to travel to the outer reaches of its impressive network. At the age of twelve my pocket money of one shilling a week, albeit supplemented by the half-crown from Uncle Gerald, was just not enough!

I had become the Dinky toy dealer of my class in Lower One and this lucrative commercial activity had expanded in Upper Two. Within my desk, in place of exercise books, were neat rows of cars and planes. One model I should have retained but sold on was the Imperial Airways "Mayo", an airliner with a small plane attached to the top of the fuselage which was and undoubtedly still is much sought after. I cannot help feeling it must have been an Englishman who devised this aeronautical "piggyback" arrangement! It had the touch of Heath Robinson about it. It obviously never really caught on but someone must have had the concept in mind when, in one of the Indiana Jones films, a small light aircraft was attached to the underside of an airship!

I was, of course, terrified that one of our form masters would ask me to open my desk and tried to give the impression of being attentive at all times. Not that I was necessarily concentrating on what he was saying, and I can recall being soundly slapped round the head by Hector Higgs during a Latin lesson for failing to decline a noun correctly after he had explained it to the class.

Hector was what one might describe as "old school", having arrived at Brentwood as a teacher in the third term of 1910. Beating knowledge into the brain of a schoolboy whose mind was clearly on other things was still quite acceptable in the 1940s. I will refer to the techniques adopted by other masters to encourage assimilation of what was being taught by them in a later chapter.

As mentioned in a previous chapter I had been extremely impressed as a "just five" year old in January 1941 when Grannie Somers bought me back from the Old Church Hospital in Romford, on my recovery from scarlet fever, in a big red double decker bus with its outside staircase to the upper deck and its "tinging" bell, and my fascination with these huge machines and their "Green Line" express counterparts burgeoned from the moment we moved back to Essex in 1946.

As indicated in an earlier chapter some young boys in my day became "train spotters" and frequented platforms at major rail termini but I preferred the "thrill of the open road" and travelled with single minded determination all over central London and to far flung garages in the Home Counties. When spotted I would draw a line through the number of the bus in my "Ian Allan, ABC of London Transport", a small book which fitted easily into a schoolboy's jacket pocket.

The enthusiasm of young boys for going out in all weathers to collect bus or train numbers may, in this day and age, be difficult to understand when most of them nowadays spend their time at home on the internet or playing computer games. The same might be said of their erstwhile enthusiasm for collecting cigarette cards or postage stamps. But to us, at the time, all these hobbies opened a window on a wider world, an interest outside our domestic surroundings.

Collecting something appeared inherent for many years in young boys generally. My two sons and their school friends went through a phase of collecting cards bearing the names, photos and club emblems of famous footballers which they stuck into albums. Of course, many people carry on collecting into middle or old age as Museums across the country bear witness.

As with trains there were buses of all shapes and sizes. Some were highly unusual like the split-level coaches that went out to the new Heathow Airport with a raised observation deck over a capacious hold for luggage at the rear of them. Others were manufactured in their hundreds or thousands as workhorses on popular routes.

There were red buses and green buses, double deckers and single deckers. The red double-deckers inhabited "inner London" as also did most of the red single-deckers. The green variety of both were, for the most part, to be found in the Home Counties, either express Green Line or London Country. Most of the London Country buses were single-deckers and their numbers more difficult to collect.

The type and number of each bus appeared in gold below the driver's cab on one side and on the side of the bonnet on the other. They could therefore be spotted from either side. Between March 1946 and early September 1948, just before I went into Classical Three, I visited, according to my battered ABC, 43 garages in central London and 18 in the Home Counties, ranging from Dartford, Tunbridge Wells, Sidcup, Guildford, Reigate, Dorking, Croydon and Staines in the south to Amersham, St. Albans, Hertford, Hitchin and Epping in the north. Garages were like honeypots to a young collector of bus numbers, like myself, who had the motivation to travel to them.

Of the red double deckers there were many variants. The majority had AEC engines but others had Bristol, Guy, Daimler or Leyland engines. Some had route numbers in boxes on the front of the roof but most just had indicator boards giving the number of the service, the destination and some of the stops "en route". The two best known routes were those of the number 9 and number 11 buses of which it was said that one could wait a long time and three would turn up together. Apocryphal perhaps but their erratic appearances with two often turning up at the same time gave rise to many jokes about them.

The knowledge I acquired about them all enabled me, much to the surprise of one of my Classics teachers, to hire a brand-new TF, luxury single decker, for a Classical Society trip to Rye and Winchelsea in 1953 when I was in the Sixth form. It is not really surprising, in the circumstances, that my late wife often commented on how well I knew my way around London and the Home Counties. My days of bus spotting had not entirely been a waste of time!

Our move to Billericay in January 1948 and my concentration on "extracurricular" activities did, of course, divert my attention from academic study and I plummeted from 13th in my last term in Lower One to 31st out of 34 in the summer term in Upper Two. As a result, Charles Allison the new Headmaster indicated to my parents that if I did not buck up my ideas, I might well have to leave the school.

It was therefore with some reluctance that I gave up "second hand car dealing" at the end of my second year and, as a result, came ninth out of 34 boys in my first term in Classical Three. My days of bus spotting were also over, much to my disappointment.

In fact, in my report for that term, my housemaster noted "a most gratifying improvement on last year's showing on which he is to be congratulated. He has developed fast". If only he had known the real reason for the turnaround! Even the Headmaster noted "this report makes good reading". From that moment on I felt that I should pay more attention to schoolwork, albeit reluctantly, after a decision was made by my form master in Classical Three that determined the trajectory of my entire life. It really was as significant as that as you will learn from later chapters.

37

My Father's Operation

In an earlier chapter I mentioned how gaunt my father looked when he drove me to school from Hornchurch in 1947. Although his mind was active and although he had shown foresight and initiative in many ways, for example, in bringing his family back to Essex, obtaining a better paid role in Local Government, dealing with the repair of our war damaged house in Hornchurch, purchasing a woodland plot and having a bungalow built upon it, his body was steadily deteriorating. By mid-1948, some two years after our move back from the Midlands, he was down to just over six stones in weight, looking skeletal and clearly heading towards an early grave. His prospects of long-term survival were looking very dismal indeed.

He had never enjoyed good health. He had suffered from persistent chest problems from an early age. They may have been inherited from his mother, Ada, who died of cardiac asthma in 1940 at the age of 63. He had been invalided out of the Royal Air Force on the grounds of chronic bronchitis some nine months after being called up in February 1941 and, although my mother ensured that he did not smoke on a regular basis, he had not helped himself by smoking the occasional Wills Woodbine or John Player cigarette when offered to him by friends and male relatives.

It was undoubtedly the chest weakness he constantly displayed, also apparent for some years in my younger sister, that prompted me to develop my lungs as much as possible by running everywhere. There is little doubt that the praepostors (prefects) at Brentwood school unwittingly helped me to do this and to instil in me a love for cross country running by putting me into "drill" on a regular basis. Drill was one of the punishments for cheek that they could impose. It entailed getting into a singlet and shorts at 4 pm, whatever the weather, and running in plimsolls on a set day of the week twice round the school playing fields. Inconvenient but not inconvenient enough to stop me being cheeky! I will mention the outcome of this punishment in a later chapter.

But his chest was not the underlying reason for his poor health and loss of weight. He had had his appendix removed in 1939 and whether or not appendicitis or a botched operation caused it, he developed a duodenal ulcer which manifested itself in 1942.

Over time a colic fistula had developed, a hole in his intestines through which he lost much of the nutrition that should have been absorbed into his body. He inevitably got thinner and thinner and less resistant to inflammation of his lungs. He could not have afforded hospital treatment in 1946 or 1947, given the expense he had incurred in building a new home for us and paying my school fees for two terms, and it was only the introduction of the National Health Service on 5 July 1948 that rescued him. His Doctor, Dr Gunter, alarmed by his deterioration and being aware of the possibility of an operation for which he would not have to pay, had him admitted to the Royal London Hospital in Whitechapel.

At the time there was no established procedure for dealing with a colic fistula and my father's future prospects looked bleaker still when the Hospital established what was wrong with him. But, at that point, a brilliant and innovative surgeon by the name of Hermon Taylor approached my father and gave him two options.

The first option was that, at the rate he was declining, he could refuse treatment and die from natural causes within three or four months. Alternatively, he could allow the surgeon to carry out an operation of which he had no previous experience and either die on the operating table if the operation was unsuccesful or survive if it was. Moreover, if it was successful he could expect to live for many years.

Naturally my father wanted to know what was involved in the operation. Mr Hermon Taylor explained that he would cut open my father's stomach, remove all his intestines, join together such parts of them as were not diseased and unaffected by the hole that had developed through them and re-insert the good bits. My father would probably finish up with just over half of his intestines but sufficient to extract nutrition from the food he was eating. My father would be a "guinea pig". What was his choice? Certain death in a few months' time if nothing was done, possible death during surgery but a chance of survival.

In an earlier chapter I commented on the fact that my father was always, almost inexplicably, cheerful, good natured and optimistic despite the poor state of his health. He had learned to live with his bad chest and the effects of his duodenal ulcer and, although it might be unfashionable to say it, I feel sure that his deeply embedded Christian faith had a lot to do with his attitude towards life.

My father must also have been impressed by the reputation and professionalism of Mr Hermon Taylor. With death staring him in the face he opted for the operation that at least offered hope of survival. I cannot imagine what was going through his mind as he fell unconscious prior to it but, being a religious man, he had undoubtedly said a prayer and left it to God to decide whether he should live or die. In the event Mr Hermon Taylor performed an outstanding feat of surgery, now called a colectomy, and my father survived. After a brief period of recuperation in hospital and at home he returned to work in his office at 98 High Street, Billericay.

He later told me that, while he was recovering in hospital after the operation he noticed a dove fluttering at the window opposite his bed just above an elderly male patient who, like himself, had recently returned to the ward after an operation. It was at that moment that my father believed the man had died. He wondered whether the dove had appeared to take the man's soul to heaven. It was a comment I have never forgotten.

All one can conclude from his "near-death experience" is that, had it not been for the election of the Labour Government in 1945 and the introduction by it of a medical service free at the point of use by everyone in Britain, my father would not have survived.

It is almost inconceivable nowadays that a national health service should not exist. The fact of its existence, in the shape of the NHS, shows how much the attitudes of society have changed since I was born.

38
Billericay High Street: 1947 to the Present

As a 10-year-old who had lived, until March 1946, in a bustling Midlands town I found Billericay a very sleepy place when we first arrived in Ramsden Bellhouse. In character it was more like a village. In fact, I can remember that, during the 1940s, people living on the outskirts of the town would say they were going "up to the village" to do their shopping.

To all outward appearances it had remained unchanged between the two World Wars. In 1946 the town was still surrounded to a very large extent by green fields and open spaces. There was little sign or expectation of the massive development that would take place from 1953 onward. The population of the surrounding area had, nevertheless, grown steadily and almost imperceptibly during that period.

As mentioned in a previous chapter the economic depression of the early / mid 1920s brought about by the First World War, had forced many families to sell their homes in London, move to their "out of town" holiday plots and live, in straitened circumstances, in the modest bungalows they had built upon them.

During the 1930s the hourly steam train service to Liverpool Street had also encouraged a number of well-to-do workers in the City of London to purchase newly built red brick houses on plots reasonably close to the High Street and the railway station.

Although mains drainage, gas, water, and electricity facilities were available within Billericay High Street this was not, however, necessarily the case elsewhere. A young child, let out to play in the garden of a Victorian house in Chapel Street which connects to and is immediately at the rear of the High Street, drowned in its cesspool in the late 1940s.

There were cesspools or septic tanks in the gardens of many properties irrespective of when they had been built.

Some ten months after the end of the war in Europe, Billericay, in general, had a drab and "down at heel" look with unmade and, in some cases, deeply rutted side roads off the High Street and off the roads leading into the town where speculative residential development had taken place in the 1930s.

The exteriors of most buildings in the High Street had been neglected from the outbreak of the War due to lack of the money and manpower necessary to repaint or repair them. This neglect had inevitably detracted from their former appearance.

There were, admittedly, one or two new buildings in the High Street in good condition, namely the red brick Post Office, the red brick Police Station and the red brick Magistrates Court behind it, all constructed in 1938. A cinema, the Ritz, faced with red bricks had also been built in the same year in Chapel Street to cater principally for the maturing offspring of those who had moved into the area in the 1920s and 1930s. I became a regular attender buying my tickets at the kiosk inside the cinema from Beryl Wormald, the thin faced and grey haired lady who later brought ice creams round at the interval!

The construction of these buildings would appear to indicate that, in the years immediately prior to the Second World War, Billericay had been regaining some of its civic pride and it did, of course, have the advantage of brick works producing red bricks close to the centre of the town! Their colour would have been fashionable at the time and pressure to use them may well have been brought to bear by the recently formed Billericay Urban District Council, successor in 1934 to the former Rural District Council.

The outbreak of the Second world War had brought to an end any aspirations there may have been for further expansion or improvement. The town's former glory days as a coaching hub were long since over and the properties that lined both sides of the High Street reflected past, but not present, prosperity.

My first memory of the High Street, therefore, was when at the age of ten I walked down it from the bus stop at Sun Corner at its southern end. It was a hot July afternoon towards the end of my term in the Prep and just a couple of months before we moved from Ramsden Bellhouse back to our home in Hornchurch.

I intended to get a lift home from my father who worked at Barnsley House, a fine Georgian building opposite the Red Lion, the historic focal points of the town and former venue of the Manorial Courts Leet and Baron for the copyhold tenants of Baron Petre, the Lord of the Manor of Great Burstead. I have previously referred to the abolition of copyhold tenure by the Law of Property Act, 1925.

Barnsley House, at 98 High Street, was occupied by the legal department of the council whose various departments had, since 1934, outgrown the Tudor building housing the former Rural District Council at 108 High Street. His office was on the first floor, and he shared it with his exceptionally capable Secretary, Joyce Carpenter, a member of a well-known farming family in Great Burstead. Some years after the death of my father she was awarded, in her married name of Norris, an MBE for her outstanding service to the community.

Prior to our return to our temporary home in Homestead Road I was going to visit Howards, the Newsagents, to see whether they had any Dinky toys in stock. The manufacturers of them had recently taken some of their metal dies out of wartime storage and had started to produce model cars and aeroplanes once again. After that I was going to Mrs. Arthy's sweet shop in the centre of the High Street in the hope of finding, maybe, some "off ration" sherbert gobstoppers, my favourite, or similar, and then spend time in the immediately adjacent second-hand book shop owned by the man with the permanent drip on the end of his nose where I could browse through his stock of pre-war adventure stories until my father was ready to leave work.

I passed the Police Station and the Magistrates Court in which, as a Solicitor, I would later defend Clients charged with motoring and other offences. It may or may not be true that, until they were removed, the town's stocks stood in the meadow upon which these embodiments of law and justice were constructed. As previously mentioned, I saw the stocks or a very convincing replica of them in the late 1940s on the small area of greensward at the entrance of Deerbank Road, close to the site of the Battle of Billericay, fought and lost by the Essex supporters of Wat Tyler in 1381.

Beyond the Police Station was "Moore's stores", a Georgian building with a couple of front rooms converted into a grocer's shop where Miss Moore who was, I believe, an elderly spinster, and her family before her, had sold tinned food and a limited range of household items, including glass and china. Immediately next door was Dr Bowesman's residence, built with the same red bricks in 1939, from which he conducted his general practice.

Crossing the road at this point I came to "Purdys", a shop with sacks of what appeared to be millet and corn on the pavement outside and, very much to my surprise, two ladies' corsets boldly displayed in the window! As a child I was unable to see the connection between these contrasting items but an old photo which I studied recently reveals that there was a sign over the door which said, "Grocer and Draper." It was doubtless a matter, in 1946, of displaying for sale anything that other shopkeepers had not thought of selling, in order to make ends meet.

The High Street was so quiet. It was almost as if the heat had driven everyone indoors. In those days there might have been the odd car parked in or driving up the High Street but, on this particular afternoon, I could only see one solitary car parked outside the Red Lion. The owner of it must have had one beer too many at lunch time and decided to walk home and collect it later. There were no parking restrictions in those days, and everyone would have known whose car it was.

From the sound of metal striking metal, it was obvious to me that a car was being repaired in Ralph Ellis's garage. His garage, really a large workshop, was separated at the time from the Red Lion by a large Seventeenth century house with a Georgian brick façade. The house, demolished in the late 1940s, had, in the past, been a Girls' teaching academy and, latterly, the Burstead House Temperance Hotel. It had a very shabby appearance when I saw it and it is not really surprising that, in the onward march of post war progress, it was pulled down and the site redeveloped.

There was, of course, a reason for the absence of cars and, for the same reason, sweets like sherbert gobstoppers. Petrol and sweets were rationed. From 1942, as mentioned in an earlier chapter, until the end of the War in 1945 petrol had only been available for work that was deemed essential, and a special work permit had been needed to obtain it.

Shortly after our victory in Europe, however, petrol became available for private use, but it was strictly rationed. In fact, petrol rationing lasted until 1950. My father may have been fortunate in this respect because, as an employee of a Local Authority, needing to travel to his place of work and around the area in the course of it, he may have received a slightly more generous allowance than others.

Not even Ralph Ellis, with his solitary petrol pump on the forecourt of his garage could have imagined the exponential growth in car ownership that has taken place since. Car use was confined to the few people who had cars and the necessary petrol coupons. Nor can our "car-oriented" twenty first century society have any idea how far, in the light of petrol rationing and the vast number of people who did not own cars, people had to walk in those early post war years.

As children and adults alike, it was either take a bus, if there was one, or walk or cycle to whatever part of Billericay one wanted to reach. No wonder we were so healthy! It was bicycle or "shanks's pony" for us children who could not afford a bus fare, with no obliging lifts to school or to social events from parents, as nowadays, or travel by car, in the case of the parents themselves, to shops in the High Street or elsewhere. Driving any distance beyond the immediate vicinity of the town would have depended on how carefully the few car owners used their precious petrol coupons.

But I digress and must now return to my walk down the High Street!

In July 1946 there was, on both sides, a virtually unbroken view of Tudor, Georgian and Victorian properties stretching out into the distance right down to the northern end of the High Street. There could only have been five or six twentieth century buildings in the entire street, three of which I have already mentioned.

Many of the larger Tudor timber framed houses had been faced with brick in Georgian times by prosperous owners who wanted to keep abreast of the times. Others still retained the black and white beamed facades they had ben given when they were built. Smaller Tudor buildings had been weather-boarded or dressed in roughcast or pebbledash, both of which disguised their original appearance and, sadly, led to their being demolished before anyone could appreciate their age and history.

In the case of the smaller Tudor buildings these cheap and easy ways of keeping the exteriors weatherproof had undoubtedly been undertaken when the economy of the town and the farming community around it hit a low point in the 1860s. Although it occurred a century later than that, I can vividly recall watching the demolition of Mr Wells, the clock maker and watch repairer's shop with its anonymous pebble-dashed exterior next to the new Post Office, and noting the blackened roof timbers of this 16th-century property where a chimney had been inserted in the nineteenth century.

Before then, there had just been a hole in the roof through which smoke from a fireplace had escaped. That former dwelling could have had a story to tell but it was superseded by bland, characterless shop premises, the fate of so many other historic buildings in the High Street.

The Georgian properties, in 1946, were to a large extent family homes. In some cases, as in the case of Moores Stores, the ground floors, or part of them, had been converted into shops with the families of the owners living behind and on the floors above. This adaptation had taken place as the erstwhile village grew in size in the late 1800s and as the increasing population had called for greater local access to food, clothing and household items. Those that remained residential, including the magnificent Burstead Lodge, belonged to comparatively wealthy families who had maintained them well until the outbreak of the War and had done their best to keep them looking respectable during it.

In this respect, for example, the three doctors, one of whom I have already mentioned, practised from well-maintained private houses, either in or set back from the High Street and I can see, in my mind's eye even to this day, Dr Gunter, our family GP, descending the graceful Georgian style staircase of Crescent House, a mid-18th-century property, set back behind a wall from the High Street, to his consulting room on the ground floor. Dr Gunter was a tall, elegant man, immaculately dressed in a dark suit and a black tie with his sleek black hair brushed back in what I can only describe as a 1930s style. He looked every inch the professional he was, and it was his referral of my father to the London Hospital in 1948 that saved my father's life.

Dr Wells, the third Doctor, lived in "Sheredays", a 15th-century house, subsequently encased in brickwork during the eighteenth century, on the opposite side of the street. He used the original kitchen of the property as his surgery and the red and gold edging around the base of the Georgian half pillars on either side of the front door was irreverently referred to by some as "blood and pus"!

I hope the good Doctor never heard that attribution to the colours!

The most prominent Victorian building in the High Street, was St. Ediths, built for a local and obviously wealthy Solicitor in 1863 some twenty years after the construction of the Billericay Workhouse. It was in a Gothic style and its brickwork had weathered into a grey colour. It had subsequently come into the hands of the Roman Catholic Church which used it as an Ursuline school and a place of worship until 1920.

After reverting to family ownership, it had a chequered history until the workhouse was converted into St. Andrew's Hospital. It then became a Nurses Hostel until 1958 and was demolished in 1960. Because it was so imposing it had, in fact, been earmarked for conservation. But it met the fate of other historic buildings and was replaced almost one hundred years after its construction by an immense red brick office building which sits uncomfortably among those that remain. But, at the time, in July 1946, the whole High Street had an air of somnolence about it. It had not changed since 1939 and the pace of life of its inhabitants appeared slow and measured, perhaps as a result of the deprivation they had had to endure during the War and had to continue to endure until conditions improved. I must now return to my peregrination of the High Street on that hot and sunny afternoon!

After visiting my father and finding out when he intended to leave his office, I set off down the High Street in order to visit the shops I had in mind. I had not gone more than a few steps down the street towards Howards, however, when I passed an elderly lady. She musts have been in her mid-70s and wore a long black dress and a black bonnet. Her hair was drawn back in a bun under the bonnet, secured by a large hat pin which, to my young and untrained eye, appeared to go right through the back of her head, protruding as it did from both sides of the bonnet. I discovered later that she was Mrs. Cottis, the wife of the owner of Cottis's Bakery, outside whose premises she was standing, and that she dressed in the fashion of a bygone era until she died.

While wondering about the lady with the hatpin through her head and only a few yards further down the street I heard a voice call out "C'mere boi." I looked up and saw a short, tubby and elderly little man sitting on a kitchen chair just inside the door of his shop, beckoning me to come over to him. He wore carpet slippers, a pair of baggy black trousers, a white shirt without a collar and a black waistcoat. On his head was a flat cap.

I dutifully complied. This was to be my first encounter with Fred Eales, saddler and harness maker, who stopped me on at least two subsequent occasions and probably any other young school boy who was wearing a Brentwood school blazer and sporting a plum-coloured school cap. Fred was well known for watching the world go by when he had nothing else to do and turned out to be one of the real personalities of Billericay, having lived in the High Street from Victorian times.

"Did yer know there were a Billy Ricky Grammar school?" he asked me.

"No Sir," I replied.

"C'mere." With that he reached into his shop and produced two large books with brown leather covers. Inside the cover of each was a frontispiece with the words "Billericay Grammar school" printed on it. I was duly impressed and pretended to be on the subsequent occasions! I only realised some years later that "Foxcroft", my stately Georgian office at 100 High Street, had been the Billericay Grammar school in the 1860s. I had been forced to sell the property when Lloyds of London, of which I had been a member for only three years and which had apparently been profitable for the previous three hundred and twenty, incurred losses of £8 billion, towards which I was, of course, obliged to contribute!

The High Street was not so very different when we, as a family, returned some sixteen months later in early January 1948 in one of the coldest winters on record.

The pace of life had definitely quickened, and the town appeared to be busier, even though there was still not a great deal one could buy in the shops. There was a feeling that the town was getting back on its feet and that, as a result of the Labour Government's ambitions for reform, momentous change was in the offing.

The real change took place, of course, in 1953 when the railway line between London, Liverpool Street, and Southend was electrified. From that moment Billericay literally exploded in terms of size and population with dramatic consequences for the centre of the town and the farmland around it. The tragedy of the High Street, since 1953, is that as a result of electrification and the attractiveness of the town to people working in the City of London, so many charming Tudor, Georgian and Victorian buildings, whose appearance had previously been concealed, have had to give way to steel and concrete structures, albeit that some are faced in red brick, and that the few residential properties which existed in 1948 have either been demolished or converted into retail shops, restaurants and offices.

Precious little thought has been given, moreover, to harmonising the old with the new and this lack of foresight has to be attributed to the local Planning Authority which could have ensured a more pleasing outcome. In fact, at one stage in the early 1960s it was felt by many residents that allowing unsightly redevelopment was deliberate rather than just plain thoughtless. Whatever the reason or motive many of these unsightly structures still remain.

The tranquillity of the town in the 1940s is a far cry from the activity and the bustle one encounters nowadays and there can be no denying that the High Street has changed out of all recognition in the years since I first walked down it as a 10-year-old. Much of its original character has been lost and the unacknowledged history and attractiveness of so many buildings have gone forever in the pursuit of consumerism and profit. Whether those that remain will also be lost is for future generations to decide but I hope that they will survive long after I have gone and that a more thoughtful approach to harmonisation and conservation will be adopted in the event of future applications for change of appearance or use.

39
Classical Three: A Fateful Decision

Although I have mentioned in an earlier chapter that our genes, family environment, historical timeframe and the attitudes of those closest to us in childhood determine the trajectory of our lives, there is one other factor that cannot be ignored. That is what I would describe as *fate* or chance. The ancient Greeks were firm believers in it and, as a result of the extraordinary things that have occurred during my life, so am I. In this chapter I will give a striking example of how fate or chance can affect one's life.

Towards the end of our second year in the Main school the teachers we had encountered during those first two years made assessments of our aptitude for the subjects we might study from that point onward.

As previously mentioned most of us had passed the "eleven plus" and notwithstanding the fact that, at first, there was a distinct divide between the boarders and the dayboys whose parents paid fees and the "Grammar bugs," like myself, whose education was paid for by the State, our teachers were only interested in making sure that we all followed courses of study that would be beneficial to us in our future careers.

What, therefore, should we study from the beginning of our third year, at the age of thirteen, until we left the school at sixteen or eighteen? For them and for us it was decision time. Some boys, in their view, were clearly "maths and science" minded, some more oriented towards the arts and languages, while others who were not so academic were considered more likely to benefit from a broader and less intensive education.

It was the members of this latter cohort who, ironically, finished up better off financially than the rest of us! On leaving school many went into property development, surveying, banking, stockbroking, the insurance and commodity markets and other types of occupation in the City of London where a Public school education would improve their chances of advancement and a rise to partnerships or positions in senior management.

I, for whatever reason, was marked out as more suited to arts and languages, basically English language and literature, history and foreign languages and consequently found myself, on arrival at school for the autumn term in Classical Three with 33 other boys.

A decision was made, at that point, by my new form master, Mr Martin ("Polecat" to the boys) which completely determined my future. After he had introduced himself to us and had informed us that he would also be our Maths teacher he stated that his very first task was to divide the class in two as far as languages were concerned.

Mr Martin was a man of medium height, with aquiline features: he looked very much a senior member of staff in his suit and tie, rather than in the sports jacket and flannels favoured by the younger teachers. He exuded authority but was not overbearing in any way. One just sensed that he was not to be trifled with and he gained the respect of us all from the outset.

"There are 34 boys in this class," he said, "and 17 of you will have to learn German and 17 of you Greek. So, first of all, how many of you want to learn German?" Thirty-three of us put our hands up.

One boy, John Rist who during his stellar career became Professor of Classics at both Toronto and Aberdeen Universities wanted, not surprisingly in retrospect, to learn Greek. Nobody else did!

He was the only undergraduate I ever met who had read all the set books for the first year of his degree course during his National Service while, at the same time, mastering Russian and working for Military Intelligence in the Middle East. He came top in virtually every subject in class and, to cap it off, achieved high grades in playing the piano. It was difficult not to feel somewhat in awe of the intelligence and ability of someone with whom I was a friend not only at school but also at university.

"In that case", declared Mr Martin, "I will have to go down the Class Register and allocate every alternate boy to German or Greek". "Hughes, you will study Greek". When he had finished his allocation, he concluded by saying "and if any of your parents object, tell them to write to me within the next couple of days and I will see what I can do to switch you".

I was disappointed by his decision, but my parents were concerned that, if they objected, I might be expelled. I had not exactly distinguished myself academically during my second year. As previously mentioned, my father spoke good German and would have preferred me to learn the language. But there was to be no going back on Mr Martin's decision. Greek it had to be whether I liked the subject or not.

For those who wonder how he acquired his nickname, Polecat is the alternative name for a ferret-like creature called a Foul Marten. That is absolutely true and an undeserved attribution to a very decent schoolmaster!

Little did I realise at the time the significance of that decision and how allocation to learning Greek would affect everything that happened to me in later life. It led to a Scholarship in Classics, to a place at Cambridge, to being seconded to work with Military Intelligence in Cyprus, to organising student travel to Greece for many years, and to meeting the love of my life on a train returning from Athens in 1960.

But for a random number of surnames of boys in the class before he came to my own, this book would not have been written. I would doubtless have gone to another University and had by no means as many remarkable experiences. Fate had clearly taken a hand.

To me the torture of having to assimilate Latin and Greek from the age of thirteen was pretty intense. On the other hand, Latin teaches one to be logical and to think straight and Greek helps one to explore human frailty. To anyone who has read my first book I have to apologise for an element of repetition, but it is necessary to give continuity to my narrative.

It was not until we reached the sixth form at the age of sixteen that we were introduced to Ancient History. That subject switched on an intense light in my brain and illuminated and justified all those arduous years of study of the Classics.

Ancient History was amazing. When studying the histories of Greece and Rome one could see how the mistakes made by past civilisation had been repeated throughout history. One could also absorb the thoughts and reflect on the ambitions of men who, more than two thousand years ago, were as clever and gifted as we are today.

Through a combination of Latin, Greek and Ancient History one enters the world of gods and heroes, of fate and hubris, of great art and architecture, of power and the corroding influence of it. Just as significantly it generates a huge desire to visit Italy and Greece and to see, at first hand, what remains of Greek and Roman civilisations. An opportunity to do so occurred, thanks to the school Scout Troop earlier than I expected. I will cover this groundbreaking trip in a later chapter.

So enthused was I by Ancient History that when my form masters decided to enter everyone else in the class for three "A" levels at the age of sixteen, one year ahead of usual, I insisted on being allowed to take the same papers with them even if my parents had to pay the Examination Board's entrance fees.

They reluctantly agreed to do so, stating that, in my case, it would be a complete waste of money on the part of whoever paid them. Although they had correctly assessed the precocious talent of the other boys, most of whom, I recall, successfully passed Latin and Greek at "A" level, I managed to surprise them by passing Ancient History. Although that particular examination fee had not been wasted, they were absolutely right about my ability to pass the other two subjects!

As the reader will already have gathered, however, the social history, of whatever period, was and has remained, an abiding interest. My form masters were not to know that at the time.

40
Healthy Mind in Healthy Body

In a previous chapter I mentioned my admiration of the Great Wilson and my desire to be like him. Brentwood school also believed in the encouragement of sporting prowess and academic achievement. But this belief was not just confined to the school. From the mid-Victorian era onward an emphasis on sport had become embedded in the culture of all public schools alongside a particularly muscular form of Christianity.

Team games became a major part of life because many in Government and in the military saw them developing the skills and determination that would help preserve and extend the Empire. When I arrived at Brentwood in 1946 the culture still existed despite the fact that the Empire was coming to an end.

Dr West, a former Headmaster in the 1860s and 1870s, had been a great enthusiast of this aspect of education and the school produced its first international footballer in 1871, it's first international Rugby player in 1873 and a cricketer called Charles Kortwright, who developed a national reputation for being the "fastest bowler ever". Others have followed in their illustrious footsteps.

While on the subject of Dr West his somewhat quaint precepts or rules, written in 1858, include the following: "Join social games with spirit keen, nor loitering round the porch be seen" and "no angry words invade your sport nor malice prompt a quick retort". It is a pity that his precepts are not wholeheartedly observed today!

There was consequently, in 1946, emphasis on every pupil having a healthy mind in a healthy body, as the Romans succinctly put it, "Mens sana in corpore sano". In addition to compulsory sport or athletics on

Wednesday and Saturday afternoons, there were also physical exercise periods for every boy in the school from the first form to the sixth form.

On my arrival in the Main school in September 1946 there were two gymnasia, one Victorian and another built between the First and Second World Wars. The periods 1910 to 1914 and 1919 to 1939 must have seen a steady expansion in the number of pupils because an ambitions development programme was initiated in the early 1920s and continued well into the late 1930s in order to accommodate them all.

The Victorian gymnasium had been built in 1891 and was intended to meet the requirements of the boys in what was called "The Old Big school" namely the original (1568) school and the classrooms that had been tacked onto it over the three centuries in between. It stood some distance away from the Old Big school and would have been adequate for the physical education of the pupils at the time

Although quite substantial in construction, and doubtless as well designed for its purpose as others in public schools in the Victorian era, the gymnasium was, in reality, nothing more than a modestly sized hall with basic physical exercise equipment attached to the walls and ceilings.

In fact, I have no doubt it was used for other school functions until the imposing Edwardian style edifice known as the Main school, fronting the Ingrave Road, filled the area between it and the Old Big school in 1910 and a proper hall, known as the Memorial Hall, capable of accommodating a much greater number of pupils, was added to it in 1923/1924.

It had climbing frames on two walls, ropes hanging down from the ceiling, long, low, moveable wooden benches along the side walls upon or under which we placed our clothes and shoes and a solid wood floor. It did not appear to be heated and, with its windows high up in the walls, was very cold in the winter months and somewhat gloomy throughout the entire year. All I can recall, in terms of freestanding equipment, were piles of coconut matting and a couple of antiquated vaulting horses over which the older boys were intended to leap.

The emphasis in Victorian and Edwardian times may well have been on the type of physical exercise one would encounter during basic army training. The low temperature inside the gymnasium from 1891 to the date I arrived at the school may also have been intended to act as a spur to energetic warming up exercises!

The philosophy of the various Headmasters may have been "we have to toughen up these young and privileged boys from comfortable, middle-class homes in order to give them the hardiness they require to maintain every part of the Empire". If so, it is no wonder that explorers and mountaineers between the 1860s and the outbreak of the Second World War were so hardy!

Being small and not very muscular in our first year we were only expected to do a few knee bends and press ups, swing our arms and upper bodies and run round the gym in an effort to keep warm. Having to leap over the vaulting horses which were taller than ourselves was beyond us. Fortunately, we 11-year-olds only had to endure physical exercise in it once a week for a comparatively short time before, in our second year, we moved to the newer lighter and better equipped gymnasium, built in 1938, at the rear of the swimming pool.

The new gymnasium was at the Ingrave end of The Chase, a wide track between the school buildings and the playing fields, and close to the Common and even closer to the Artichoke Public House. This was fortunate for Mr Shortland (Shortie), the physical training and gymnastics master who, like many other members of the teaching staff, was a habitué of the establishment.

In addition to wall ladders on all four walls the new gymnasium had cross beams which, if one possessed a good sense of balance, would enable one to traverse the gym from side to side. These cross beams were particularly helpful when we played "Pirates" at the end of each term.

A boy chosen by Mr Shortland would be given the task of catching every other boy in the class by using the wall ladders, the cross beams and the ropes hanging down from the ceiling. Once caught, usually by a tap on the shoulder, you were "out" as you were if you put a foot on the floor of the gym in an effort to escape. It was one of the highlights of our periods in the gym.

The new gymnasium was the domain of Mr Shortland and his assistant, Miss Trott, a young lady probably in her late twenties or early thirties by whose figure we, and possibly Mr Shortland himself, were impressed! She was dark haired, good looking with a shapely pair of tanned legs which she displayed under her dark blue hockey skirt. However feminine and attractive she may have been she was a "no nonsense" teacher in our first year in the Victorian gym and she put us thorough our paces with enthusiasm. There was to be no slacking with her while we puffed and panted our way through our exercises. She was particularly keen on good posture and encouraged us to keep our chins up at all times and not to slouch.

In fact, I am told that while demonstrating good posture to an older class during the summer term she inadvertently fell into the school swimming pool. She apparently thanked the boys for not laughing at her and for helping her to get out of the water. But that is apocryphal. I know I would have laughed!

The same rigorous exercise regime was imposed by Mr Shortland in our subsequent years. Both were intent on ensuring that we stayed supple and both succeeded in this respect.

Physical exercise outside in the open air included swimming in the school pool, running and athletics, and every year there was a school Sports Day when the various houses competed against each other. I can recall that, in one year, my house, North, was lucky enough to have an outstanding athlete by the name of R.A.C. Davies who won virtually every event in which he had been entered. He almost single-handedly propelled us to the top of the leader board, to the smug satisfaction of everyone in the House. It was a moment of fleeting glory, never again to be repeated once he had left the school.

I did not take part in athletics but, like my father, always enjoyed being in the water once I had got over my original experience of slipping underwater in the swimming pool in Kettering. I have already narrated the fact that I was caught in the school pool with my friend, John Farrant, when neither of us could swim more than a few feet and when the water temperature was 42 degrees F.

Swimming and swimming lessons took place in the summer term when the weather had improved and the water temperature in the pool was sufficiently high. I swam my first length in the pool in the summer of 1949 and never looked back until my serious brain haemorrhage at the age of 71 while doing my usual thirty lengths in the new school pool in 2007.

Running, however, was an "all weather" form of exercise and although it is barely conceivable in this day and age I can vividly recall, as a 13-year-old, being summoned with the rest of my year to do a cross country run in early March. We gathered in the large playing field next to the Essex County Cricket Ground, on the north side of the road leading from Brentwood High Street to Chelmsford (the old A12), just after lunch on a Wednesday afternoon. This was, of course, many years before the construction of the Brentwood by-pass.

It was bitterly cold, and we appeared, shivering, in singlet, shorts, and plimsolls, without socks, for a four mile run. There were no custom built running shoes in those days.

We left the field and headed north along a series of farm tracks in the direction of Pilgrims Hatch. After about one and a half miles we came to a farmyard which was a least four inches deep in mud and dung from the cattle on the farm. As we plunged into it the thin sheet of ice covering it cracked and scratched our unprotected ankles.

The suction experienced when one tried to take a step forward was so great that more than one boy lost one of his plimsolls and had to plunge his hands into this sludgy mess in order to find and retrieve it! Why no one succumbed to a tetanus infection I will never understand but we all eventually, and safely, made our way back to the school where cold taps were available in the Old Cloisters to wash the mud and dung from our legs before we dressed back into our normal school clothes. That particular run was an experience I am unlikely to forget!

Running and building up stamina was one of the key methods employed by the school in keeping us fit, and from my fourth to upper sixth form years I would run four or five miles from the school to Eagle Way in Warley and come back via the Ingrave Road on Wednesday afternoons, come rain or shine. It was a good time for thinking and the exercise did me no harm. My Saturday afternoons were devoted to playing rugby union football or cricket but during the autumn (Michaelmas) and spring (Lent) terms many boys played soccer at which the school excelled at the time.

It is not really surprising that, as a result of being put in drill on a regular basis by the prefects and by having to run even more by virtue of the school curriculum, I should finish up as Captain of my House cross country team, a lifelong running enthusiast and founder of the Billericay Striders Running Club which currently has over two hundred members. It is only recently, since the age 85, that I have had to curtail for the time-being my regular five mile run on Sundays but that is another story!

41
Extramural Activities: 1948-1951

"What is the time, Dad?" I would ask my father as I got ready for school. Time you knew better", was his stock response and, in time, my sister, Angela, and I would refer to this often-repeated comment as his "number one joke"!

He would then proceed to tell me what the time actually was. The reason we both asked was that the wind-up clock on the mantel of the tiled fireplace surrounding the two bar electric fire in the dining room at Pink Cottage was invariably set at fifteen minutes ahead of real time!

This could be extremely confusing. I believe the general idea was to prompt us to get on with whatever we should be doing before we left home but all this stratagem achieved was to introduce an element of uncertainty into our minds. Neither of us had a wristwatch nor could we be sure whether he had reset the clock back to Greenwich mean time.

My father always had our best interests at heart, however, and in order to channel my restless energy into something worthwhile, encouraged me to follow in his footsteps and join the Boy Scouts when we arrived in a freezing cold Billericay in January 1948. It is such a long time ago that I cannot remember why I joined the 2nd Billericay Sea Scouts who met at the Mayflower Hall in Chapel Street.

Perhaps it was the attraction of the black and white naval head dress and the warm dark blue, knitted pullover we wore as our uniform or, more likely, the fact that two young boys, Colin and Brian Hunt, living in Jubilee Cottages, virtually opposite, were members of the Troop.

Why a small town so far from the sea should have Sea Scouts I have no idea, but I suspect that Peter Fairbairn, our Scoutmaster, and a former Petty Officer in the Royal Navy, may have persuaded the Scout Association into having the troop designated as such. I understand, in this respect, that some time before I joined the Troop it had acquired a dinghy which it moored on the boating lake known as Lake Meadows.

Regrettably the dinghy had capsized when a number of "land lubber" sea scouts were getting into it and had disappeared, without trace, into the murky waters of the lake.

We received no naval training and spent our time either working towards our Second Class or proficiency badges or playing games in the fields behind the Hall. We did, however, explore HMS Kenya, a light cruiser, which had seen action during the Second World War, when it paid a visit to the Port of London and we also attended the first post-war International Jamboree at Hawkwell, Hockley, near Southend on Sea in the summer of 1948. All I can remember of the Jamboree is that we spent several days under canvas and that it was unseasonably wet and miserable most of the time.

Scouts from many countries in Europe attended the event and the food on offer, albeit frugal, was probably no worse for the majority than that enjoyed in their own homes. The whole continent was poverty stricken and life and diet for everyone were pretty basic.

During the Jamboree I made friends with a charming young Italian boy scout, the same age as myself, who, to my surprise, spoke reasonably good English. We exchanged names and addresses and two or three weeks after the jamboree had ended, I received an impressively embossed letter inside an embossed envelope. Somehow the letter, the content of which I cannot now recall, vanished shortly after its arrival. I do not know what happened to it. Conceivably my parents took fright at the sight of the green monogram on the letter and decided that it might be best if I did not respond to it. The boy was clearly from an aristocratic and wealthy family, and they would have been concerned at the prospect of accommodating him in our three bedroom bungalow if he came back to England or the cost of my travelling out to Italy to stay with him should I enter into correspondence with him.

We also had regular Church parades at the Congregational Church in Chapel Street. The Sermons given by the Reverend George Walker, a grandfatherly figure and author of "The History of a little Town", (Billericay, of course) were always interesting and enjoyable. He had the ability to connect to every member of his congregation and it was not until I reached Cambridge that I encountered sermons or addresses by celebrities in Great St. Mary's, the University Church, that compared with them.

The scout master ("Skip" short for Skipper) was, frankly, a rather suspect character. He seemed to enjoy taking young sea scouts to his flat in Southend and "entertaining" them. I received such an invitation myself and was taken by Skip to see Bert Ossirrati, Southend's champion wrestler at the Kursaal, a huge entertainment complex built for visiting Londoners in the early 1900s. Bert Ossirrati was like a rubber ball, bouncing up off the canvas as he was hurled onto it by his Irish opponent who clearly won the bout. When Bert Ossirrati was given the decision, a riot broke out, with chairs being thrown into the ring and the Irishman giving an impassioned harangue to the furious crowd.

"This foight has been fixed," he shouted, as he stood on the ropes, and it was clear that most people agreed. I was led outside as bare-knuckle fights broke out and spread from the ring towards the back of the hall. As a 12-year-old I thought this was really exciting.

It was when Skip offered to dry me after a swim that I felt something was amiss. I politely declined and dried myself. I left the Troop shortly afterwards but not before I had gained my second-class badge and had been presented with a splendid sheath knife in a leather holder for being top fundraiser during "Bob a job" week (a "Bob" was a shilling). It was salesmanship rather than effort that enabled me to bring in 37 shillings and six pence, substantially more than anyone else!

The troop was disbanded a few months after I left it. There were no CRB checks in those days. Too much trust, and perhaps, naivety was shown in the appointment of Scout Leaders. During my later 40-year spell as President of the local District Scout Association I felt that the pendulum had swung rather too much in the opposite direction, insofar as a number of perfectly respectable and enthusiastic parents were prevented or discouraged from offering their services to the Scout movement. But the Association doubtless considered it better to be safe rather than sorry, notwithstanding the fact that committed leaders of Cub packs and Scout troops have always been in short supply.

As previously mentioned, my parents were keen Christians and, when we moved to Billericay took Angela and me quite regularly to the Parish Church, St. Mary Magdalen in the High Street, where, I have to confess, the Reverend Smith, in contrast to the Reverend Walker, gave what seemed to me to be incredibly boring sermons.

In fact, I prevailed on my parents to let me join the Kings Own Bible Class. It was interdenominational and led by Peter Braun, a keen evangelist who, with his companion, Normal Wilson, told us stories from the Bible, taught us how to pray and got us to sing "happy hymns"! Most importantly these two men taught us to be kind to others and not to ignore or look down on people less fortunate than ourselves. For example, they welcomed to the Bible Class an older boy, Joe, who shook uncontrollably all the time, keeping his left arm as close to his body as he could while walking with a permanent shuffling limp. Whether he had had a stroke or similar I cannot say. It was clear that, although he was years older than us, he loved coming to the Bible classes. He was a regular attender and was accepted by us all.

There was no television in most people's homes until 1953 and I do not recall my parents renting a television set, the cost of an outright purchase being well outside my mother's budgetary calculations, before I was called up into the Army. By way of alternative entertainment there were books from the Public Library in the High Street and magazines, and visits to the Ritz Cinema or to school friends. When I was not doing homework the bulk of my leisure time was, of course, taken up with bus spotting.

My parents had a regular subscription to Readers Digest and, being a voracious reader, I would sprawl across the dining room floor, much to everyone's annoyance with the magazine "face up" on the seat of a low easy chair, reading it as soon as it arrived. The books of many well-known authors were serialised, of whom Neville Shute was a personal favourite. His serialised works included "A Town like Alice" in 1950, "The far Country" in 1952 and "In the Wet" in 1953.

My mother would also occasionally buy "Old Moore's Almanac"

with horoscopes and a good deal of astrological "hocus pocus" in it. It is difficult to believe that the Almanac has been published continuously since 1697 and is still going strong in Ireland where I suspect there is a greater belief in all things mystical. It was originally written and published by Francis Moore, a self-taught physician who served in the Court of Charles II.

According to its current promotional material it contains its "usual mix of scarily accurate predictions and thought-provoking articles" Perhaps my mother, like many other mothers, wanted to gain some insight into what lay in store for her family!

One prediction she could not have read in it is that, at the age of thirteen I would escape death by a whisker! As I have mentioned earlier in this book I had to cycle almost everywhere, whether it be to the Scouts or to the Kings Own, to the homes of my friends and on outings of various kinds. One summer's afternoon I nonchalantly rode my bike out of the drive of Pink Cottage, only to be aware at the last moment that a car was approaching fast from the direction of Ramsden Heath on my right. As I frantically applied the brakes, wobbled and fell off my bike in the process, I was certain the car was going to hit me. Miraculously, and to my great relief, the car had already started to swerve and missed me by inches.

The driver who stopped to make sure I was all right told me that somehow he had sensed that someone was coming out of our drive and had already started to take evasive action. I had been incredibly lucky. If he had not had that premonition, I would have been killed.

This is only one of the many occasions during my life that I have survived a life-threatening situation, and I am deeply indebted to my "guardian angel" for enabling me to do so.

42
The Teachers at Brentwood School

According to a School Inspector's Report published in 1952, after an intensive five-day visit, the word that best described the educational environment at Brentwood school in the late 1940s and early 1950s was "vigorous". Schoolmasters were undoubtedly trying in their different ways to bring out the best, mentally and physically, in a high spirited and intelligent intake of boys, the majority of whom had passed the "eleven plus" examination and who were experiencing and enjoying life in a public school for the first time.

The schoolmasters themselves varied a great deal in age and character. Some of them were fresh out of the Armed Forces, following demobilisation and others were longstanding members of staff who had not had to endure the rigours of military service. Some wanted longstanding methods of education to remain rooted in the Pre-War past while others were looking for more enlightened ways of teaching. Several of the younger teachers were themselves new to the public school system even though they had been to what we would now call Russell Group Universities.

The more capable schoolmasters imbued us with enthusiasm for their subjects and drew us into a better understanding of them. Others, mostly older generation, taught by rote, like production line managers processing us for our forthcoming "0" level examinations. "This is your text book," they would say, "and you must learn everything in it by heart, even if you do not fully understand what it means." Fortunately, there were not too many of this sort.

In the school prospectus for 1946, printed during the war, it is stated that, "House masters may administer corporal punishment" presumably for serious misbehaviour." Although there is clear reference to house master, as opposed to form master, it would appear that form masters also felt that they could do the same where not paying attention or annoying them in other ways was concerned.

Some, therefore, resorted to physical punishment in pursuit of their teaching objectives and I have already mentioned the expert blackboard rubber thrower, Miss Haynes, in the Prep, the plimsoll wielding Mr Kershaw in our first year in the Main school and Hector Higgs, who, in our second year, as I have previously mentioned, believed that smacking boys soundly round the head was the best way of knocking Latin into them!

Hector was one of the "teaching by rote" variety. In fairness to him, however, he had arrived at Brentwood, as a young teacher, in the Autumn term of 1910 and had been subjected to Victorian methods of teaching which he must have endured when a schoolboy himself in the late 1890s and the early 1900s. One master was, in fact, quite gratuitous in his use of the cane, whether one was misbehaving or not, and I will refer to him later in this chapter.

Many had idiosyncrasies which, for the most part, endeared them to us and others were just plain eccentric. I will refer to some of them later in the chapter. But, before I do so, I have to refer, once again, to the headmaster who presided over them.

As previously mentioned, Charles Ralph Allison ("Chas") arrived at the Main school at the beginning of the Autumn term in 1945, two terms before I entered the Prep. He replaced James (Jimmy) Hough, M.A., late Exhibitioner of St. John's College Cambridge., hence doubtless the heavy emphasis on graduate teachers from that University, although four masters at the time were from the "other place", three were from London University and a couple from elsewhere.

Mr Hough, who had been Headmaster from 1914 to 1945, and Second Master from 1903 to 1913 before that, had presided over the rapid expansion of the school from 1910 onward. In addition to being extraordinarily capable he had also been extremely popular with staff and pupils alike.

In fact, in 1935, on commemorating his first 21 years as head, he was described as "a man of such simplicity of life, so kindly, so human that the longer he is among us the more fortunate we count ourselves". He was awarded an OBE in 1958 for his services to Education and, in 1945, was clearly a hard act to follow. The Governors wanted someone of equal calibre to step into his shoes.

Charles Allison was that person. A distinguished-looking man whose manner and presence was commanding, he fitted the role perfectly and remained as Headmaster during another impressive growth spurt in the development of the school. As previously mentioned it was he who introduced "Allison serge" in the interests of uniformity, the "tradition" of boaters in the summer term and the flowing royal blue gowns for House Praepostors, a somewhat pretentious name for senior prefects.

He raised the profile of the school by inviting the late Queen Elizabeth II to visit the school in 1957 on the inaccurate, but unchallenged, basis of it celebrating its 400th anniversary in that year and he did his best to give us an awareness and love of literature and poetry by issuing "Memoranda" (things to be remembered) to every boy in the school during my third year.

Memoranda was a pocket size booklet in a magenta cover which contained a selection of well-known poems and extracts from the books and plays of famous writers. Sections of it were intended to be learned by heart each year as we moved upward through the school. I absorbed everything in it and still possess my copy in a battered and distressed state, more than 75 years after I received it. It contains such inspirational thoughts and reflections on humanity and nature that I would not be without it.

Charles Allison also believed in making us socially aware and promoted the Docklands Settlement Scheme, a charitable East End of London project and gave lessons to Upper Sixth formers on current domestic and foreign affairs. A keen supporter of the United Nations and its related agencies, his observations were impartial and objective.

He encouraged the concept of democratic government and arranged for us to hold our own Mock General Election. I recall that a sixth former by the name of D.A. Dallas stood as a candidate. His election slogan

"Vote for Dad", plus the fact that he represented the Conservative Party, ensured his victory!

However progressive and enlightened he was he could not, at first, eradicate the punitive regimes of some teachers. One of the first things he did, however, was to discontinue the Black Book.

If a boy was misbehaving in class and his form master did not wish to disturb the flow of his lesson, he would tell the miscreant that he was putting him in the Black Book. The offending boy would then have to present himself to the Duty Master at midday on that or the following day for a caning. Having to wait, often overnight, for punishment must have been unnerving and was unnecessarily severe. Charles Allison appreciated this.

He had to bring about a gradual transformation in this respect by replacing the more sadistic ones when they retired with teachers of the same mindset as himself. Of the punitive variety I encountered two prime examples, namely Mr Rennie and Mr Nicholls and I give twenty first century readers pause for thought over the methods they employed.

At the beginning of each lesson Mr Rennie, who taught us in our third year, would place nine old pennies on his desk and ask for a 12-inch wooden ruler which he would lay beside them. Pennies in 1949 were larger and heavier than the current 50p piece and would clink as he put them down. That sound acted as a forewarning of what might be in store.

Like a coiled, unblinking cobra, Mr Rennie would teach quietly enough but if any boy misbehaved, he would strike. "Come out, Smith," let us say, and the wretched child would reluctantly shuffle to his desk. "Put out your right hand, palm down." Once the hand was in position, Mr Rennie would pick up the ruler and bring it down hard on the boy's unprotected knuckles. If the blow was too hard it would break the wooden ruler at which point Mr Rennie would give the nine pence to the boy from whom he had borrowed it and tell him to use the money to buy another. Like every other boy in the class I did my best to avoid confrontation with that ruler!

Mr Nicholls, who taught Biology, called Nature Study in the 1940s and whose nickname was "Dammy Nick" had a different technique.

If he heard boys talking among themselves while he was teaching, he would step out from behind his desk and walk slowly towards the boys in question. When he reached the boy judged by him to have been the instigator, he would stand behind him and grip his hair just above the right ear and twist it, saying, "Bee sting, boy, bee sting." It felt as if one's hair was being pulled out by the roots and I assume he learned this sophisticated form of torture from his own school days. Being talkative, before I knew better, I experienced the pain.

He used the expletive "Damn me" a lot when he first arrived as a teacher, and it was adopted and slightly abbreviated thereafter as a nickname. If one is charitably inclined it is possible that he, like some other teachers, was affected psychologically by traumatic experiences during the war and that this led to more brutality than one might normally expect.

The same cannot be said, however, of Geoffrey Kidd, another teacher whom I will mention again in another chapter. I was never taught by him but, according to a former pupil who entered the school in the mid 1940s and with whom I have discussed the matter, he would come into a class at the beginning of the school year and ask the two biggest boys to come to the front, whereupon he would beat each of them soundly on their backsides with a cane. "That is for nothing", he would say. "Just wait until you do something".

Apparently, this method of exerting authority was not confined to Mr Kidd alone. It was common practice in the 1920s and 1930s to do this in Public schools. No wonder relationships between the pupils themselves were "power based". There are echoes of "Tom Brown's school Days" in the attitudes prevalent at the time.

There were many eccentric teachers but, for me, one stood out. He was Mr Fisher, the Physics Teacher, with his shock of grey hair and whose nickname was "Funf" after the character in the comedy radio programme, I.T.M.A. He was the proprietor of a shop called Radiogram in Brentwood High Street selling vinyl records, to which he retreated after school. He drove a 1926 "bull nose" Morris which was already an antique when I entered the school in 1946.

Other teachers had foibles. When I was in Classical Five, for example, our form master, Mr Barron (nickname "Spud") would check our fingernails before we went into assembly in the Memorial Hall. If there was any dirt under them he would send us to the Cloisters to remove it and return for re-inspection. He was, however, an amazingly good English teacher. He produced the school's dramatic productions and taught so many boys to appreciate literature and poetry.

I have to confess that I did annoy him occasionally by letting school boy humour intrude into what one might otherwise describe as quite a decent attempt at prose composition. I think I did it out of a sense of embarrassment at letting my hair down and expressing myself in an imaginative way. I was not the only boy to do this and sometimes his exasperation with us showed. But he carried on regardless and I have been ever grateful to him for giving me, in particular, a lifelong love of poetry.

By contrast, one of our Classics teachers, Mr Cluer, nickname "Tom" was never too bothered about his appearance and would often turn up in class with small pieces of toilet paper stuck to the sides of his face by congealed blood where he had nicked his skin while shaving with a cut-throat razor. The toilet paper staunched the trickle of blood that would otherwise have worked its way down to his shirt collar. Why he used such a fearsome object we could never understand but it presumably saved him the expense of buying razor blades! I will mention his "bon mots" later.

Another teacher with, in his case, a refreshingly unorthodox approach to his subject was the Reverend R. R. Lewis, ("Tusky" to the boys because he had two pronounced molars)! He was the only ordained Church of England priest I have ever encountered who did not believe in miracles and who taught us to be wary of them.

Of the parable of the five loaves and fishes, for example, he would say: "I was out in Palestine during the war and if any Arabs had been asked to go out into the desert they would not have been so stupid as to go without food and water. The same precaution would have been taken by the Jews at the time of Jesus and he and his disciples would easily have been able to find sufficient spare food from those who had it to feed those incautious enough not to have done so. The so-called miracle is easily explicable in those terms".

One of his responsibilities was to prepare those of us who were members of the Church of England for Confirmation and we attended talks in the Chapel after school about the significance of the ceremony and our need to practise our Christian beliefs in our daily lives.

I liked the Reverend Lewis a lot and joined his Red Cross Section in the Third form. He and the school Nurse taught us how to clean and dress wounds, staunch bleeding, make slings, and quarter the ends of beds. I put what I had learned to good use during my National Service, particularly when patching up fellow members of my Royal Artillery Regiment who had been involved in late evening confrontations with drunken Scotsmen in Leith, the port and principal pub area of Edinburgh!

One of the most popular for his irreverence was Mr Hodgson, "Joe" to the boys. He was Housemaster of Mill Hill, a boarding house and had been an accomplished footballer in his earlier years. He had arrived at the school in 1934 and was loved by the boys for his bluff and forthright manner. Although he never taught me History or English I can recall him presiding over school lunches in the newly built dining hall.

The staple element of our lunches was "stodge", essentially a form of suet pudding, which came in three basic forms. There was plain white stodge for one's first course, which one covered with gravy, alternatively a sort of "off white" stodge with currants in it, and brown stodge, flavoured with cocoa, for dessert. The latter were accompanied by a yellow glutinous substance which was described as custard!

Grace was said every day before the meal. For any presiding master with a classical turn of mind it was "Benedictus benedicat." For every other it was "For what we are about to receive may the Lord make us truly thankful". On one occasion, however, Joe who was by no means a Classicist, had taken a look at the food on offer that day and intoned "Benedictus, bury the cat" as we all stood with heads bowed.

His version of Grace was met with peals of laughter. It did rather sum up what we felt about the unimaginative and unappetising food which was a far cry from that served to pupils in the twenty first century!

As Classicists we had the benefit of worldly advice from our teachers, Messrs Cluer (Tom) and Riddiford (Bubbles), and two or three of us witnessed a striking, in the true sense of the word, example of how to impose authority on a recalcitrant pupil from our third Classics teacher, the bespectacled and outwardly placid, Mr Benson. I will record this incident later in the chapter.

In terms of extracurricular education, for example, Tom came into our classroom one day, when we were in the Lower Sixth and said, in grave tones, "Boys, I want to tell you all about matrimony." We wondered what he was going to say. "When you get married, you will look into her eyes and what will you see?"

"Don't know, Sir", we replied.

"You will see marital bliss. And when she looks into your eyes what will she see?"

"Don't know, Sir".

"Three square meals a day". We came to the conclusion that poor Tom was not happily married!

Whatever the state of his marriage, he did appear to be happy in his role of Head of Classics and certainly knew how to get the best out of us. When, for example, on a scorchingly hot July afternoon in 1953 our inclination would have been to doze off at our desks rather than study Thucydides, he came into the classroom and said, "It is far too stuffy in here to be able to concentrate on school work. Pick up your textbooks, we are going outside".

Without further ado he led us out onto the school playing fields where, fanned by a cool breeze and sitting on the grass in the shade of a massive oak tree, we were able to enjoy the lesson. It was a pleasant and unforgettable experience.

Regrettably we did sometimes take advantage of his good nature and he could be provoked into extreme, almost irrational, behaviour. On one occasion, for example, he came into the Bean Library which acted as our classroom at the time and saw, on the shelf at the far end of the library, the revered marble bust of John Milton with a school cap on its head and a school scarf round its shoulders.

"Who has done this?" he shouted. "If he is a Praepostor, I will have him "de-preed," - stripped of his role as such. "If he is not, I will have him expelled." We all looked at him in amazement. "I am keeping you all in after school until I find out".

"What, without food?" inquired one boy.

As junior librarian at the time, responsible in part for the good behaviour of pupils in the library, I could have been in trouble but, by a stroke of luck, Mr Alan ("Daddy") Brooks, the master in charge of the library walked in and burst out laughing. He could see the funny side of what one of us had done. Tom was forced to subside by the reaction of a fellow master, but it was not the last prank we played on him.

Although, as Housemaster of East House, one of the day-boy houses, some of its members found him rather "wet", and there is no doubt that he did not have the commanding presence of other Housemasters he was a thoroughly decent man and an exceptionally good teacher. As editor of the Classical Society Journal I came into contact with him a lot during my compilation and production of each edition and found him kind and helpful.

Although his life and circumstances would not have been the same as those of "The Crock" in "The Browning Version", (referring to Browning's translation of the Agamemnon of Aeschylus) a phrase in the translation is probably apposite: "God, from afar, looks graciously upon a gentle master".

Mr Riddiford, by contrast, was a different and completely irrepressible teacher. He had an effervescent personality, hence the nickname "Bubbles"! He would, for example, come into the classroom for an Italian language lesson and say "Let's forget about textbooks for the moment. I am going to tell you about Italian coffee bars". And off he would go, striding round the classroom, pointing out an imaginary Gaggia coffee machine "over here" and wines and spirits behind an imaginary bar "over there" while we sat entranced by his enthusiastic description of life in Italy, particularly life in coffee bars!

Coffee shops or bars now proliferate in England, but did not feature in the early 1950s, and the whole concept of them was intriguingly foreign and novel to us at the time. As an aside we were equally unfamiliar with Italian food. Travel abroad for a family holiday was virtually unheard of. The mass market in holiday travel to the Continent of Europe was years away.

Such, in fact, was the naivety of the general public and their ignorance of foreign cuisine that, in the early days of black and white television, the BBC showed an April Fool's Day programme on the gathering of the spaghetti harvest in Italy.

Richard Dimbleby, a famous and much respected commentator who normally covered State events, solemnly showed men and women climbing ladders to pick long strips of spaghetti from the branches of what must have been olive trees! And many people watching the programme actually believed him! What modern generations tuck into nowadays with relish was once treated with suspicion. Our taste buds have since been liberated!

He also had worldly advice for us. "If you want to do anything in the Army tell them you can already, do it", he said. "If you want to drive a truck, tell them you can already drive a truck. They will then put you on an M.T (Motor Transport) course. It is how the Army operates".

"Take my example. I wanted to go out to Italy during my National Service so I told my CO (Commanding Officer) that I could speak fluent Italian. It was an absolute lie but before I knew it I was in Trieste and up before a Major in the Intelligence Corps.

The Major was not impressed and said "Riddiford, I am going to give you a month to learn Italian. If you do not, I will send you on the first flight back to England".

Bubbles continued: "so I really set myself to the task of learning Italian. I put an ice pack on my head as I sweated over the words and phrases, I had to be able to pronounce. At the end of the month, I went before the Major desperately worried that I would be flown home".

"Not bad, Riddiford," said the Major. "You have done well but you need to brush up your colloquial Italian. Get yourself a woman."

"So I did," said Bubbles, "and now have a wife and two bambini. I married the daughter of an engineer in Mestre, near Venice, and my life could not have turned out better for me."

We boys were impressed and I made a mental note of his advice.

I used it to good effect during my National Service when, fed up with acting as Guard Commander overnight at Edinburgh Castle and Redford Barracks at least once a week, with the loss of sleep that responsibility entailed, I told the C.O. of my Regiment that I could speak fluent modern Greek and wished to be posted to active service in Cyprus as an interpreter.

Of course, I could not speak Greek any more than Mr Riddiford had been able to speak Italian but I had been to Greece with the school Scout Troop, of which more anon, had ancient Greek at "A" level and had mugged up on some standard questions and answers in a modern Greek phrasebook I had purchased in a book shop in Princes Street. His advice was "spot on" and I quickly found myself, promoted to Sergeant and attached to Military Intelligence in Cyprus. But that is another story!

Our third Classics master was Mr Benson. His nickname was "Ivy", after the well-known female band leader during the Second World War. He taught us Latin and Ancient History, was in his mid-thirties, softly spoken and very Christian. He deserved and obtained our respect for the friendly and encouraging way in which he imparted his obvious knowledge of his subjects to us.

It would be unheard of nowadays for a schoolmaster to engage in fisticuffs with one of his pupils and would probably result in the master's dismissal. This might have been the case in the early 1950s if the school had come to hear about it. It is all the more remarkable, in the circumstances, that the mild-mannered Mr Benson should have been provoked into doing so.

There was just one occasion, however, when one of the boys in the first year of the Upper Sixth form took unwarranted advantage of his easy-going nature.

For the sake of anonymity, I will call him Thurgood. He rather fancied himself as a Ladies man and as a sportsman. What he did during his lunch break I have no idea but he consistently turned up late after lunch for Latin lessons in the Bean Library. He was not in Upper Six Classics and I suspect that, being in another sixth form, he needed to brush up his Latin in order to gain admission to one of the Oxbridge Colleges. "O" level Latin was still a requirement for a place in many of them despite the fact that it would not necessarily be relevant to the Degree course one hoped to follow.

After he had done so on three or four occasions without offering any explanation or apology, Mr Benson told him that his patience with Thurgood's lack of time keeping was exhausted. He must turn up on time in future or else. "Or else what?" replied Thurgood". You don't frighten me. I could beat you into a pulp any day". "Really", said Mr Benson. "In that case you and I will meet at 4 pm at the back of the Bean Library and we will see about that".

I am absolutely positive what Mr Benson meant by "or else" was that he would ban him from further lessons, but Thurgood was all about exerting his masculine ego. I was aware that Mr Benson had been in Military Intelligence during the War, breaking down and translating Japanese coded messages. Although outwardly mild and studious he had kept himself fit and had played squash regularly. It is a physically demanding game as anyone who has ever played it will confirm.

Not wanting to miss a good fight several of us appeared behind the Bean Library at 4 pm, followed shortly thereafter by Thurgood and Mr Benson. Thurgood took off his grey school jacket. He was well built and quite muscular. No wonder he appealed to young ladies! Mr Benson turned to me and said. "Brian, would you please hold my glasses and my jacket". With that he rolled up the sleeves of his shirt and squared up to Thurgood.

It was obvious to everyone present that it would be a "no contest". Mr Benson was all muscle under that unpretentious brown tweed jacket and clearly one hundred percent fit. His spectacles belied his real athleticism – a bit like Clark Kent and Superman! One short sharp jab to the solar plexus saw Thurgood buckle and go down on one knee. "Had enough, Thurgood?", said Mr Benson.

Thurgood rose, put on his jacket and retreated without saying a word. I handed Mr Benson back his jacket and glasses and that was the end of the matter. But from that day onward Thurgood never turned up late!

The only time I saw real anger on the face of Mr Benson was when we drew in chalk on one of the patio windows looking out from our classroom over the garden of Roden House the outline of a jagged hole, the size of a football and the cracks that spread across the glass in all directions.

From any more than twenty feet, as he walked down the patch towards us it looked very convincing. His thunderous expression changed as he realised that the glass had not been shattered after all and was replaced by a broad grin. We rubbed off the chalk and equanimity was restored. This was only one of a number of innocent jokes we played on our masters, most of which they took in good part.

One master by whom I was influenced and whom I have already mentioned was Alan Brooks. He apparently acquired his nickname, Daddy, by having three daughters! Not only did I come into frequent contact with him as my housemaster when captain of the house rugby and cross-country teams but also as senior librarian.

I have always had a love of books and gravitating to this latter position was a natural progression. It not only entailed referencing and keeping track of all books taken out of the library by pupils and masters but also ensuring that pupils behaved themselves within it. The library was a popular spot during the lunch break for the serious senior and not so serious junior members of the school.

Shortly after being appointed Senior Librarian, Mr Brooks chided me for being a trifle hard by expelling a noisy third former from the library without compunction one lunch time. My response was that it was better to be firm and decisive at the outset rather than be soft at the beginning and then try to impose good behaviour later. My strict approach to noisy juniors would make the library quieter for those who wanted to work in it. He appreciated and accepted the point I had made. After a month or so everyone knew what standard of behaviour was expected and I could afford to be lenient, where appropriate.

As senior Librarian I was able to persuade Mr Brooks to purchase the famous Latin and Greek Dictionaries (Lewis and Short and Liddell and Scott, copies of which our Classics masters already possessed) for the reference section, also a number of books on Ancient History, including Syme on Inscriptions. The information contained in these additions to the library enhanced the knowledge and abilities of our very gifted Upper Sixth form. They also made it easier for me to prevail on members of my class to write learned articles for the Classical Society Journal on Roman and Greek culture and history which, even to this day, I find remarkably interesting and well informed.

Having discussed the teaching staff with someone who entered the school as a Catholic during the War years I would add two of his memories of "prejudice" which I did not encounter, but which are entirely believable.

Mr Shortland had a dislike of boys whom he considered too fat or too cheeky. There could not have been many fat boys at the school during the War years because food was rationed but for those that were he devised a challenge which would result in a beating if they did not meet it.

He would make them jump over a bar set at two feet six inches above the ground. If they knocked the bar off its supports, they would be punished! Cheeky boys received the same punishment. Because he was keen on archery he would beat the boys on the backside with an arrow shaft. It had less bend in it than a cane.

Mr Jacottet, the teacher of French and Commander of the local Home Guard during the war, had an intense aversion to Roman Catholicism as a result of his Huguenot origins. He would mark down the written school work of boys who met for the weekly service at Brentwood Cathedral rather than in the school chapel. Apparently, a Catholic boy would receive the same mark for three mistakes as a non-Catholic boy would for several more. The memory of this unfair treatment has remained vivid in the recollection of the former pupil after more than eighty years.

Fortunately, I never encountered those types of prejudice, although I was regularly punished for misdemeanours during my early years in the school by masters and prefects alike. The post war period was a tough one in every way but for children who had lived through years of deprivation and hardship there was not a great deal during it that affected us long term.

We recall most masters with affection but some we recall for their prejudice and what one would now describe as sadism. But harshness and prejudice probably stiffened our resolve to enjoy all the more what came after our school days.

43
The Festival of Britain 1951

Britain had just about recovered from the devastating effects of the First World War, the Spanish Flu epidemic that followed it, and the depression of the 1920s when it was plunged, once again, into conflict.

The mid/late 1930s had, as previously mentioned, witnessed the restoration of a sense of comparative wellbeing but the nation's hopes and aspirations for a peaceful and prosperous future had been rudely shattered by a titanic and a massively life and resource consuming struggle to defeat Germany and Japan and to bring peace of a kind to Europe.

At the end of the Second World War in 1945, the economy of the country was in a parlous state and the relatively modest pre-War standard of living of just about everyone except, perhaps farmers, and the landed gentry, had been reduced to a much more basic level.

There had been two major political parties and two alternative choices competing for the votes of the electorate in the General Election of 1945, namely a measured and somewhat uninspiring programme of legislative reform proposed by Winston Churchill, our war-time Prime Minister and Leader of the Conservative Party, and a "new vision" of society offered by Clement Attlee, Deputy Prime Minister in the coalition Government and leader of the Labour Party. The "new vision" included immediate radical reform, full implementation of the proposals in the Beveridge Report and the sweeping away of many traditional, but much disliked, aspects of class and privilege.

Not surprisingly, the Labour Party won by a landslide, much to the chagrin of Winston Churchill, and expectations were high. But in 1950, five years after the end of the war, the government and the people were still struggling with the legacy of it.

The Labour Government, to its immense credit, had laid the foundations of the Welfare State, including the introduction of a much-needed health service, available and free of charge to all irrespective of means, known by its initials, the NHS.

The Government had also done its best to re-house those whose homes had been destroyed by building over one million Council Houses and erecting over 150,000 temporary prefabricated homes, known as Prefabs. In fact, by 1951, fifteen per cent of all dwellings in the UK were owned by the Government in one way or another, more than the proportion in the Soviet Union at the time!

As mentioned in an earlier chapter it had introduced far sighted Town and Country Planning legislation to create new towns for those displaced during the War, had reformed the Law of Landlord and Tenant and had passed other legislation which assisted the poorer members of society.

There was no getting away, however, from the fact that the Government and nearly everyone in Britain was really hard up. There was great austerity. Food (including sweets and chocolate) was still rationed, petrol rationing had only recently come to an end, and signs of the devastation caused by German bombing were everywhere. The whole country looked "down at heel" and people were wondering if and when things would ever improve. Recovery from the war was still a "work in progress".

It was against this background and, in an effort to give the country a sense of renewal and optimism for the future, that the Labour Government decided to promote a Festival of Britain in 1951.

It was going to be nationwide and would have its epicentre in London in the form of an Exhibition on the South bank of the Thames between the London County Council offices and Waterloo Bridge, opposite the Embankment.

The festival in London was going to mirror the Great Exhibition of 1851 and the hope behind it was that it would represent a turning point in the century. It would mark the end of a dispiriting fifty years and the introduction of a revitalised and forward-looking Britain.

Prince Albert, Queen Victoria's husband, had been the driving force behind the Great Exhibition which had acted as a showcase for British manufacturing prowess in 1851. It had been held in the Crystal Palace, a massive iron framed building into which sheets of strengthened glass had been inserted. It was a glittering and spectacular structure and a proud landmark for Londoners until, sadly, it was destroyed by fire in 1936.

London had to have something equally impressive for the South Bank Exhibition and Hugh Casson, a famous architect was appointed Director of Architecture and commissioned to design and supervise the construction of one permanent building, the Royal Festival Hall, and two temporary structures on the Exhibition site. These were the Dome of Discovery and the Skylon. Although temporary they were intended to have a life span of several years. The relevance of this observation will be explained later in the Chapter.

The Dome of Discovery, an exhibition hall, was the largest domed space in the world at the time and the Skylon was a futuristic slender "cigar-shaped" steel cylinder three hundred feet in height suspended some fifty feet above the ground. It was clad in aluminium louvres and lit from the inside at night. It appeared from a distance to be hovering in the sky but it was, in fact, held up by steel cables. A popular joke was that the Skylon was like the British economy. It had no visible means of support!

The South Bank Exhibition, as it was called, which opened on 4 May 1951, proved to be an immense attraction for young and old alike and over eight million people visited it. I can remember that, as a family, we travelled up to London with my friend, Peter Preston, for a special day out. It was on the 10th September 1951 because Peter and I sent each other free greetings on that date from the Dome Colonial Telegraph Office run by Cable and Wireless Ltd. I still have the telegram!

In the words of the festival brochure "the Exhibition is a new sort of narrative about Britain. It tells the story of British contributions to world civilisation through the medium of tangible things – the illustrations themselves being taken primarily from science, technology and the products of contemporary British industry".

"Each pavilion provides a chapter of the story which is in three parts: the upstream circuit of buildings describes the natural wealth of Britain and what, in skills and achievements, the British people have derived from their land. The Dome of Discovery shows the different spheres in which our natural bent for exploration has been expressed, and the practical outcome of many great discoveries".

"The Downsteam circuit of buildings relates the story of the people of Britain in the context of their more domestic life and leisure". In the Festival brochure the people of Britain were described as "people of mixed ancestry and a blend of different qualities." But in 1951, nearly everyone was white and most subscribed to Christianity. We did not have the multicultural society that exists in the 21st century.

In one Downstream display entitled "The Lion and the Unicorn", which gave glimpses of British character and tradition, the traditional heraldic representation of the lion as England and the unicorn as Scotland was changed, the lion symbolising action and the unicorn imagination. One wonders how the Scots felt about the implicit characterisation at the time!

In an effort to display the nation's ingenuity, adaptability and forward thinking there were areas in the Downstream circuit devoted to solutions to problems of space in the home, equipment and classrooms for new secondary schools, recent achievements in public health, medicine, surgery and nursing.

There was also a display of sports which originated in Britain and which, in the words of the festival brochure, "we have carried around the world". It is worth pointing out in this respect, that at the time we were better at the sports we had invented than other nations. The same cannot be said of today!

As a 15-year-old I was captivated by the new invention of television, with "telecinema" and large screen television on the horizon. The thought of being able to watch films and entertainment in one's own home was mind boggling. Most people could not afford to buy a television set and those who could watched TV through a screen that was about twelve inches across and showed pictures in black and white. The first TV I watched was in 1953, two years later, when many people, including my uncle Gerald, bought one for the Coronation of Queen Elizabeth.

Being quite keen on food, as a growing teenager, my only disappointment was that, apart from beer and cups of tea, the twelve pubs and cafés on the site could only come up with the most basic of lunch menus! I can remember us all sitting rather despondently on a low wall eating my mother's fish paste sandwiches and some cheese and tomato rolls and packets of Smiths potato crisps, with their little blue bags of salt inside, which my parents had been able to purchase from one of the cafés. Austerity was still ever present!

There is no doubt that the Exhibition gave a shot in the arm to the long-suffering masses who had worked so hard and who had sacrificed so much during the War. Overall, it was also a good promotional tool for British industry and for a financially straitened Government, notwithstanding the fact that neither had the resources to develop many of the visionary projects on display!

Moreover, the Royal Festival Hall proved a great success. It has excellent acoustics and was opened with performances conducted by Sir Malcolm Sargent and Sir Adrian Boult to public acclaim. It continues to be a popular venue for events of all kinds.

Unfortunately for all the temporary structures on the South Bank Exhibition site including the Skylon and the Dome of Discovery, which would have given enjoyment and imparted knowledge to the public for many years, Winston Churchill ordered their removal when he was returned to power in the 1951 General Election. He saw them as "a symbol" of the previous government's vision of a new Socialist Britain!

It was an act of wanton destruction, probably as a result of pique that anything so popular should have taken place under the auspices of a Labour party that had so unceremoniously bundled him out of power in 1945!

It is sobering to reflect on the fact that, although the Exhibition site could be unnecessarily demolished, little attention was being paid to restoring or rebuilding other devastated parts of the City of London. In fact, some remained derelict for a very long time. I can recall that when, in 1960, I used a Secretarial Agency near St. Paul's Cathedral for my student travel circulars and, even later, when between 1964 and 1966 I used Lionel Rapkin, a firm of printers near Ludgate Circus for my travel brochures, I skirted on my way to them a number of overgrown bomb sites which had not been redeveloped. There are now, of course, smart offices and blocks of flats upon these once desolate areas.

The South Bank Exhibition was only one of the many events the Government hoped would be held across the country and Billericay was not going to be left out of the festivities if Alma Hatt, the dynamic Town Clerk, and the citizens of Billericay had anything to do with it!

Alma Hatt, who was subsequently instrumental in Billericay coming to national attention as the first constituency to announce its results in the 1955 General Election, set up a Festival Committee whose first task was to devise a programme for a large scale "one day" event in Lake Meadows, the local park on Saturday, 4 August 1951.

In addition to a Ladies hockey match (the "over 30s" versus the "under 30") a bowls match, sideshows, boating on the lake, fishing, putting, pitch and putt and a pub crawl competition, which was, in fact, a sort of treasure hunt with clues in a number of local public houses, it was decided that the principal Festival event had to be light-hearted, humorous and draw attention to the town. It was at this point that some bright spark suggested borrowing and adapting a centuries old tradition from a town on the north side of Chelmsford.

Dunmow, the town in question, had for centuries held a Flitch Trial at which a cured and smoked side of bacon, virtually half the body of a medium sized pig would be awarded to couples who could prove that they had been happily married for a year and a day. Couples claiming the Flitch had to submit themselves to a trial in which they were both cross-examined by a sceptical Counsel for the Flitch and defended against such scepticism by Counsel for the claimants. A jury of maidens and bachelors would decide on the couple most happily married. Each trial obviously provided a lot of entertainment for the large audience who would thoroughly enjoy the probing of the couple's married life. Each husband and wife, open to such public scrutiny, would have to be prepared to be subjected to close examination of every aspect of it, however embarrassing that might be!

Awarding a Flitch to those who could prove marital harmony was not unique to Dunmow. There is evidence that the tradition existed outside Britain in mainland Europe, and some would put its origins as far back as Saxon times.

It appears to have been initiated in Dunmow in 1104 when an Augustinian Priory was founded in Little Dunmow through the good offices of the Fitzwalter family, and there is a nice, but undoubtedly apocryphal, explanation for its existence.

The Lord of the Manor, Reginald Fitzwalter and his wife, are said to have dressed themselves as "humble folk" and begged the blessing of the newly arrived Prior a year and a day after their marriage. The Prior impressed by their devotion bestowed upon them a flitch of bacon. Upon revealing his true identity Fitzwalter gave the Prior land on condition that a flitch be awarded to any couple who could claim and prove that they were similarly devoted.

Whatever the origin, news of the Dunmow Flitch trials spread far and wide over the next two hundred years. The author, William Longland who lived on the Welsh borders mentioned them in his 1362 book, "The Vision of Piers Plowman" in a manner that implied general knowledge of the custom among his readers.

Chaucer himself writing less than half a century later alludes to the Dunmow Flitch trials in "The Wife of Bath's Tale" and again does not see the need to explain it to his readers. When speaking of three of her five husbands, good men but older, who could scarcely keep up with her nightly demands, she says, "The bacon was not fet for hem, I trowe, that some men han in Essex at Dunmowe." I leave the reader to translate but the gist is clear and the reference to Dunmow demonstrates that he and his contemporaries knew all about them.

The custom had also been imposed upon Sir Philip de Someville in 1336, who acquired the Manor of Whichnoure near Lichfield in Staffordshire from the Earl of Lancaster for a small fee on condition that he kept "ready arranged at all times of year, except Lent, one bacon-flyke (flitch) hanging in his Hall at Winchnoure, to be given to every man or woman who demanded it a year and a day after marriage, upon their swearing they would not have changed for none other". One assumes that the successful claimant or spouse would "take home the bacon"!

This historical Dunmow Flitch is known to have been successfully claimed only six times although there may have been more that are unknown. It was not until 1445 that they are officially recorded. The earliest recorded successful claimant is Richard Wright from Norwich in the twenty third year of the reign of Henry VI, and the last was John Shakeshands in 1751 in the reign of George II.

It was clearly not easy to convince juries of ongoing marital bliss and an anonymous, humorous and fictional account appeared in Joseph Addison's Spectator Magazine in 1714 poking fun at what appeared to be the Wychnour Flitch trials. In the article one couple were at first successful but then had the flitch taken away from them after they began to argue "how it should be dressed". Another couple failed when the husband, who had only reluctantly attended, had his ears boxed by his wife during questioning. While a third couple, who applied shortly after their honeymoon, passed the questioning but were only awarded one rasher because insufficient time had passed to win a complete flitch! A sea captain was successful because he and his wife had not actually seen one another for over a year since their marriage!

In 1832 a retired cheesemonger and his wife tried to claim the Dunmow Flitch but were rebuffed by the Steward to the Lord of the Manor who said he regarded the trials as "an idle custom bringing people of indifferent character into the neighbourhood." The Wichnoure Flitch Trials had ceased a century earlier, a replacement for the flitch having been carved in wood and displayed over the mantle of the fireplace in the main hall of Wychnor, presumably as a token acknowledgement of the condition of the original purchase of the land by Sir Philip de Somerville.

And that might have been the end of them, but in 1854 William Harrison Ainsworth wrote a tremendously popular novel "A Flitch of Bacon", subtitled "The Custom of Dunmow: a tale of English home".

At the centre of the novel is a scheming character, intent on claiming a flitch by marrying a succession of women in an attempt to find one who might enable him to win it. However far-fetched the story, making fun of the tradition must have appealed to the Victorian sense of humour as it had to the anonymous writer in the Spectator magazine, and the Town Council of Dunmow were quickly prevailed upon by Ainsworth himself to take over the Trials from the Lord of the Manor and reinstate them as a Civic event. In fact, he actively encouraged them to do so by donating two flitches for the first of the revival ceremonies in 1855!

The Trials have been held ever since! The first, after the Second World War, were held in 1949 despite rationing being in force and are now held every fourth year on Leap years - 2028, and 2032 being the next Leap years at the time of writing this book.

Aware of the success of the Dunmow Flitch Trials two years previously a much more humorous version was advertised in the local Billericay Press and four couples bravely volunteered to be put on trial. They were not, however, young couples who had only been married a year and a day: In their case they had to aver "that they had nothing but a happy married life, had never offended each other, nor repented their marriage, nor had a cross word". A tall order, one might say!

The judge was, of course, Alma Hatt and the Clerk of the Court was, not unsurprisingly, my father. Counsel for the Claimants was a Mr Charles Wyman, a gentleman much involved in Operatic productions in the town while Counsel for the Flitch was a Mr Terry Thomas, not the famous film star, but a prominent member of the Billericay Folk Players, the amateur dramatic society. Strangely I got to know them both well in the 1960s. The Jury of maidens and bachelors comprised young men and women from the town, several of whom I also got to know well in later years!

Claimants could bring witnesses and documents in support of their claim and Counsel for the claimants could sympathetically present them, their documents and their witnesses to the jury. Having laid bare, figuratively, their mode of life, the claimants and their witnesses were at the mercy of Counsel for the Flitch who had no intention of losing it because he got a share of it if the Claimants were unsuccessful! The Judge also got a share in this event!

During the cross-examination, counsel for the Flitch was allowed "Three sneers, two coughs and one chuckle!" According to the festival programme, counsel for the Flitch would then make a heart rending appeal to the Jury "to save his bacon!"

Counsel for the claimants was then allowed with (lawful) passion "to carry the Jury in great flights of oratory (or imagination) to scenes of nuptial bliss where he would show that angels were no better than the claimants and that the devil himself was a very angel compared with Counsel for the Flitch"! The Judge, Alma Hatt, being a barrister, would then sum up each couple's chances. then instruct the members of the jury to retire and consider their verdict.

The Flitch was awarded on the day to the couple adjudged to be the most happily married but I cannot recall which of the four claimants it was. The winning couple then had to kneel upon the kneeling stone and take an oath which was more or less identical to that imposed upon the winners of the Dunmow Flitch Trials.

After the oath was sworn, Alma Hatt then intoned:

"Since to these conditions, without any fear, of your own accord you do freely swear, a gammon of bacon you shall receive and bear it away with love and good leave. For this is the custom at Billericay known, though the pleasure be ours, the Bacon's your own".

I suspect that this awful doggerel was produced by my father who liked to compose humorous poetry, as mentioned earlier in this book. The winning couple were then lifted shoulder high in ceremonial chairs and carried round the enclosure in which the Trials had taken place.

The whole event was very lighthearted and, like festivities in other towns across the country, intended to lift the spirits of people in the locality. Whether these nationwide festivities succeeded in every region is difficult to tell but, from 1951 onward, there was definitely in Billericay at least a feeling of looking forward to the future rather than back to the past.

44
Leisure-Time Activities 1949-1952

Filling in my leisure hours has never been a problem whether it be by reading books or magazines or by joining in activities with others, young or old, who share the same interests.

Not long after I left the Sea Scouts I met a boy my own age who went to KEGs, the King Edward VI Grammar school which, as you will doubtless recall, had been rescued from oblivion by the citizens of Chelmsford when, as a Chantry school, it had been forced to close on the dissolution of the monasteries by Henry VIII.

His name was Peter Preston. We immediately became firm friends and spent a great deal of time in each other's company for many years. In fact, I was best man at his wedding to his first wife, a Vicar's daughter, when he was going through his religious phase.

It was only when he left Billericay and moved, after his divorce, to a remote corner of Scotland that our friendship had to be confined to letters and telephone conversations. At the time of writing this chapter I still correspond with the widow of his second marriage, a remarkably philosophical lady whom I have never met but who clearly has a deep well of kindness, humour, and understanding of human nature within her.

A single child, he lived with his parents at 158 Norsey Road, only a couple of hundred yards further up the road towards Billericay. Peter's parents were a charming couple with relatives living in properties between our respective homes. His father, Eric, was an engineer by profession who worked, I believe, for the Ministry of Defence and his mother Cis (Cecilia) became my teenage confidant. I would spend ages chatting to her when I was not doing things with Peter.

I say that 158 Norsey Road was distinctive because, within its large garden with its long frontage to the road, were the remains of a Bronze Age tumulus behind the deerbank that once enclosed the woods. The tumulus had been excavated in the 1880s and it contents lodged in the Colchester Museum at the time.

It had been re-excavated at the beginning of the Second World War to house an air raid shelter, lined on its base and sides with concrete. I understand that during its conversion a cuff link belonging to one of the gentlemen who had carried out the original excavation was discovered, but nothing more!

Sadly, it has disappeared, having been razed to the ground as a result of the transformation of the former garden into three building plots upon which now stand three somewhat pretentious houses, albeit very much in keeping with all the other houses that back onto the woods.

While still a garden Eric Preston had a garage at the lower end of it with access directly onto Norsey Road. In it he kept a magnificent 1937 SS Jaguar, in immaculate condition. He would spend hours dismantling and reassembling parts of the engine. In fact, he was so enamoured of this admittedly beautiful looking car that he hardly ever took it out! It was a standing joke in his family that, even after the end of petrol rationing, it was kept more as a show room model than as a vehicle that should be driven on a road!

Before he passed the scholarship examination that won him a place at KEGs, Peter had been to a private school, St. John's in Billericay. He had been a very bright pupil and had obviously impressed David Cook, the Deputy Headmaster, who, on 3 January 1951, took Peter, me and another boy whose nickname was "Slick" to the Scholboys Exhibition in Olympia.

In retrospect there was quite a large military presence at the Exhibition. The Royal Navy offered guidance on sailing a dinghy and demonstrated cross sections of one of the mines that sank our ships during the war and one of the torpedoes that sank those of our enemies. The Army, in the shape of the Parachute Regiment, offered a controlled leap from an aircraft fuselage some 25 feet above the ground while the

Royal Air Force let young lads, like me, climb into a mock, but realistic cockpit of a fighter aircraft.

These displays and activities were, perhaps, designed with a view to encouraging school leavers to seek permanent careers in the Armed Forces because, as a nation, we still regarded ourselves as a world power with commitments to protect our remaining colonies from invasion and insurgency.

There was a splendid "go kart" track and an immense railway layout which caught the imagination of Peter and me. There was, for some reason, an impressive large-scale model of a merchant ship in a water tank and also, bizarrely for an audience of young school boys, there were farm animals and demonstrations of basket weaving!

In addition to the above there were men dressed as Hairy Monsters and Robots wandering round the Exhibition Hall, and all the toys, games and other things one could buy that appealed to youngsters like us. David Cook was a kind and decent man, and I am afraid that Peter and I did rather test his patience by our high spirits during a memorable and enjoyable visit.

Enthused, no doubt, by the visit Peter and I, who shared a love of models, would subsequently spend hours during the following summer holiday in a rather dilapidated greenhouse in the Preston's garden laying out, on shelving that ran at waist level around it, a model town with houses and shops made out of shoe boxes, and similar and a road for our Dinky cars and lorries in the same way as model railway enthusiasts lay out landscapes for their trains.

Being handy with Harbutts plasticine I made miniature figures to populate our town, many in uniform, to give a semblance of realism to it. We even prevailed upon Peter's parents to purchase model trees and mock grass. We had previously, in the Easter holidays, built a Meccano bridge across the air raid shelter which had, by then, been converted into a fish pond. When one of our Dinky cars fell in, sank into its murky depths, and proved irrecoverable, we decided that the green house was a far safer place for our activities!

We later moved on to making Airfix model aeroplanes, painting them and adding the roundels and other stickers that made them look so authentic. There were few sedentary pastimes that attracted us, apart from Monopoly and doing large jigsaw puzzles.

We were creative all the time and did not rely on outside stimuli. The fact that Peter was studying science at school and I Classics had no impact on our friendship or on what we did. I can recall that we went on, in later years, for example, to create a six-foot-high Easter egg, illuminated with fairy lights, from which the then Billericay Beauty Queen emerged in a swimsuit at a Young Conservatives dance in the Archer Hall, the town's principal entertainment venue.

Two incidents from this period stand out in my mind, one unpleasant and one educational as far as the psychology of the female sex is concerned.

For the first two years after our arrival in Norsey Road there were no houses between Pink Cottage and Bowburn Cottage, the home of John Strong to whom I have referred in a previous chapter, but, in 1950, a Mr and Mrs Gould who had purchased one of the intervening plots and had built a house upon it, invited us over. They wished to introduce themselves to us. It was on that occasion that Mr Gould, a successful businessman in his late fifties, did something I will never forget.

He proudly took us around the former woodland, which he had converted into a back garden, and showed us his vegetable patch and the area in which he was growing strawberries.

A sparrow had caught its leg in the netting over the strawberries and could not extricate itself. Mr Gould picked up a spade and took a swing at it. At that very moment another sparrow arrived and started fluttering on the ground next to its stricken mate. It was trying to divert Mr Gould's attention while the other desperately tried to escape, but to no avail. Mr Gould systematically clubbed both to death. I was horrified. The man clearly had no soul. I felt that anyone else, including myself, if it had been my garden, would have released the sparrow. I never went into his garden again.

On a less serious note, I took little interest in girls during this period of adolescence, although I was of interest to three young ladies of my own age who accosted me one day at the garden gate of Pink Cottage and asked me which of them I liked the most! We had all travelled regularly to Brentwood where they attended the County High school for Girls and had sat on the back seats of the bus chatting to each other. Their names were Margaret Hatchard, Pat Candler and Daphne Dawkins.

Although all three were very pleasant to talk to, and good company on the journey to school, I made the fatal mistake of naming the one I liked most, Daphne Dawkins! From that moment the other two never spoke to me again and all three moved to the front of the bus! Moreover, shortly after this incident, Daphne, the only one who would talk to me, moved with her parents out of the area. I was not overly concerned because, with everything I was doing at school and elsewhere, I really had no time for girls. But that encounter taught me the value of diplomacy in relationships, however casual or distant!

School and homework from Monday to Saturday during term time and Church or Bible Class on Sunday mornings meant that my activities with Peter were confined to a large extent to the Easter and Summer holidays. Apart from the time spent with him the highlight of the summer holidays was the annual 14-day venture into the unknown with my parents and my sister, Angela.

My parents did not have the money to pay for hotels or bed and breakfast accommodation and from 1951 to 1954 we camped out wherever we went, whether it be in a farmer's field on the way to or back from our holiday destination, or on land overlooking the sea whenever we headed to somewhere with a beach.

In 1950, however, my father, ever the optimist, decided that his 1937 eight horsepower Morris Minor, registration number KV 8557, which had transported us, before petrol rationing, from Kettering to Dagenham, could tow the caravan that had been kindly lent to him by an office colleague to Suffolk. He must have been under the mistaken impression that Suffolk, like Norfolk, was very flat!

The poor little car, not even as big as the world-famous Volkswagen Golf, managed, remarkably, to tow it to Lowestoft with my mother, sister and me as passengers and with everything we needed, except food, for a fortnight's holiday inside the caravan.

When we reached the Caravan Park at Corton, just outside Lowestoft, we had to descend about forty feet to it and the caravan literally pushed the car down the slope until we reached ground level with my father frantically applying the brakes to no effect.

The problem then facing my father was how to get it back up the slope when we left for home. Fortunately, I made friends with a pretty young thirteen year old by the name of Maritza Jackson whose mother was, I believe, Hungarian. Her father, Peter, owned a six-wheel amphibious vehicle used by the United States Army, principally during the D-Day landings in the Second World War, to transport troops and goods from ship to shore.

Its nickname was a "Duck", its official army designation being a DUKW. It was shaped like a boat and was over thirty feet long. It had an extremely powerful engine and Mr Jackson not only took us children across the beach and into the sea in it (as he did for many a thrill-seeking holidaymaker) but he was also kind enough to tow our caravan effortlessly back onto the main road at the end of our holiday.

After that and a couple of other nail-biting experiences on our next holiday to Devon and Cornwall, including its inability to get to the top of a steep hill in Polperro, my father decided to sell the Morris Minor and buy a 1936 Austin Ascot de Luxe, registration number CEV 420, complete with starting handle, from a fellow employee in Billericay Council.

The "deluxe" aspect consisted principally of dark blue leather seats, faded cream interior lining and woven string containers close to the rear side windows in which ladies might place small items such as gloves, scarves, etc. Although a starter motor had been fitted, it still needed hand cranking on occasion.

It was a 12-horsepower model and Mr Harry Mayhew, the seller, being an employee, had been able to drive it round the area on Council business for some years. Because he was so short, and usually wore a hat, all one could normally see, when he owned it, was a car being driven, it would appear, by a hat! His eyes were just above the bonnet!

In this amazingly reliable car, which my father sold to me some years later, we travelled as far as Anglesey in the West and Loch Lomond in the North. It did, however, have its unpredictable moments and I can vividly recall that, when returning from Sheppey Road one Saturday evening, the head gasket on the engine block began to leak, causing the engine to lose power.

My mother, sister and I had to get out and push the ailing vehicle all the way up Brook Street Hill in Brentwood, past Honeypot Lane, the former site of Redrow (see the Chapter on the founding of Brentwood school) while my father, like a jockey urging his horse to gallop, was rocking backwards and forwards in the driver's seat! Once over the top of the hill the car coughed, and spluttered, its way back to our house in Billericay and, of course, on the following Monday to Ralph Ellis's garage in the High Street.

My father was no stranger to camping. He had been a Boy Scout in the 1920s and an Assistant Scout Master in the 1930s. The Austin did not have a boot, as such, but a section of the rear, behind the back seats, opened up and folded down to form a platform for suitcases. We also had the two wheeled trailer which had proved too heavy for the Morris Minor in hilly country and into which we put all our camping gear.

Late every afternoon my father would select and approach the owner of a farm likely to allow us to camp in one of his fields and from whom we might buy fresh milk in the morning. Once the field had been located we would unload the tents, the groundsheets, the bedding, the primus stoves and the cooking utensils and set up camp.

I have to confess that, as a budding 15-year-old chronicler of the day's events and the places we had visited, I let my father put up the two tents while I wrote my log before it got too dark to do so! That, I regret, was my excuse for not helping out as much as I should! It was very "teenage" of me at the time to avoid anything that resembled real effort, but my father never seemed to mind and it would not be long before my mother had produced a cooked meal for everyone. My father was always meticulous in leaving the field as he found it, ensuring thereby that others would be permitted to camp in the same spot.

Although camping might strike many readers as a primitive way of holidaying we always had great fun as a family doing so and it prepared me for sleeping out on the roofs of hotels, on the decks of Greek inter-island ferries and on places like the hillside at Delphi, and the beach at Mykonos, when, in my undergraduate days I managed to survive on as little as £23 for a twenty four day holiday in an, as yet, unspoilt Greece.

During our travels we passed through many towns well before motorways by-passed them and after viewing what each had to offer in terms of a Cathedral, a castle, a nearby stately home, or any other interesting feature, I would buy a postcard of it to remind me of my visit. It was a relatively inexpensive hobby, particularly when my parents shared the cost, and I quickly built up a large collection. It did occur to me, after a time, however, that instead of using my precious pocket money on cards I could go into the local Council Offices and obtain the latest Town Guide free of charge with all the relevant information and pictures in it.

This stratagem proved so successful that I started to write to Local Authorities for them irrespective of whether we had visited the town in question on our holidays. By studying a road atlas I could pick out places with fascinating names and write for their guidebooks. I picked out, for example, Rhosllanercrogog, which sounded wonderfully Welsh and was somewhat disappointed when I received the Guide Book for Wrexham!

I persevered from the age of fifteen until the age of twenty, shortly before going up to Cambridge, and now possess a comprehensive overview of what towns in England, Scotland and Wales, were like in the 1950s, and of the aspirations of the Local Authorities that existed at the time. The changes in the fortunes of many of them have been profound over the past seventy years and some, including Billericay Urban District itself, have disappeared and been merged into larger authorities. Moreover, guidebooks have been dropped by them in favour of bland websites and tourist office leaflets.

I kept writing for them during National Service, particularly so when on active service working in Military Intelligence in Northern Cyprus. My parents would know I was still alive by the fact that at least one guidebook dropped through the letterbox every week!

We were invariably lucky with the weather on our camping holidays, and I can only remember one or two occasions, including one at Wollacombe in Devon where we had to "sit out" the rain in one of the tents. Fortunately, my father, being an experienced camper, never set up camp where we would have to experience wet conditions under our groundsheets.

In retrospect we travelled long distances and visited a great many places, three of which stand out in my mind. I can also recall how we all held our breath as our trusty Austin laboured in bottom gear, with trailer attached, to the top of the Kirkstone Pass in Cumbria, one of the steepest ascents for a motor vehicle in England. As previously stated, my father was ever the optimist. The car just made it!

The three places, Tretower Court, near Crickhowell, a tiny fish and chip restaurant in Alnwick and Hopetoun House are memorable for different reasons.

Tretower Court, with its adjoining castle set in green countryside, lying to the south of the Black Mountains, the eastern range of the Brecon Beacons National Park was our first encounter with somewhere unique. We had visited castles and stately homes, but this was different. It had been the home of the Vaughan family for many centuries and after falling into disrepair had been bought for the nation in 1934. The initial restoration of it took forty years and it was still being restored when we came across it. The atmosphere was magical. There was nothing ordinary about the wonderful group of heavily timbered mediaeval buildings, which I understand have been substantially enhanced over the following decades. It was an unforgettable experience.

The fish and chip restaurant in Alnwick in Northumberland was like no other. We descended a flight of stone steps in a street of old buildings and entered a cosy room with an open fire in the corner. A smiling elderly lady who insisted on calling everyone "Pet" greeted us. The restaurant only had one room with, perhaps, four tables in it. It was all very Dickensian. The lady who must have been the owner served us the best homemade fish and chips I have ever tasted before or since. It was, in many ways, my introduction to the warmth and hospitality of people in the north-east of England.

Hopetoun House, again, was an unforgettable experience. After camping out close to the sands at Gullane, and a morning visit to Edinburgh and the Forth Bridge, we headed for Linlithgow. The road from Queensferry took us past a magnificent stately home and we wondered whether it was open to the public. Somewhat overawed by its size we nevertheless decided to go and ask. We went down the long drive and drew up in front of it. There was nobody about.

At this point my adventurous father said "there may be someone at the back. Let us go and have a look". We walked round, I seem to recall, the left-hand side of the building and came across a middle aged gentleman sitting, in the afternoon sunshine, on a double size swing lounger with a canopy on top. By his side was a small table with a drink on it.

He looked somewhat taken aback to see this ragtag group approach and told us that the house was not open to the public. My father apologised profusely for disturbing him. He accepted the apology and very graciously offered us cups of tea. He went off to produce them and, while he was out of sight, my neat and tidy mother picked up the cushions lying on the ground and replaced them on the lounger.

Our host duly returned with the tea and went to sit down but, instead of the lounger, he sat with an agonising thud on the paving stones in front of it. It was at this point that my parents realised that the cushions had been placed on the ground deliberately to soften any fall. He must have missed the lounger regularly!

In the circumstances we bid him a quick farewell, thanking him for his kindness and beat a hasty retreat. It was a highly embarrassing incident and I will always remember the look of pain on the poor man's face. Hopetoun House was the ancestral home of the Hope family and, in retrospect, the unfortunate gentleman may well have been the Earl of Hopetoun, the Marquis of Linlithgow. He never said who he was, and we never asked.

They say that travel when young is an education and travel when old is an experience. But we always seemed to have both on these "seat of the pants" holidays. And that is what made them so memorable.

45
The Brentwood School CCF

At the end of the Second World War the Labour Government was very much aware of its overseas commitments and of the threats that faced the nation. Military manpower would not only be necessary to ward off any communist aggression, but also to control any manifestations of a desire for independence from British colonial rule and to guard or police places as far apart as Christmas Island in the Pacific, Berlin in Germany and Trieste on the Mediterranean coast of Italy.

On the other hand, servicemen who had been involved in protecting the country during the Second World War wanted to be demobilised and to be able to return to their families and dependants and look for work in "civvy street" without delay.

In the circumstances the Government, in 1947, introduced National Service for every 17 to 21-year-old physically and mentally capable of being conscripted into the Army, the Royal Navy or the Royal Air Force. Some would be granted deferment or exemption, temporary or permanent, but, basically, everyone who left school at the age of seventeen or eighteen had to serve in the armed forces, initially for eighteen months until 1950 and for two years from the outbreak of the Korean War in 1950.

It was not an attractive proposition for school leavers. Pay started, for a Private at 28 shillings a week (£1.40p), rising only if one gained a Commission or a higher rank as a Non-Commissioned Officer (NCO). Living conditions during National Service were basic, almost primitive in some places, and death was an ever-present risk. In fact, 395 National Servicemen were killed on active service in Malaya, Korea,

Kenya and Cyprus between 1947 and 1963 when conscription ended. We, at Brentwood school, were well aware of the imminence of National Service and had a good idea of what might be involved in being called up, especially those, like me who had been on training courses of various kinds with the regular army.

Combined Cadet Forces (CCFs) had existed in Public and many Grammar schools well before the Second World War and constituted the pool from which most Officers, on permanent or temporary Commissions, were drawn while Army Cadet Force and Air Training Corps Units in towns and cities across England, Scotland and Wales existed primarily to provide Non-Commissioned Officers (NCO's) and full-time regulars.

In the early 1950s Brentwood school CCF was one of the largest in England and I believe that this is still the case. When I left school in 1954 there must have been in excess of 500 of us who donned army or air cadet uniforms and turned up to school in them on Thursdays.

The army contingent was at battalion strength divided into the equivalent of three rifle companies and a combat support company containing a Signals platoon. There could not have been far short of seventy Air cadets as well. When we were all on parade on the playing field closest to the school for our Annual Inspection by a senior ranking Army officer, we must have looked an impressive sight, provided the inspecting officer did not look too closely at some of the uniforms worn by the fourth formers!

We entered the CCF in the fourth form, most wearing baggy uniforms that were too big for us, presumably to allow for growth, and progressed through to looking like real soldiers or airmen in the Upper Sixth form. I can still remember the hours I spent in the outhouse at Pink Cottage brushing my corps boots and polishing with Brasso my belt buckles and cap badge, after homework, on Wednesday evening, ensuring that they shone.

For most pupils the CCF was an introduction to military discipline before conscription and gave an insight into what we would be expected to assimilate during National Service. We learned a lot about drill, field craft, using and maintaining a rifle and a light machine gun, known as a

Bren gun, map reading, battle procedures, etc. These were taught in two parts of a "Certificate A" syllabus, and we took proficiency exams at the end of our fourth and fifth form years respectively in order to gain the appropriate "Certificate A" signification on our uniforms.

With several hundred uniforms, belts with brass buckles, berets and badges to store and with such a lot of military hardware to keep safe, there had, of course, to be a large and secure building in which to put it all. It was painted green, almost camouflaged, and located in the grounds of the school, opposite the new gymnasium and on the other side of The Chase, the private road that bordered the school buildings on one side and the playing fields on the other.

The Corps Hut, as it was known was manned in my time by Regimental Sergeant Major (RSM) Stevenson and subsequently by RSM Mason, both former regular soldiers with a wealth of experience behind them. It was not only their responsibility to issue and recover all the uniforms and other items, but also to protect and maintain the radio sets and the Lee Enfield rifles from the First World War which, deactivated, were used for training and ceremonial purposes. The strong smell, principally of oil, as one entered the windowless Corps Hut was quite different from any other, I have experienced: it is one I will not forget!

After passing my "Certificate A" I decided to go into the Signals Platoon in Support Company and, in order to improve my knowledge and skills, volunteered to attend Training Courses offered by the Royal Corps of Signals in Colchester during the summer vacations. I wanted to emulate my grandfather who, as previously mentioned, laid telephone cables in "no man's land" between the front-line trenches and Forward Observation Posts (FOP's) for the Royal Artillery during the First World War.

I also attended, over the next three years, Corps Camps at Pirbright in Surrey and Fingringhoe in Essex. It was at Pirbright in my last year at Brentwood that I had a memorable experience, details of which I will relate later in this chapter.

Being "wet behind the ears" and unused to speaking to an audience I have to confess to an embarrassing thirty minutes during my first Signals Course at Colchester. About six of us were detailed by the Officer in charge to give a five-minute talk on a subject of our choice. I was first to do so and, for some reason, decided to talk about English Cathedrals many of which I had visited with my parents. Once into the subject I panicked and did not know how or when to stop! To the great relief of the other cadets, I was still speaking twenty five minutes later when the Officer called a halt to proceedings. We had run out of time! It was a valuable lesson in learning how to speak for only five minutes and I have never exceeded my allotted time slot since!

During these courses I learned all about telephone cable laying and how to operate radio sets used by the British Army at the time. After qualifying as a signaller on one Course I then qualified as a Signals Instructor on another and was rapidly promoted to Sergeant in charge of the Platoon. The way in which I gained promotion to Colour Sergeant with a crown above my Sergeant's stripes was very amusing.

On one of our CCF "away days", after I had qualified as an instructor, we were taken to an area of open countryside between Debden and Chigwell and I set the Platoon the task of laying telephone cables to various points on the scrub land around us.

I was standing talking to Captain Jack Higgs, the Officer in charge of Support Company, whose father, Hector Higgs, used to beat me and the other boys in Upper Two around the head if we could not decline Latin nouns or verbs, when Major Kidd, another schoolmaster and second in command of the CCF turned up in his car and asked us what we were doing.

"We are laying telephone cables to Forward Observation Posts, Sir", I replied. He peered at the ground. "Well, you don't seem to be making a very good job of it. The line of this cable is obvious", he said.

"Would you care to follow it, Sir," I replied and off he went pulling the cable from the ground until he entered a very large blackberry bush. When he tried to extricate himself he got hopelessly caught in the brambles and we had to help him get out.

"That was a decoy cable, Sir, and in a war time situation a landmine would have been attached to the end of it. You would have been blown to smithereens. The actual cable is over here, Sir." I pointed to a barely discernible line running across the ground about 20 feet away.

I had been taught by the Royal Corps of Signals to dig diagonally into the ground when laying cables and not vertically. It was easier to conceal the cable. You can imagine Major Kidd's embarrassment! Jack Higgs could scarcely conceal his mirth and insisted on driving me back to school in his car rather than on the bus that had been hired for my platoon, chuckling to himself all the way and asking what else I had learned on the signals courses.

Within a couple of weeks and doubtless as a result of Major Kidd's discomfiture I was promoted to colour sergeant, the only person in the entire CCF entitled to wear a splendid red sash across my chest. I could not be promoted to CSM, Company sergeant major, in charge of Support Company until Roger Voss, the then CSM was promoted to RSM of the entire Army contingent. I then stepped into his place.

The only cadet in my platoon upon whom I was obliged to keep a very close eye was David Irving, subsequently author of books denying the Holocaust. He was truculent and not inclined to accept any form of military discipline or attempts to train him in the use of Army wireless sets. He must have opted to join my platoon thinking that it was a soft option.

Another cadet whose enthusiasm, on the other hand, I had to curb was David Maynard Smith. After I had taught him and a number of others how to lay and protect a telephone cable, crossing a tarmacadam road, he asked if could carry on and lay a few more.

He had noticed that when a flatbed lorry went over the first protected cable the load on it had jumped in the air and moved a few inches backwards. He was trying to calculate how many bumps and at what frequency the cables would have to be laid to shake a load off a lorry. I told him that this was not the purpose of the lesson, and he reluctantly dismantled his two other "speed bumps"!

The memorable experience to which I have already referred was at the end of my last term at the school and occurred during a week-long Corps Camp at Pirbright in Surrey. The Army element of CCFs across the country attended these major annual events with up to fifteen hundred cadets of all ranks from a variety of Public Grammar schools. We were all under canvas in what I recall were "eight-man" tents and took part in exercises and lectures on various military subjects on five of the seven days.

A CSM, from each of seven schools was appointed Camp Marshall for a day and, being a CSM, I happened to be one of those selected! Being the Camp Marshall involved getting up early, before 6 am, and going to bed very late, after 11 pm, and dealing throughout the day with logistical and organisational issues of various kinds. One of my duties, for example, was to ensure that orderly queues formed outside the massive Dining Hall for meals, there being so many cadets to cater for.

On my "Camp Marshall Day" I was standing at lunch time by the doors of the Dining Hall, supervising the entrance of cadets into it. To my left, down the side of the building was a long orderly queue of cadets from the various schools patiently waiting to be admitted when, to my surprise, a platoon marched up from my right-hand side and headed straight for the entrance

I immediately approached the Sergeant at the head of it. "Excuse me", I said to him. "But you must take your platoon to the end of the queue. Cadets are admitted in order of arrival. You cannot barge in at the front."

"But we are Eton," he replied, "and we go straight in."

"No, I am afraid, you do not. You are late and, I repeat, you must take your platoon to the end of the queue and await your turn."

"But this is preposterous,, expostulated the snooty sergeant, "I will have to report you to the camp commandant if we cannot go in straightaway as we normally do."

"Then you will have to do that," I replied, "but in the meantime, march your platoon to the back of the queue." Realising that he was getting nowhere, he reluctantly ordered his platoon to comply.

Eton is undoubtedly an excellent school from the academic point of view but I felt, at the time, that it might have taught its pupils to temper their obviously inbuilt sense of superiority with respect for cadets from less privileged backgrounds who had actually turned up for lunch before them. Since those days one can only hope that the school has done so. I leave the reader to assess whether respect for those less fortunate than themselves is reflected in the behaviour of old Etonians currently in the public eye!

In 1953, a year earlier, the school had been invited to send six representatives of the CCF to the Coronation of Queen Elizabeth II. With cadets from a limited number of other schools they would be allowed to stand on the Albert Memorial in front of Buckingham Palace and have a grandstand view of the Royal Coach and the Household Cavalry as they left and returned to it.

The Officer in charge of the CCF, Lt. Colonel Jones, another schoolmaster, decided that the fairest way of allocating the six places on offer was to select one cadet from the fourth form year, one from the fifth, one from the Lower Sixth and the other three by rank, Lance Corporal, Corporal and Sergeants, including the CSMs and the RSM. I was lucky enough to be allocated the one place for the latter category. We had to present ourselves in uniform, looking our smartest, to the Officer in charge of the Memorial by not later than 7 am on 6 June, Coronation Day.

Coronation Day was overcast and somewhat damp, but I arrived in time and positioned myself with the others on the lower part of the Memorial. Above us were the television and film camera crews and at the same time as they subsequently panned their cameras across the magnificent sight of the Royal Coach and the Household Cavalry they could not help showing the backs of the heads of the cadets below them.

Uncle Gerald had, as previously mentioned, purchased a television set for the occasion and my parents, who did not own one, drove over to Sheppey Road to watch the coverage of it on the BBC. My mother proudly said that she saw me on the Memorial. She recognised me by my ears which were sticking out from under my beret!

Of course, I had an excellent view of the palace and watched the Queen depart for her Coronation in Westminster Abbey and return, also her appearance on the balcony of the Palace afterwards. There was, however, an unfortunate end to a really amazing day. After very much enjoying the pomp and splendour of the occasion and feeling somewhat overawed by it all I travelled on the District Line to Becontree and joined my parents for the journey back to Billericay.

We arrived home at about midnight and as we turned into the drive the car's headlights revealed that the front door of Pink Cottage was wide open. We were being or had been burgled. I leapt out of the car and ran into the house. There was still cigarette smoke in the lounge and the dining room rear window was open. The thieves had been ransacking the house and must have heard our car coming up the drive.

Our back garden, at the time, comprised a small area of lawn beyond which lay two hundred feet of woodland and thick undergrowth. Beyond our unfenced rear boundary were Norsey Woods. The burglars had bolted through the dining room window with my mother's jewellery and had disappeared in the darkness. The happiness of the day changed immediately into shock and distress at the brazen theft of items which, whatever their monetary value, were of considerable emotional significance to her.

My own house has been burgled since and I have experienced the same stomach-turning sensation at seeing one's possessions strewn about rooms in the search by thieves for items of value which they have found and taken with them.

The Police were informed immediately but there was little they could do. However, fortunately, the thieves jettisoned the jewellery they considered worthless and threw it over the wall of the cottage rented by Alec Boughtwood, caretaker of the Billericay Urban District Council's offices, in Chapel Street. Alec, whom I got to know quite well when using the yard of one of the Council buildings as the departure point for my Billericay to Kathmandu "bus service" in the 1960s, handed it in to the Police and my mother recovered it.

The camp at Pirbright in July 1954 marked the end of my involvement in the school CCF, apart from returning my uniform. Conscription into the Royal Artillery, and the acquisition of less prestigious battle dress, followed two months' later at the end of September.

Being an Army cadet was a worthwhile experience as I have no doubt it will continue to be for pupils of the schools that still have a CCF. I learned a lot that was of use in later life. One can only hope, however, that, as a Nation, we will not have to contemplate or actually face up to another war in which future generations of cadets will have to apply the skills they acquired in them.

46
Lullingstone Roman Villa 1953

I knew when I did badly in my Latin and Greek "A" levels at the age of 16 that I would, once again, have to "pull my socks up" and concentrate on achieving "A" levels at seventeen and "S" levels at eighteen if I was to win a place at one of the Colleges in Cambridge.

I was spurred on to do so by Mr Riddiford's sarcastic comment, "Hughes, on those results you might just as well give up any idea of passing Greek at "A" level". It was only later that I realised he was deliberately winding me up! He knew exactly how I would react to a comment like that!

My determination to succeed and prove him wrong did not mean, however, that I had to spend all my spare time studying Greek. I could find other outlets for my energy and one of them proved to be unusual and particularly interesting.

Such was the enthusiasm generated by my introduction to Ancient History that when, at seventeen, I became Secretary of the school's Classical Society, Editor of its Journal and organiser of its activities under the watchful eye of Tom Cluer, the Chairman of the Society and senior Classics master, I asked him whether a group from our class could conceivably go down to Lullingstone in the summer holidays and help excavate the Roman Villa there.

He had read or heard that the Ministry of Works, being short of money for the project, were looking for volunteers to assist with the work involved and had mentioned this to us, in passing, during one of our history lessons.

I do not think, for one moment, that he had expected us to react to his comment in the way we did. Nevertheless, he was impressed by our willingness to participate and, not wishing to put us off doing something similar in future, he promised to write to the relevant authority and ask whether permission would be forthcoming.

Lullingstone, a civil parish until 1955 and currently in the Sevenoaks District, is a small village, near Eynsford in Kent, in what is known as the Darent Valley and was, until late summer 1939, best known for Lullingstone Castle, occupied for centuries by the Hart Dyke family, and for the silk produced within a wing of the Castle.

Lady Zoe Hart Dyke had decided in the early 1930s, for whatever reason, to create a silkworm farm within her 6,000-acre estate. Maybe she had a lot of mulberry bushes in the grounds and wanted to put them to good use! So remarkably successful was she that, by late 1935, she had produced half a ton of silk that year from silkworms hatched from eggs she had purchased in France, Turkey and China. Unbelievably, each one was making a silk thread half a mile long!

Queen Mary, the wife of George V, got to hear about the farm and visited it. She was so impressed by the high quality of the silk that she ensured it was used for the Coronation Robe of her son, George VI. Having gained royal approval, it was subsequently used for the wedding dress and Coronation Robe of Princess/Queen Elizabeth II and, when the farm was relocated, for the wedding dress of Lady Diana Spencer, later Princess Diana, the mother of Princes William and Harry Windsor.

When I say "best known," the Government had announced in 1937 that it proposed to build an airport the size of Heathrow there! Fortunately for Lullingstone Castle and the Roman Villa the project was abandoned on the outbreak of World War Two. An airport the size of Heathrow would probably have spelled disaster for one or both.

The existence of a Roman Villa was discovered by a preliminary archaeological survey during the summer of 1939 but it was only some time after the War that anything could be done to reveal the true scale and importance of it. The Villa, located in the low-lying fields beside the River Darent, was found to possess some of the finest mosaics in England, virtually complete and unaltered by time.

What was even more amazing was the discovery of a rare "house church", what we would now call a Chapel, within the building dating from the Fourth century, containing Christian inscriptions, the least equivocal of any Roman site in the country.

The Villa had begun its life in around 100AD at a time when the Romans had finally brought most of the unruly tribes in the south and east of what they were to call their new Province of Britannia under their control and had introduced a period of relative peace and prosperity. It was pretty luxurious from the start and had developed over the centuries to suit the tastes and beliefs of successive wealthy owners, reaching a peak of luxury in the mid Fourth century.

It could possibly have been the family home of Pertinax, the Roman Emperor, for just 87 days, in 193 AD. It was finally destroyed in around 420 AD shortly after the Romans left the Province for good.

The chapel provided the earliest evidence of Christianity in Britain dating to about forty years after Emperor Constantine adopted it as the official religion of the Roman Empire in 313AD, thereby ending the all-too-common persecution of Christians. It was decorated with a "Chi-rho" monogram, one of the earliest symbols of Christianity, also with a set of wall paintings that have been interpreted as showing a group of Christians at prayer.

The chapel was built above a Cult house and a hypocaust which provided heating to a bath suite inside the Villa. A niche in the wall of the Cult House had a painting of three water nymphs and it is quite likely, therefore, that before Christianity was adopted by Imperial Decree, the Villa was associated with a water cult and probably had been since it was built. It is also likely that the owners of the Villa in the Fourth century were "hedging their bets" by worshipping some of the old Gods as well as the God Constantine had imposed on them.

The spectacular mosaics to which I have referred above depict ancient myths and can now be viewed inside a specially designed building. The site is open to the public and, according to English Heritage, the villa "comes to life in a film and "light show" that illuminates the excavated areas and reveals how they were once used".

Surprisingly permission was given and John Rist, John and Graham Pilling (twins), Roger Rehahn, Graham Little and I were dropped off at the site by our parents, plus tents and camping gear at the end of the summer term. We introduced ourselves to the Archaeologist in charge who, to our relief, was expecting us and pitched our tents, where directed, in a field close by on the village side of the excavations.

Of course, the Archaeologist was not going to let a bunch of inexperienced schoolboys loose on anything that might be of significance, but he did set us to work the next day on an outhouse, adjacent to the Villa where we could cause the least damage! For several days we trowelled and brushed where instructed by a keen young assistant. None of us found anything of note, a few broken pieces of Roman pottery, but that was all.

Nevertheless, we learned a lot during our stay about the techniques employed in excavating an archaeological site, had a privileged peek at what had already been revealed by others and a thoroughly enjoyable time because the weather was fine and the company good natured and entertaining.

What I remember best, however, is the visit we paid to the village pub on our second evening. We had to walk down a long, wooded lane to it. The branches of the trees arched high over us, giving the impression that we were in a foliaged Cathedral. I seem to recall that the pub was called "The Plough". Research reveals that the village had a population of 127 in 1951 and, whatever its name, it was, in 1953, very much a country "local" with few pretensions.

Before we went in, we decided to tease the barman by pretending to be foreign. Graham Little who wore glasses and looked very studious ordered the first round in a strangely guttural and halting accent and we all sat in a corner speaking gibberish, mixed with a bit of Latin, for about five minutes, pausing only to laugh at some non-existent joke. We could see we were attracting the attention of the regulars who were looking at us with a mixture of suspicion and incomprehension.

With the consent of my companions, I then walked up to the bar and ordered another round in perfect English. It was at this point that the penny dropped!" "You have been having us on, then," said one of the regulars. "We thought you was Polish". Everybody had a good laugh at our harmless deception and we settled down in the pub to enjoy ourselves and have a good chat about our experiences during the day.

It was when we left the pub and set off to return to our tents that we began to be affected by the eeriness of the route back to them. It was almost pitch dark and the leaves on the trees were rustling in the light breeze above us. We had, admittedly, had quite a lot to drink, and this could have heightened a sense of alarm or foreboding. I did nothing to ease their apprehension by telling them about the ghostly old lady my grandfather had encountered when his car had broken down one moonlit night on the outskirts of Doncaster!

As a result, we all gathered in one tent on our return telling each other ghost stories and being thoroughly spooked by them, also by the way only our faces were visible in the light of the Tilley lamp in the middle of us while the shadows of our heads and bodies were moving behind us on the tent walls! Suffice to say that I was the first to decide to go to bed at 1.30 am in the morning leaving the rest of them huddled round the lamp! I cannot recall our going back to the pub again after that distinctly scary night!

On the back of this intriguing glimpse into the Roman occupation of Britain, I was able in 1954, to persuade all the members of my class and sufficient numbers from the other upper sixth forms to fill a coach for a full day excursion to the remains of the massive Roman fort at Richborough, near Sandwich, and then along the coast to Rye and Winchelsea. My extensive knowledge of London Transport buses enabled me to hire TF7c, a sleek and impressive single deck, glass roofed, coach used for sightseeing tours. Being used, moreover, to visiting classrooms to recover books from pupils and schoolmasters who had not returned them to the Library, I had no problem in collecting the cost of the trip from the participants in it!

The Roman fort at Richborough, whose Latin name was Rutupiae was the most important in the Province. It had been constructed close to the point at which the Emperor Claudius had launched his invasion of Britain in 43AD and had witnessed the departure of the last Roman legions in the Fifth century.

In 1954 Rye and Winchelsea were old-worldly and fascinating places to visit. They possessed, at the time, a quiet charm and their appearance was more reminiscent of the end of the Nineteenth rather than the middle of the Twentieth century. The boys on the excursions thoroughly enjoyed exploring them and I was pleased and relieved that this was the case.

The weather was kind to us and everyone, including Tom Cluer who accompanied us, appreciated the arrangements I had made for the day. In retrospect it was the start of my organising travel for students, an activity which burgeoned in later years.

47

To Greece as a Boy Scout, 1954

Study of the Classics and, in particular ancient history, had generated in me an intense desire to visit Italy and Greece. As soon, therefore, as I learned, in late 1953, that the school Scout Troop would be making a ground breaking visit to Greece in the spring of 1954, as the first British Scout Troop to do so since the end of the Greek Civil War in 1953, I approached Mr Rowswell, the school Scoutmaster and asked him whether I could participate in the trip as an "ex boy scout".

Mr Rowswell ("Perk" to the boys) was short and stocky and full of energy. Not only was he a teacher, but he also controlled the issue of textbooks to every boy in the school. One would often find him in a large room next to the Cloisters in the Old school behind huge piles of books which he issued to classes and retrieved at the end of each school year.

"No", he replied. "You have to be a member of the school Scout Troop and to be a First Class Scout. You are only a Second Class Scout". "OK, how do I become a First Class Scout?" "You have to pass a number of tests and undertake a two-day twenty mile hike, and write a log on what you saw and did during those two days. It is November now and we are going in April. I cannot see you being able to do the hike before then". "If I do the hike and pass the tests, will you take me?"

He looked at me quizzically. "If you do, I will let you join the trip."

Fortunately, I had three things in my favour, namely, wonderful parents, determination, and the fact that another boy who had been in the school Scout Troop for two years, but who had not yet achieved his First Class, also wanted to go to Greece.

My mother who, as previously indicated, controlled the family finances with the precision of an Accountant decided that she would help me raise the cost of the trip by going out and doing a post round. Such was the volume of Christmas cards in those days that the Post Office advertised for additional temporary staff in December to assist in the delivery of them.

Moreover, I was used to the cold. My bedroom in Pink Cottage was like an ice box until central heating was installed some years later. Having to sleep out in a tent in a quilted sleeping bag, albeit in the middle of winter, would not be a deterrent.

And so it was that in February 1954, with my 13-year-old companion, I was driven down to Kent and deposited in a country lane not too far away from Cobham. It was a sunny but intensely cold day, and I have to admit to being probably the first Boy Scout in the country to abandon shorts for corduroy trousers!

As the sun began to set, we stopped at a farm and decided to ask if we could camp in the farmer's field. He was somewhat concerned by our request and offered to put us up for the night, but we bravely declined his kind offer. What would Perk think if we had "cheated" by spending the night in a comfy farmhouse?

We nearly froze to death that night and when we tried to fold the little green bivouac tent in the morning it just would not fold. It was like a board, frozen solid! We ultimately managed to pack it and set off again on our hike.

During the morning, we came to a hamlet, with a church and about four or five houses close by. In the grey stone walls of one of the houses, set back from the Church and close to the field we had just crossed, I noticed some thin red tiles. The house had a Georgian front door but was obviously much older than that. I thought the tiles might be Roman and we decided to knock on the front door and ask if they were. It would be something to add to our log.

The door was opened by a slim, blond, young lady in a long grey dress with a white collar. She looked about 25. "Sorry to bother you, but do you know if the tiles in the walls of your house are Roman?"

"Yes, they are," she replied. "You both look cold. Would you like to come in and have a cup of tea? I can then show you one or two other interesting things about the house."

We gratefully accepted the offer and went inside. She was, apparently, the governess to four young children whom we never saw. After the cup of tea she led us down a corridor, on the north side of the house, into a room which had a large round hole in the floor about six feet across and about five feet deep. From the centre of it protruded, a couple of feet above floor level, a very solid upright wooden beam upon which were what appeared to be iron shackles.

"Do you know what this is? It is a bear pit and on the wall over there you can see an Anglo-Saxon window. But that is not all. Follow me".

She led us into what I recognised as a mediaeval hall and pointed to the wall. There, etched into the surface of it, were pictures of what looked like Thirteenth Century ships with wording beneath them in what must have been an early form of French or English. These pictures and wording had obviously been made by children. We were absolutely gobsmacked by what we saw and thanked the young lady effusively for what she had shown us.

After I wrote the book in which I first described this extraordinary house I decided that I must try to find it and look around it again. By poring over the Gravesend and Rochester Ordnance Survey Map, and by driving up and down a number of country roads and lanes, I eventually located it. It appeared to have lost its former Georgian style front entrance and to have acquired a covered porch, but it was definitely the same house with the Roman tiles in its walls.

Through the Vicar, whose name and telephone number was on a Notice Board within the entrance to the Church, I contacted the owner who, very kindly, agreed to show me, and my lady companion, around it in January 2022. The owner, an extremely pleasant and charming young lady, confirmed that the Hall, with its minstrel gallery could even have been built in the Twelfth Century and that parts of the house were reputedly the oldest domestic living spaces in the country.

At this point, you, the reader, will doubtless be wondering where this house is! I promised the owner of what is still a private residence that I would not name it. However, a real sleuth can doubtless identify it!

Of the ships etched into the wall one was still visible and has been dated by the National Maritime Museum at approx. 1340 AD. The Museum went on to add, however, that the ship represented could have been sailing a century earlier since its basic shape had not changed in a hundred years. The room in which we, as boy scouts, had our cups of tea looked very much the same.

The owner asked me where the "bear pit" had been and I led her down a corridor to the room in which I vividly remembered seeing it. The pit had been filled in and tiled over at some point in the past, and there is now no visible evidence of it, but I know, from my photographic memory, that it was under the floor surface of that room!

When, in turn, I asked her about the Governess she said that she had not heard of a family with a Governess within living memory. Although it had been 67 years since my original visit I did wonder whether, at that point, my fellow scout and I had entered into a "time warp". The young lady had, admittedly, been dressed strangely for the twentieth century. In that case, to what century had we been unwitting visitors? I feel certain that further research will reveal the identity of the young woman and the period in which she lived, if not in 1954!

Having braved the elements and submitted my log I was allowed to travel to Greece with the school Scout Troop. Prior to departure, Perk sent everyone duplicated, handwritten, sheets of information listing the arrival and departure times of the trains and ships upon which we would travel, the items we had to bring with us and the estimated cost of meals en route to Athens. They were comprehensive and very specific.

For example, the food to be taken with us was two packed meals for lunch in Milan and Brindisi respectively and two weeks' ration of butter, preserved meat, sugar and a one pound (1 lb) bag of porridge oatmeal. Taking butter on a trip like this and expecting it to remain edible for perhaps a fortnight was optimistic and possibly based on the misplaced notion that we would be taking the cooler English weather to Greece with us!

From a later experience of students putting bars of chocolate in their rucksacks, having them melt, soak through their packed clothes, and drip onto their heads from the luggage rack above in the heat of summer

I would not have made this a requirement, even in April. I ignored that requirement, in any event! Moreover, bread in the form of sandwiches put in a greaseproof paper bag, as would have been the case in 1954, would have dried out and tasted like cardboard after a couple of days! I doubt whether any of us would have relished eating them in Brindisi on the third day after our departure from England! But in all other respects the instructions were excellent.

We were informed that a "Tommy Cooker" for solid fuel, a sort of primitive primus stove would be provided by the school, but that we would have to equip ourselves with all necessary clothing, including a complete uniform with Baden Powell Scout hat or beret, eating utensils and camping gear, apart from a tent, mending materials and last, but not least, a shoe brush!

What Perk did not appreciate at the time was that men and boys would sit in the streets of Athens and brush and polish one's shoes for a few drachmas. The country was in a desperate financial state, having recently devalued its currency. Apart from its shipping industry it still had a rural economy and unemployment in towns and cities was rife. It had not yet recovered from the Civil War.

In the notes Perk sent us he stated that his intent was to ensure that we were "a well-trained, exemplary party of scouts because all Britain will be judged in the Greek mind by the standard we set". A bit of an exaggeration perhaps but he was quite right in assuming that we would attract a lot of attention, as indeed we did. I will mention this aspect of matters later in the chapter.

As for our travel arrangements Perk was a veritable "Thomas Cook" with his precise details of our itinerary in each direction, times of arrival in and departure from a number of cities en route, also of what we would eat and how much we should pay for each meal.

For example, from our departure point in Gravesend we would have lunch in Maidstone, cost two shillings and six pence (12 ½p), travel to Folkestone, have tea on board the cross channel steamer, cost two shillings and three pence (approx. 11½p), take a train across France via Lille, Metz and Strasbourg and have a meat breakfast in the dining car at Basle, cost six shillings and six pence (32½p) in Swiss currency before travelling via Lucerne and the St. Gotthard Tunnel to Milan.

There we would find shower baths in the Station. After a quick wash-and-brush-up and a sightseeing tour of the city we would have supper in an Italian restaurant, cost five shillings and six pence (27 ½p) in Italian currency before heading by train, once again to Brindisi.

The depth of information provided by him was extraordinary and I have to admit that I copied his example when sending some fifteen thousand students on this and the Belgrade route to Greece between 1957 and 1972.

However, I put details of restaurants, cheap accommodation, transport facilities to popular island and inland destinations, and other essential information in a separate "Handbook on Greece" which grew substantially over the years as a result of contributions to it by students who donated useful tips to pass on to future travellers.

The group was quite large with 33 scouts and four accompanying adults, namely, Perk, Tom Cluer as Assistant Scout Master, Keith Benson, our mild mannered Classics Master, and Mr Barron "Spud", (examiner of fingernails), Head of English. Twelve of the scouts were from the Third Gidea Park Troop of which Perk was also Scoutmaster and travelling with us and them was a Romford Rover Scout by the name of Geoff Higgs.

Geoff Higgs, an extremely pleasant man in his mid/late twenties, was returning to Athens where he worked as a teacher. I believe it was he who had liaised with the Greek Scout Association in connection with our visit. He was, however, going to disembark at Corfu and make his way by boat to Cephalonia for a very poignant reason. Athens gets very hot in July and August and while he was visiting England in 1953, his young bride had decided to spend a few weeks during the school summer holiday with her parents on this beautiful and much cooler island.

On 12 August 1953 four massive earthquakes, 7.2 on the Richter scale, had demolished the house in which she was staying: she and her parents had been killed when it collapsed on them. In fact, most houses and nearly all the impressive Venetian buildings that once adorned Cephalonia were destroyed and between 500 and 800 people died. The earthquakes were so violent that the island was raised 60 cm, nearly two feet, above its original level. The event was called "The Tragedy of Cephalonia" and Geoff was going there to visit his wife's grave and pay his respects to the surviving members of her family.

Notwithstanding his reason for disembarking at Corfu he was cheerful and helpful in his manner towards us and taught us to sing "Zeeto Ellas" (long live Greece) to the first few bars of "London's burning" which we all performed with gusto on a visit to "Radio Athens" during our stay!

Having arrived in Brindisi on the third day we boarded the M.V. Miaoulis, a brand new and very beautiful but small passenger ship operated by Nomikos Lines.

It had been presented to Greece as part of the reparations Italy made for occupying parts of the country, including, incidentally, Cephalonia, during the Second World War.

Regrettably I left my mark on the ship by lighting my small Tommy Cooker facing downwards on the pristine planking! Hopefully, the crew never realised how the burn marks appeared on the foredeck upon which we slept and did our cooking.

After calling in at Corfu Town, where it is said cricket had once been played in the main square possibly by the crew of a visiting British warship, we travelled on to Patras and the Corinth Canal. I went through and over it many times in later years and never ceased to be impressed and awed by this massive cleft in the solid rock of the Isthmus. The towering walls of the canal appeared to be so close to the sides of the ship as we passed through it. The half-light at the bottom of this great chasm and the regular echoing sound of the ship's engine in an otherwise silent world emphasised its unique nature.

On arrival in Piraeus we were met and taken by coach to our campsite in the middle of an Army Commando camp at Vouliagmeni, set among pine trees bordering the Aegean sea. Our sand-coloured army tents had already been erected for us and we were greeted warmly by the officers in charge. It is hard to imagine an army camp on the site of this now popular holiday resort populated as it is by massive hotels and expensive villas, but in those days the area was totally undeveloped.

Mass tourism was unheard of at the time and apart from the gentry who undertook the mind-broadening Classical Tour in the 18th century and the passengers on luxury liners who, until the outbreak of the Second World War, stepped ashore for a brief excursion to Athens, few foreigners set foot in the country. On our visit to the Acropolis, shortly after our arrival, we were able to wander freely around the Acropolis and the Parthenon and climb, for example, into the Erectheion, a less robust temple building and view the famous Caryatids, female stone figures supporting the stone masonry above them from the inside of it. There were no guards or Tourist Police and none of the restrictions, regulations and hordes of tourists one would encounter a few years later.

Little rebuilding or redevelopment had taken place in Athens between liberation from the Nazis in 1945, and the end of the Civil War in 1953, the main street, Venizelos Street, was still called "Winston Churchill Street" and one could buy two kilos of fresh oranges for roughly 2 ½p. At the time there were 85,000 drachmas to the pound sterling and, as youngsters, we felt quite rich with these high denomination notes even though they were worth so little. The 12-mile journey by bus into Athens cost, for example, 11,000 drachmas, approx. 14p, return!

On the second day after our arrival the scouting authorities arranged for us to be taken to a local Secondary school to meet the senior students there and, somewhat to our embarrassment, to participate in a game of basketball even though none of us had ever played it before. Not only that, the entire school turned out to watch us!

We were no match for them, as they quickly realised, and they reacted by giving us as many chances to score as possible! But it was all good fun and they were all very keen to try out their English on us. As far as they were concerned we were celebrities and it is true to say that we were treated as such, wherever we went.

Our visit was featured in the City's newspapers and, as previously mentioned, we appeared on Athens Radio.

The City authorities decided to give some of the senior students at the school an opportunity to practise their English on us by allowing them to accompany us, as honoured guests, on our visits to Athens. Among the students was an attractive young lady by the name of Lydia Hadjidakis, with whom I was able to converse – she in her faltering English and me in my faltering Greek.

One of the things that interested me in her, apart admittedly from her good looks, was her name. "Hadji" is Turkish, and her family must have been part of the Turkish population which dominated Greece until 1820.

Lord Byron was one of the champions of liberty during the Greeks' struggle for independence, hence the popularity of the name in Greece, and most Turks were driven out of Greece at the time, in the same way as the long-settled Greeks were driven out of Turkey a century later when Kemal Attaturk came to power.

Some Turks, including Lydia's family, must have stayed in Greece and become assimilated into the Greek population. I was later to experience the antipathy of the Greeks towards the Turks and vice versa while working in military intelligence during my military service in Cyprus.

Because it was such an unusual visit to Greece the British Ambassador, Charles Peake, attended our camp late one afternoon with a number of Greek dignitaries whom we had to entertain with renditions of scouting songs. The dignitaries would not have understood, or even recognised, the tunes of most of them, particularly "Ging Gang Goolie", a gibberish song written by Robert Baden Powell himself, but they were friendly and polite and we, hopefully, contributed to cordial relationships between our respective governments! All I can remember is that we gave an energetic and full-throated performance and that we were thanked politely by the Ambassador at the end of it!

During our "action packed" stay we went on excursions to the picturesque Monastery at Dafni, to Mycenae and to the ancient open-air theatre at Epidauros. We were astonished by its acoustics. One could literally hear a pin drop on the stone in the middle of the stage from the seat furthest away from it. Mr Barron had, of course, to declaim some Shakespeare from the centre spot. The opportunity to do so was too good for him to miss!

Returning from Piraeus, this time on the MV Achilleus, but by the same rail route from Brindisi, I was full of enthusiasm for Greece and probably to the surprise of my teachers achieved a State Scholarship in Classics and a place at Cambridge.

I do not, however, claim credit for that success. The credit goes to our extraordinary teachers. Five, out of the eight boys in the Upper Sixth form, second year, achieved Scholarships in Classics. That has to say as much for the quality of the education as for the abilities of the pupils who were taught.

Although I did not appreciate it at the time Mr Martin's fateful and completely random selection of the course of study I was to follow proved, in the event, to be of immense and life changing significance to me and I can have no complaint whatever at the outcome. It took me to places I would not have visited, to experiences I would not otherwise have enjoyed and led to the success I ultimately achieved.

It is a matter of regret that Latin, Greek and Ancient History are no longer as popular subjects as they once were because they provide such a remarkable foundation for later studies and enable one to think logically and put life into perspective.

I can only hope that one day this is appreciated, and that study of the Classics makes a comeback. I have my doubts, but one can always live in hope!!

Epilogue

In the third paragraph of the Preface I stated that in my first book, *A Law Unto Myself*, I left a lot unsaid about my childhood. Even now there is a lot more to tell but I trust that what I have revealed in the preceding chapters will have given you, the reader, a broad-brush picture of the life and times of one very English schoolboy between birth in 1936 and his departure from school in 1954.

My aim has been to shed light not only on the places in which I have lived and the state of the nation during those eighteen momentous years but also on my family background, the schools I attended and on the evolution of the communities of which I have been a member.

My journey to adulthood has been that of a young boy from a lower middle class background whose grandparents and great grandparents saw better days financially during the latter part of the nineteenth and the earlier part of the twentieth centuries. The perspective, therefore, is personal, and not necessarily representative or descriptive of the impact that the events described may have had on other young boys during this period.

My outlook has also been profoundly influenced by the decision of Mr Martin that I should enter the Classics stream and study the works of Plato and Aristotle, Euripides and Sophocles instead of Goethe, Kant and other German writers and philosophers.

At the end of my school career, which came all too quickly, my only regrets were that I had not had sufficient time to complete the re-labelling of all the shelves in the Bean Library to show the subjects covered by the books on each shelf, and to participate in the Docklands Settlement Project. But I made up for these omissions in later years by engaging "pro bono" in many community activities.

The reason for these being "unfinished business" was the fact that I had to devote an indecent amount of time to the study of Latin, Greek and Ancient History, particularly during my last two terms! It is not as if I wasted any time at school or in doing hours of homework in the evenings. In my earlier years it is probably true that my father's constant warning about "procrastination being the thief of time" was appropriate and necessary but from the Lower Sixth form onward my hands were full. There was no time I could afford to waste.

During my progression to senior librarian, Praepostor, editor of the *Journal of the Classical Society*, signals instructor and company sergeant major in the CCF, captain of House rugby and cross-country, participant in or organiser of events, including an appearance in one of the school's productions on the stage of the Memorial Hall, there were few hours left for anything but study. In this connection I was gratified to receive a letter, dated 10 September 1954, from Michael Benson in which he wrote as follows:

"Dear Brian, I do want to congratulate you most warmly on your GCE results which I learned yesterday have earned you a State Scholarship. That brings with it, I believe, a place at Downing College, Cambridge. It is a thoroughly well-deserved reward for your efforts. Of all the pupils I have taught at Brentwood you have made the largest and most consistent progress in the Sixth From. If you continue to improve in the same way at Cambridge you may well achieve a First Class. You will only do so by steady effort, but it is a possibility."

It was generous of him to say that, and a First Class might conceivably have been a possibility, had I been prepared to forsake the thoroughly enjoyable activities in which I immersed myself at University. As at school I had no desire to become an egghead and just concentrate on study. There were far too many pleasurable distractions and so many other avenues to explore.

He went on to say, "You can look back on your school career with great satisfaction for you have achieved not only academic success but positions of responsibility which have brought you experience of handling other people. What is more, you have given the school your service without stint in many directions and this brings its own reward".

Once again, it was kind of him to say so but academic success was as much attributable to the excellence of the teaching as my ability to absorb what was being taught. I did, of course, have a secret weapon namely my photographic memory which stood me in good stead at the time and has done so throughout my life. It made passing examinations so much easier insofar as I could, in effect, refer to pages in a textbook by looking them up in my mind's eye. That facility proved equally valuable when I appeared in many plays and operatic productions during my twenties and thirties.

I also have to acknowledge that my parents contributed to any success I had at school by their unwavering support and the assurance I received, in particular, from my father, with his many words of wisdom which I bear in mind to this very day.

When I was being a judgemental teenager, as most teenagers are, he would say, "Brian, life is not black and white as you seem to think. It is shades of grey". It is only with maturity that one discovers how true this is.

When I was overindulging on sweets and chocolates his comment would be "Brian, you are what you eat", an inconvenient truth one should not ignore, and when I was not exactly being honest with myself, another teenage trait, "Brian, unto thine own self be true, thou can'st not then be false to any man." He was my moral mentor and guide in every sense.

I have often wondered how stable the parental relationships of other boys in the school were and how their attitudes and achievements must have been predicated on the atmosphere within their own homes. To the extent that most of my fellow pupils in Upper Six Classics did so well, their family environments must have been equally supportive and stress free, thereby enabling them to concentrate on achieving good grades in what they were being taught.

To my father's "bon mots" I would merely add the following: "Live life to the full, make the most of your talents, do not think you are better or worse than anyone else, and be kind and honest in your relationship." On that basis you will have nothing to regret when you pass on to 'wherever we all go'.

The reader will not be surprised to learn that I have tried to live up to my own, and my father's precepts, albeit with the odd hiccup on my part along the way.

My first 18 years were full of interesting experiences but were nowhere as eventful as those that followed. Life was lived thereafter on the broader canvas of family, community activities, involvement in stockbroking, running travel enterprises and engagement in many aspects of the Law. It continues at the same frenetic pace notwithstanding the fact that I am close to ninety. In this respect the fates have been kind, and I am lucky enough to have been born with the right genes without which I would not have been able to do so much.

As a result of a number of paranormal experiences my original assumption that one only lives once has been challenged and a book based on them will follow.

But that is for the future, if I live long enough in this body and century to complete it.

www.ingramcontent.com/pod-product-compliance
Lightning Source LLC
Chambersburg PA
CBHW041302240426
43661CB00010B/988